COW CREEK CHRONICLES

University Press of Florida
Florida A&M University, Tallahassee · Florida Atlantic University, Boca Raton
Florida Gulf Coast University, Ft. Myers · Florida International University, Miami
Florida State University, Tallahassee · New College of Florida, Sarasota
University of Central Florida, Orlando · University of Florida, Gainesville
University of North Florida, Jacksonville · University of South Florida, Tampa
University of West Florida, Pensacola

GREGORY ENNS

COW CREEK
CHRONICLES

The Rise and Fall of an
Early Florida Cattle Ranch

University Press of Florida
Gainesville · Tallahassee · Tampa
Boca Raton · Pensacola · Orlando · Miami
Jacksonville · Ft. Myers · Sarasota

Cover: *Roundup* by E. L. "Buster" Kenton (Used with permission
of Rose Marie Kenton Anderson and Debra Sloan.)
Cover design by Larry Leshan.

Page ii: *Cow Creek Crossing*, circa 1970 by E. L. "Buster" Kenton
(Used with permission of Rose Marie Kenton Anderson and Debra Sloan.)

Page vi: Illustration by Michelle Moore Burney.

Copyright 2025 by Gregory Enns
All rights reserved
Published in the United States of America

30 29 28 27 26 25   6   5   4   3   2   1

A record of cataloging-in-publication information
is available from the Library of Congress.
ISBN 978-0-8130-8120-5

The University Press of Florida is the scholarly publishing agency
for the State University System of Florida, comprising Florida A&M University,
Florida Atlantic University, Florida Gulf Coast University, Florida International
University, Florida State University, New College of Florida, University of Central
Florida, University of Florida, University of North Florida, University
of South Florida, and University of West Florida.

University Press of Florida
2046 NE Waldo Road
Suite 2100
Gainesville, FL 32609
http://upress.ufl.edu

GPSR EU Authorized Representative: Mare Nostrum Group B.V., Mauritskade 21D,
1091 GC Amsterdam, The Netherlands, gpsr@mare-nostrum.co.uk

CONTENTS

Introduction · The Ranch *1*

1 · The Earliest Arrivals
10

2 · The Settlers
23

3 · Florida Migration
31

4 · Fort Pierce Beckons
37

5 · Polly Parker (Emateloye)
47

6 · Frank at the Fore
57

7 · The Open Range
68

8 · The Foreman
75

9 · Seminoles Leave Cow Creek
86

10 · A New Heir
95

11 · Enter Tommy
107

12 · Cow Creek in the 1960s
115

13 · Ranch Improvements
131

14 · In the Limelight
141

15 · The Making of TL
150

16 · Leaving the Old Ways Behind
155

17 · Liquidation
176

18 · A Litany of Losses
183

19 · The Last Camp
195

Epilogue *202*
Acknowledgments *221*
Notes on Sources *225*
Index *231*

Map of Florida

- St. Marks
- Lake City [Alligator]
- Jacksonville
- Seville
- Geneva [Harney Cove]
- Orlando
- Tampa
- Egmont Key
- Istokpoga
- Basinger
- Okeechobee
- Cow Creek
- Fort Pierce
- Brighton Reservation
- Fort Myers
- Lake Okeechobee
- The Everglades
- Miami

Atlantic Ocean

Gulf of Mexico

COW CREEK CHRONICLES

Frank Raulerson and his granddaughter, Jo Ann, astride horses at Cow Creek Ranch about 1940. (Courtesy of the Sloan family.)

INTRODUCTION

The Ranch

Settlers and Seminoles

As a young girl growing up in the 1930s, Jo Ann Raulerson was happiest at her grandfather's Cow Creek Ranch. Located between Fort Pierce and Okeechobee on Florida's east coast, Cow Creek was more like a collection of woods and swamps with a few cleared pastures rather than the modern ranch of today.

On weekends, Jo Ann's grandparents, Frank and Annie Louise Raulerson, would load Jo Ann in their black Cadillac to drive the 17 miles west from their stately home in Fort Pierce along the curvy, bumpy road to Okeechobee before turning north, entering the ranch, and driving 4 more miles to their cypress cabin across from the ranch's cow pens.

Jo Ann liked to hang around the cow pens with her friend Ephraim, one of the eleven children of her grandfather's foreman, John Norman. Ephraim, who was three years older than Jo Ann, and his siblings were like family, and the Norman children felt so at ease with Jo Ann's grandparents that they called them Uncle Frank and Aunt Lou.

Friendly but businesslike, Uncle Frank always seemed to have a Tampa Nugget cigar in his mouth while the very proper Aunt Lou often donned a hat and would have hard candy ready to give the children.

Ephraim, who dropped out of school at thirteen to work full-time at Cow Creek, was an unknowing coach to Jo Ann, able to answer almost any question about cattle, riding horses, or hunting that she didn't learn from her grandfather, whom she called Granddad.

Jo Ann would learn how to throw a lariat with some proficiency, but it was her ability to crack a cow whip that was most impressive. Barely

5 feet tall, she'd raise her hand above her head, lightly flick her wrist to extend the 10-foot thong, and then, with her shoulder, elbow, and wrist in motion, rotate the whip handle counterclockwise. She'd keep rotating, careful not to let the buckskin thong or tip hit the ground, until she had enough momentum to snap her wrist in the opposite direction and produce a loud cracking sound that came from the skinny popper at the whip's end.

Jo Ann's weekends at the ranch were a stark contrast to weekdays and the formality of life in town, where Jo Ann's grandmother, whom she called Mother Lou, and an endless parade of Mother Lou's visiting sisters would school Jo Ann on being a lady. Dresses had to be worn. Places had to be set just so for the frequent and formal dinners Mother Lou and her housekeepers would produce. Proper English had to be spoken. Adults were to be addressed politely. Above all, complaints were never to be registered nor feelings expressed.

If she had been allowed to express her feelings, Jo Ann would have

An early photo of Cow Creek Ranch shows an improved pasture and the cattle raised there. Before the creation of the ranch and pasture improvements, the land was mostly swamp or hard scrub. (Courtesy of the Arnold family.)

The old Cow Creek Ranch headquarters includes the house Frank Raulerson built in 1930 for his stays at the ranch. The road through the ranch into the headquarters was 4 miles long. (Photo by Gregory Enns.)

been entitled to complain. Her father died in a boating accident when she was eight. After Granddad and Mother Lou insisted on raising Jo Ann themselves, Jo Ann's mother, Mae, moved away from Fort Pierce and remarried. Granddad and Mother Lou gave Jo Ann a life of privilege and comfort but one lacking in the spontaneity of parental love. In Jo Ann's world, everything was measured and planned.

Visits to the ranch were a big relief for Jo Ann. With the many Norman children also visiting the ranch for weekends from their home in Okeechobee, it was a chance to be with other kids and take a break from the world of older adults Jo Ann endured in town. As Jo Ann grew older and learned to ride, she and Ephraim would go off on horseback to explore the ranch. There was plenty to see. The 4-mile route down the old ranch road to the main entry gate was the easiest ride. Leaving the homeplace, they rode to the distance in the north where they could see old Blue Mountain, which wasn't a mountain at all but a forest of towering cypress trees that looked like a mountain in the morning mist.

They could stop in the old citrus grove that Seminoles had planted on the ranch road's south side. Jo Ann loved to hunt squirrels in the grove and in the oak and cabbage palm hammocks next to it. The grove's towering trees, sweet tangerines among them, had become so untended that Spanish moss, more commonly seen on oaks, had taken up residence on them. Jo Ann became a sure shot with her .22 rifle, hitting her targeted squirrel in the head, with the quarry falling from the tree and producing a satisfying thump as it hit the ground.

A little farther down the ranch road and to the north, Jo Ann and Ephraim could ride down Sandy Lane, with its marshes on the west side and its pastures filled with cattle on the east side. On school vacations, Granddad would let Jo Ann work the cattle with the cowboys during roundups.

Down Sandy Lane, Jo Ann and Ephraim could also see row after row of tomatoes on fields Granddad would lease to farmers. With much of the land covered by heavy scrub, the tomato farmers would clear the land of its ancient vegetation, raise their tomatoes, harvest them, and then repeat the process for only a few years, moving off somewhere else before nematodes began settling into the soil. With a little more effort, Granddad would turn those vacant fields into cow pastures after the farmer's lease was up.

The ride down the ranch road was fun, but the best ride to the most beautiful spot of the ranch went north from the cow pens through scrub and occasional pastures and past the tiny bent pine they called the Hangman's Tree, so named because of its curved trunk. A little later, they'd arrive at their destination, Cow Creek, a small but majestic waterway covered in ancient and towering cypress.

During the summer rainy season, they could swim in the tea-colored creek with the sandy bottom. In winter's dry months, they could walk their horses through the creek, but during the summer they'd sometimes have to swim their horses across it.

It was along the creek that extended Seminole families lived in a collection of traditional open-air homes called chickees. With frames of cypress and roofs of woven palmetto fronds, the chickees were barely noticeable in the hammocks in which they were located. Most of the chickees were for sleeping, with one for cooking and one where the Seminole women would pump the treadle of a sewing machine with their feet to produce their colorful patchwork clothing. Sometimes the women would give Jo Ann beads and necklaces they made to trade and sell in town.

Many of the Seminoles who lived along the creek were descendants of Emateloye Estenletkvte, or Polly Parker, who was a central figure in Seminole history. In 1858, Polly and other members of her clan were captured by US soldiers to be forcibly removed from Florida to Indian territory in the Western United States. Polly organized an escape in the Panhandle and led a handful of others back to freedom in their homelands. Polly lived near the creek until her death in 1922. Her descendants were credited with repopulating the tribe so that by the 1960s some 20 percent of the tribe could trace their lineage to Polly Parker.

Polly's granddaughter Lena and Lena's husband, Tushlanee, known as Joe Bowers, the English name he gave himself after a settler he liked, lived closest to the creek with their eight children. Frank Raulerson employed the Seminoles who lived along the creek as day laborers, and Joe was the Seminole whom Jo Ann's grandfather perhaps knew best. The white cattlemen recruited him for roundups because of his exceptional ability to work with cattle, especially the cantankerous ones that ran into the woods instead of herding with the others. Joe knew every trail in the woods. He also knew citrus and planted one of the area's earliest citrus groves.

After Joe was killed by a hit-and-run truck driver in 1935, Frank and his foreman, John Norman, and the other cowboys took to calling the part of the ranch where Joe and his family lived along the creek, the Joe Bowers Strand.

The friendship between Frank, Joe, and other Seminoles represented an evolution between two opposing parties who had been at war the century before. During the three Seminole Wars in Florida from 1816 to 1858, the Seminoles had resisted efforts by white settlers like the Raulerson family to lay claim to Florida while being pursued under an official US government policy to relocate them out of Florida to west of the Mississippi River. Various members of the Raulerson family had fought against the Seminoles, and some had even received Florida lands for free for their service fighting the Seminoles. Some Seminoles had undoubtedly died at the hands of Raulerson family warriors, and Frank's own kin, including a great-aunt and several cousins, had been killed at the hands of the Seminoles.

The Seminoles at Cow Creek were from a line of the tribe's most independent warriors, who resisted assimilation for more than a century. They were also among the last Seminoles in Florida clinging to their traditional lifestyle by continuing to live in chickees outside a reservation instead of in modern housing within one. They had long hunted in the cypress forest along the creek, and their ancestors likely used it as a hideaway during the Seminole Wars. The creek held such significance that this band of the tribe became known as the Cow Creek Seminoles.

The Seminoles were the last of Indigenous communities going back thousands of years on the Florida peninsula who used the land for fishing, hunting, and just plain living, all without the need for surveys, deeds, or fences—instruments of typical American settlement that had brought Frank and his family success on the Florida frontier.

Climbing to the Top

In 1930, the year Jo Ann was born, Frank Raulerson must have felt like he was on top of a mountain, if Florida ever had one. Since arriving in coastal Fort Pierce twenty-three years earlier from the interior Florida settlement of Geneva, he had opened a grocery store and was running cattle and purchasing property to create his ranches. He had built one of Fort Pierce's largest and most ornate edifices, the Raulerson Building, and was living in one of the town's most impressive houses.

Frank assembled Cow Creek over several decades. In the days of the open range, when cattle ran freely and without fences, he created one of the region's first ranches. By 1916, the local newspaper had begun referencing his "Cow Creek Ranch," and in 1923 he purchased about 600 acres to set up a headquarters. Over the next few years, he purchased more parcels around the original piece and would put together a ranch of 23,000 acres, all of which he'd enclose with fence. He'd also buy two other ranches of similar size in Okeechobee County. In 1930 he constructed his three-bedroom weekend home at Cow Creek from cypress harvested at the ranch.

As Frank expanded his cattle operations, he also was quickly moving up the political ladder. In 1918, he had begun serving as an alderman on the Fort Pierce City Council, as it was then called, and subsequently won election to the St. Lucie County Commission. In the 1920s, the governor appointed him to the state's Livestock Sanitary Board, an influential panel that set livestock health and movement requirements in the state and provided Frank with an insider's knowledge of the state's cattle industry. He had headed a syndicate that owned the local newspaper, the *Fort Pierce News-Tribune*, and, in the year of Jo Ann's birth, won a seat in the Florida Senate, henceforth being formally known as Senator Raulerson.

On the personal side, Frank's playboy son and only heir, Alfred, had finally settled down, marrying seemingly for keeps after two earlier failed marriages and running his own cattle herd in Sebastian. The family's future seemed secure with the birth of Jo Ann, and Cow Creek Ranch would play a big role in Jo Ann's life.

Window into History

In many ways, Cow Creek Ranch became a symbol for both the Raulersons and the Seminoles, a crossroads where two vastly different beliefs intersected about how the land was to be used.

The ranchland itself was a window into both Florida's geologic and human history. Before Florida's beginning, there was no land and no peninsula, just a large expanse of sea. Volcanic eruptions and carbon deposits from dead marine organisms such as coral, plankton, algae, and sea urchins built up the ocean floor, creating the peninsula 530 million years ago.

During a period in which as many as seventeen ice ages occurred, Florida was variously underwater as the peninsula was shaped and reshaped to its present form. Conch and oyster shells and white sand at Cow Creek and other locations in interior Florida are hints of the state's underwater past. The most visible reminder is the Lake Wales Ridge in Central Florida, where thousands of years of fluctuating sea levels created a 100-mile stretch of white sand mounds.

Frank Raulerson ran cattle in the open range at Cow Creek. In 1923, he purchased about 600 acres to create a ranch headquarters. (Courtesy of the Sloan family.)

In the last ice age, Florida was much drier and larger, with more savanna-like conditions, and the peninsula was home to animals such as giant armadillos, sloths, saber-toothed cats, and mastodons. But as that last ice age ended 10,000 years ago, sea levels rose, the climate became damper, and habitats such as the Everglades were created. The change in climate combined with hunting by humans led to the disappearance of large animals in Florida such as mammoths and mastodons. The recovery of mastodon bones at Cow Creek in the 1970s also revealed a time when prehistoric species roamed the region.

When humans arrived in Florida nearly 15,000 years ago during the last ice age, the southern half of the peninsula was submerged under what modern geologists call the Okeechobean Sea. When ocean waters receded from the Florida peninsula 6,000 years ago during the glacial melt, a pool of water left behind in a shallow depression created Lake Okeechobee, the second-largest freshwater lake in what would become the mainland United States. At the time, the lake had no defined edge, with water flowing seamlessly into the Everglades. Over time, decomposing detritus that became peat and muck created the lake's southern edge. Under these conditions, Lake Okeechobee served as a connector of the Everglades to the south and the Kissimmee River to the north.

Some 15 miles away east of Lake Okeechobee, a much smaller body of water, Jernigan's Pond, was formed near a wetland. Fed by this wetland and a series of sand ridges seeping water, a tiny creek was born. Today that waterway, known as Cow Creek, is actually more of an expanding and contracting swamp that runs west–east along the far eastern border of modern-day Okeechobee County into St. Lucie County.

Around Cow Creek and South Florida, other signs of the state's submerged past are the hammocks that appear throughout the landscape. When sea levels dropped, coral reefs were exposed and died, leaving behind mounds of limestone bedrock. Birds, wind, and water currents transported organic material to the mounds, which became covered with palmetto, pine, and oak and today are called hammocks. Crops could be grown on the peat-rich hammocks, or islands, and, with much of the land around them a swamp, early natives poled canoes from tree island to tree island.

In its most natural state before the construction of irrigation canals and dikes, Cow Creek was covered in towering bald cypress, creating a spectacular natural cathedral. The creek provided an ideal habitat for the growth of bald cypress, a hardwood tree that produces stumps around its trunk called knees, roots that help anchor the tree and help aerate the tree's submerged roots. The trees can reach more than 150 feet in height and live up to six hundred years, and the conditions at Cow Creek made them thrive, creating a dense forest. Native peoples and early Euro-Americans must have been awed by the sight when they first entered this natural sanctuary, feeling as if nature itself was enshrouding them.

1

THE EARLIEST ARRIVALS

Florida's First Humans

The first humans arrived on the Florida peninsula nearly 15,000 years ago, according to archaeological findings on the Aucilla River southeast of Tallahassee. The research dates the site to 14,550 years ago, making it the oldest-known site of human life in the southeastern United States.

These Paleo-Indians were descendants of people who crossed into North America from Eastern Asia during the Pleistocene Epoch, or ice age, which lasted from 2.6 million to 11,700 years ago. Nomadic hunters, they used spears and arrows of flint and stone to hunt big-game animals for their survival. They spread throughout the peninsula and the Keys. As the big game became extinct because of climate change and overhunting, food sources shifted to small game and shellfish. Human populations increased and became more stationary, with some groups growing corn, beans, squash, and other crops.

The Mayaimi and Ais People

To the south and west of Cow Creek lay a series of archaeological complexes, including circular ditches and geometrically shaped mounds, built from about 2000 BC to 1700 CE by the Mayaimi people, identified as the Belle Glade or Okeechobee culture. The Mayaimi, concentrated mostly around Lake Mayaimi, known today as Lake Okeechobee, are credited with building the mounds at archaeological sites such as Big Mound City, Tony's Mound, Fort Center, and the Ortona prehistoric village. All provided elevated locations above the waterline for human habitation, growing crops, and creating hubs for trade. These sites also had large earthworks and ponds and hundreds of miles of canals and raised causeways to connect the towns.

The Mayaimi, who are not culturally or linguistically related to the Miami people of the Great Lakes region, primarily subsisted on the bounty from Lake Okeechobee, including alligator, bass, terrapins, and snakes.

The region to the east of Cow Creek was inhabited by Native Americans known as the Ais people beginning about 2000 BC. They lived in towns along what is now called the Treasure Coast and Space Coast in small groups of huts framed with sticks and covered on the sides and roof by sabal palmetto fronds. Oysters and clams harvested from the Indian River were a mainstay of their diet, and the Ais built huge middens, or shell mounds, from discarded shells. The first Euro-American observations about the Ais come from Jonathan Dickinson's *Journal*, the account of an English Quaker who was shipwrecked north of the Jupiter Inlet in 1696.

The Ais created their largest midden, 1,000 feet long and 50 feet high, at their paramount town of Jece, whose probable location was what is now known as Pelican Island north of Vero Beach. Little evidence of the bluff exists today, as it was leveled between 1908 and 1913, when loads of shell were hauled away to build roads in the region. Two of their smaller middens farther south were at the original site of the fort at Fort Pierce and in Jensen Beach, where Indian Riverside Park and the Mansion at Tuckahoe are now located.

Although the Ais lived mostly along the coast, they were known to travel to interior Florida for seasonal hunts for deer, turkey, and bear, and artifacts recovered at digs near Cow Creek have been linked to the Ais.

Besides the Ais, other tribes on the Florida peninsula during the sixteenth century were the Apalachee, Pensacola, Timucua, Tocobago, Calusa, Saturiwa, Utina, Potano, Ocale, Tequesta, Mayaca, Jororo, Chacato, Chisca, and others. Some 350,000 Natives lived on the peninsula when the first Europeans arrived in the early 1500s. But by 1760, disease, slavery, relocation, and warfare with Europeans had all but wiped these tribes out, including the Ais and Mayaimi. At the end of the Spanish colonial period in the early 1800s, it is estimated that fewer than 8,000 people were living on the peninsula.

Spanish Arrivals

Spaniard Juan Ponce de León in 1513 became the first European to arrive at the land he would call La Florida, or the flower. St. Augustine is popularly believed to be the site of his landing, but scholars aren't in agreement on exactly where he first set foot on Florida's east coast. Incursions by Spanish explorers would provide the basics for the creation of Florida's ranch and cattle culture by introducing cattle, horses, hogs, and citrus. Even the word "ranch"—derived from *ranchero*—comes from the Spanish.

Many scholars believe cattle were introduced to the Florida peninsula during Ponce de León's final visit to Florida in 1521, when he brought Spanish Andalusian longhorn cattle with him to establish settlements on the Gulf coast, landing near Charlotte Harbor.

When the Spanish settled St. Augustine in 1565, they established other missions along the Atlantic coast, raising Andalusian cattle there. Jesuit and Franciscan missionaries near St. Augustine were early ranchers in Florida. Cattle raising was important to early Spanish colonization, since the Spaniards initial efforts at farming were not very successful. Thus, cattle raising became Florida's first industry. And from these imported breeds evolved Florida's cracker cow, also called a scrub cow, with their most useful traits being their endurance and their resistance to disease.

Joseph A. Ackerman Jr., who wrote three books on the Florida cattle industry, put forth the following scenario in *Florida Cowman*: "Although these first cattle herds were small, they were made of hardy cattle that reproduced rapidly in the wilderness. They had soon spread over many parts of the peninsula and over parts of the Southeast. Preconditioned in Spain by centuries of environmental extremes and selective breeding, they were tougher than any other European stock. While other breeds vanished, the Spanish foundlings survived."

Cattle weren't the only escapees from the Spanish. Hernando de Soto brought the first pigs to America, and escapees are thought to have created Florida's feral hog population. Today, the hogs are found throughout Florida in oak-cabbage hammocks, marshes, sloughs, pine flatlands, and open agricultural areas.

The Spanish also were responsible for bringing horses to Florida in the 1500s. This Spanish stock evolved into the Florida cracker horse, which is derived from the Iberian horse of sixteenth-century Spain and includes the blood of the North African Barb, Spanish Sorraia, and Spanish Jennet.

Besides livestock, the Spanish also brought to the Americas the custom of branding, or searing a cow's flesh, most commonly on the hind quarter. The branding process is done with a hot iron, creating a distinctive mark to establish ownership of the cow.

The Seminoles

During the period that the Ais and other Indigenous Florida tribes were being displaced from the Florida peninsula in the 1700s because of disease, warfare, and slavery, bands of Creek natives from Georgia and the part of the Mississippi Territory that would become Alabama were making their way to Spanish Florida as Euro-American settlers pushed into the Creek homelands. These new arrivals became part of the group known as Seminoles, a name whose origins are attributed to the Spanish word *cimaronnes,* meaning "runaways" or "wild ones." Initially interpreted as a slur, the name today is embraced by the Seminoles, who call themselves the "unconquered people."

Besides Creeks, the members of the Seminole Tribe of Florida say they are descendants of the original humans who arrived in Florida as well as other Native people such as the Calusa, Tequesta, and Apalachee. The Seminole Tribe of Florida, Inc., the political entity representing today's Seminoles, says Seminoles are the descendants of many Native Americans who inhabited Florida and the Southeast for millennia.

Seminoles who descended from the Creeks came from two groups: the Lower Creeks, concentrated mostly in southwestern Georgia and mostly speaking Mikasuki; and the Upper Creeks, who occupied territory in central Alabama and mostly speaking Muskogee.

The two languages defined what would become two groups within the Seminole Tribe that continue to exist today: the Miccosukee, who speak Mikasuki, closely related to Hichiti; and the Tallahassees and what later would become the Cow Creeks, who speak Muskogee. Both are from a family of languages called Muskogean. Thus, there is no Seminole language, per se. Though the two words are sometimes used interchangeably, Miccosukee generally refers to the people while Mikasuki refers to the language.

A group of about one hundred Miccosukees in 1962 created a separate Miccosukee Tribe of Indians of Florida, with many traditional Miccosukee remaining within the Seminole Tribe. There are also Seminoles who do not identify with either tribe, and they are called traditionals or independents.

Both the Seminoles and Miccosukee descended from the Mississippian cultures, known for their well-organized farming techniques, town layouts, and mound-like ceremonial complexes.

Historian and former Floridian Jason Herbert devoted his doctoral dissertation at the University of Minnesota to the important relationship of cattle to the Seminole culture. "For many outside of the Tribe, the idea that Indians—especially Florida Indians—were and are cow people runs contrary to images of lone cowboys on western ranches popularized by popular culture in the United States," Herbert wrote. "In Florida this erasure happens at a young age, when secondary schools teach historical fictions that treat settler colonists as the state's original cow people as de facto histories and then employ textbooks and standards that ignore Indigenous pastoral traditions."

Florida's early cattle history has remained stubbornly fixed on the Spanish, even though Seminole ancestors were hunting native buffalo (which became extinct in Florida after 1786), gathering feral cattle, and developing their own herds at the same time as the Spanish colonizers were first establishing their haciendas, Florida's first ranches. Through trade with the Spanish, Seminole ancestors also obtained domesticated cattle, which were easier to work with.

The Seminole Tribe of Florida's Tribal Historic Preservation Office offers this history: "While the cattle were new to Florida, the ancestors were very familiar with their relatives, the buffalo which lived in the northern and central areas of the peninsula in those times. The men and women of Florida had worked the buffalo since time immemorial, and knew how to maintain the land to keep the buffalo around. They found that these same techniques worked even better with these new domesticated European cattle, and the herd grew and spread, quickly becoming a part of Native foodways and of Native culture."

Ahaya, a leader of the Oconee, one of the tribes from which the Seminoles descended, developed a herd of thousands after settling his followers 10 miles south of modern-day Gainesville at what would become known as

Payne's Prairie. Ahaya's cattle holdings were so extensive that the British referred to him as Cowkeeper.

Herbert argues that cattle were at the center of conflict between the Seminoles, other Indigenous people, and Euro-American settlers through the end of the last Seminole War in 1858. Furthermore, he says, "control over the animals and the pastures they grazed upon were the primary causes behind both Indigenous possession and later dispossession of Florida."

"As introduced species," Herbert writes, "cattle changed landscapes and ecosystems in Florida, as they and other species did elsewhere on the globe when presented with new lands and waters to occupy. Cattle, in other words, transformed societies and ecosystems in the spaces we now define as Florida."

Cow Creek Seminoles

Before they were known as Cow Creek Seminoles, the Muskogee-speaking band of the Seminole Tribe were known as Tallahassees, a name that has no relation to the Florida state capital except its spelling. Historian Mark Boyd wrote that both "Tallassee," hometown of Upper Creek leader Peter McQueen, and "Tallahassee" are English variants of the Muskogee word for "old town." Boyd gave this explanation for how the name Tallahassee in the early nineteenth century came to refer to the band of Seminoles from Tallassee, Alabama: "As the war progressed, a tendency appears for writers to use the form Tallahassee, when it appears obvious they meant Tallassee. The substitution was natural, owing to an almost identical pronunciation, a similar significance, and an increasing familiarity with the spelling of the name of the territorial capital." Boyd concluded that those referred to as Tallahassees "are to be taken as Tallassees, alluding to Peter McQueen's band of fugitive Red Sticks."

The first printed reference to Cow Creek Seminoles appeared in 1887 in Clay MacCauley's *The Seminole Indians of Florida*. MacCauley, a Unitarian minister, had conducted a three-month survey of the Seminoles for the Smithsonian Institution in the winter of 1880–81. He identified Cow Creek as one of five Seminole settlements. His report also contained a map identifying the location of Cow Creek swamp. The other settlements were

Big Cypress, Fish Eating Creek, Catfish Lake, and Miami. "Shortly after this date, the Muskogee-speaking Catfish Lake and Fish Eating Creek settlements consolidated with that at Cow Creek, thus constituting the Cow Creek band," Mark Boyd wrote of MacCauley's visit.

Harry A. Kersey, who spent much of his academic career at Florida Atlantic University studying the Cow Creek Seminoles, wrote that the name Cow Creek became an all-encompassing term for a large part of the tribe: "In the 1880s the ethnologist Clay MacCauley had located only two northern bands of Seminoles, one of them having camps on Cow Creek; that settlement survived into this century and the term was apparently extended to include all Muskogee Seminoles."

No record exists for why the name Cow Creek was used to identify most of the Muskogee-speaking members within the tribe. Whether Cow Creek was named by Euro-American settlers or Seminoles is also unknown. The creek served as an ever-present water source for cattle roaming in the region for more than four centuries, and Seminoles before the Indian Removal Act of 1830 ran large herds of cattle on the Florida peninsula. Seminoles who lived along Cow Creek pronounced the waterway "Wa ga huch ee."

In his survey, MacCauley noted the independence of the Cow Creek Seminoles. He wrote that, unlike other settlements, they did not attend the Green Corn Dance, the largest gathering of the year: "The people of Cat Fish Lake and Cow Creek settlements live in a large measure independent of or without civil connection with the others. Tcup-ko [Chupco] calls his people 'Tallahassee Indians.' He says that they are not 'the same' as the Fish Eating Creek, Big Cypress, and Miami people. I learned, moreover, that the ceremony of the Green Corn Dance may take place at the three last named settlements and not at those of the north. The 'Tallahassee Indians' go to Fish Eating Creek if they desire to take part in the festival."

In researching the Seminoles, the biggest challenge is discerning between two vastly different methods of preserving history: the written documentation provided by US Army officers and Euro-American settlers and the oral tradition of the Seminoles. The early written accounts often depict the Seminoles as simple-minded savages, whereas later accounts, mostly after the Civil War, play into the stereotype of the noble savage.

Critiquing nineteenth-century settlement histories, scholar Kristalyn Marie Shefveland says such settler histories employed a common strategy of describing Indigenous people as savage denizens of the wild who should be replaced by God-fearing farmers taming the wilderness. In this view, complex histories of Indigenous relations are ignored, and Indigenous people themselves are erroneously declared long gone or pacified.

Nineteenth-Century Seminole Leaders

The Cow Creek Seminoles were among the most strident of the Seminoles resisting American assimilation. This line of Seminoles included such leaders as Peter McQueen, Osceola, Chupco, Tallahassee, and Tom Tiger, as well as Polly Parker, the woman considered the Evangeline of the tribe.

Peter McQueen, son of a Creek woman and Scottish trader, headed a breakaway group from Tallassee, an Upper Creek town. Known by his Creek name of Talmuches Hadjo, he and his band were called Red Sticks because they painted their war sticks red.

As a leader, McQueen was at the forefront of resistance to assimilation or trade with white people and wanted to restore traditional culture and religion, as opposed to the peace-seeking White Sticks, who created sizable farming operations, raised livestock, and were more inclined to trade with Euro-American settlers and accommodate white culture. A civil war called the Creek War broke out between the two factions, and it quickly became part of the larger War of 1812 between the United States and Great Britain.

Although McQueen's Red Sticks had success with several battles against White Stick and US forces, they were ultimately defeated by Col. Andrew Jackson at the Battle of Horseshoe Bend southeast of modern-day Birmingham on March 27, 1814, after which many Red Stick Creeks fled to Florida.

On April 12, 1818, at the Battle of Econfina, north of modern-day Panama City, US troops attacked McQueen's village, killing thirty-seven warriors and capturing ninety-seven women and children. McQueen escaped and sought refuge deep into South Florida. He died, apparently of natural causes, in 1820 at Cape Florida on Key Biscayne.

Osceola

Some historical accounts say that the Seminole leader Osceola was one of the children captured—and later released—in the US raid on McQueen's village during the Battle of Econfina. Gen. Thomas W. Woodward, one of the leaders at the battle, said in his private letters that he had held Osceola as prisoner in 1818, "and he was then but a lad." As an adult, Osceola would become the most famous Tallahassee Seminole and a national symbol of white betrayal of Native Americans.

Woodward recorded that Osceola was born in the early 1800s in a cabin in Tuskegee, in what was then Mississippi Territory and would become Alabama, the son of a Creek woman, Polly Copinger, and an English trader named Powell. Osceola maintained as an adult that he was full-blooded Creek.

Though he had a traditional Creek upbringing, Osceola grew up with the English name of Billy Powell until he took the name Ussa Yaholo, or Black Drink Singer, after a coming-of-age ceremony involving the drinking of a black purgative liquid made from the yaupon holly leaf. The name was later anglicized to Osceola.

Osceola came to prominence in the tribe just before the Second Seminole War. When the Indian Removal Act advocated by Jackson was passed in 1830, with the United States attempting to relocate Seminoles during the notorious Trail of Tears, Osceola led the Seminole resistance to relocation and opposed the 1832 Treaty of Payne's Landing, under which some Seminole leaders agreed to removal. But the treaty was later exposed as being obtained through fraud and coercion. Osceola stridently opposed removal and viewed the signing of the treaty by his fellow Seminoles as a betrayal. Osceola's opposition to relocation made him a symbol of Seminole independence. But he also became exemplar par excellence for betrayal of Native Americans by the US government.

In the fall of 1837, US Army leaders under the command of Gen. Thomas Jesup reached out to Osceola to carry out discussions under a white flag of truce, which carried the expectation that all parties were free to leave at the end the meeting. But when Osceola and seventy-five of his warriors arrived near St. Augustine on October 21, 1837, to begin peace negotiations, they instead were taken into custody and imprisoned at Fort Marion, originally St. Augustine's Castillo de San Marcos built by the Spanish.

Two months after their imprisonment, some twenty Seminole warriors escaped but without Osceola, who was stricken with illness and unable to scale the fort's walls. The escape prompted the army to ship Osceola and 237 of his people to Fort Moultrie on Sullivan's Island in South Carolina, where Osceola died on January 30, 1838.

Chupco

Another young member of McQueen's band who would become a leader of the Tallahassees was Echo Emathla Chupco, whose name also appears as Chopka and most widely as Chipco. The Seminoles who are descended from him refer to him as Chupco.

Chupco was born in the early 1800s in what is now Alabama and fled to Florida with his family after the Battle of Horseshoe Bend. Chupco and three brothers and two sisters reached the Peace River, near Bartow, and then settled at Thonotosassa Lake northeast of Tampa after 1823.

Chupco was one of the Seminole leaders in what became known as the Dade Massacre, which occurred on December 28, 1835, as 107 men under Brevet Maj. Francis Dade marched from Fort Brooke on Tampa Bay to shore up the garrison at Fort King in present-day Ocala. Chupco and a band he was leading were living nearby.

Fifty miles before their destination, near present-day Bushnell, Dade's troops were attacked in a pine forest by 180 Seminole warriors. Dade and more than one hundred of his men were killed by Seminoles under Chupco and other leaders while only six Seminoles died. The battle sent shock waves throughout the nation and strengthened the US resolve to continue the wars against the Seminoles. Chupco died in 1881 at his camp at Catfish Lake (now Lake Pierce), northeast of Lake Wales.

Chief Tallahassee

While the Seminoles were not at war during Tallahassee's chieftainship of the Cow Creeks, his reign was more ceremonial. He was perhaps best known for improving relations with white people. In the 1880s, under pressure from settlers and ranchers, he led the migration of the Muskogee-speaking Seminoles from Catfish Lake to places east of Lake Okeechobee such as Cow Creek, Hungryland, and Bluefield.

Some settled on a popular trading site on high ground that became known as Indiantown, where the US government purchased a 2,200–acre tract of land for the Seminoles. The tract was later traded in the 1930s for land adjacent to reservations in Hendry and Glades Counties. Tallahassee's last camping ground was said to be in Hungryland, now part of Martin and Palm Beach Counties. During Tallahassee's leadership, the Cow Creek band increased to thirty extended families who were part of five clans. Tallahassee died in 1909 at the age of 90.

Tallahassee's wife was Martha Tiger, sister of Tom Tiger. Tallahassee was the father of six sons and three daughters: Billy Buster, Belle Willingham, Mr. Dennis, Chipco II, Tommy Hill, Emma Martin, Charlie Martin, and Susie M. Several of them were listed in St. Lucie County Census surveys of Cow Creek during the 1920s and 1930s.

Perhaps Tallahassee made his greatest mark as a postwar chief by helping to preserve the Seminole way of living. Anthropologist Alexander Spoehr said the Cow Creek Seminoles' retreat into Florida's interior helped them hold on to their customs and resist change.

Tom Tiger

Tom Tiger, or Thlocklo Tustenuggee, captured headlines in both life and death. Born to a Miccosukee father and a Tallahassee mother, Tiger was an industrious and early citrus grower. He fought in the Third Seminole War (1855–58), and he planted some two thousand citrus trees at Cow Creek, which he later sold to cattle king Eli O. Morgan. Tiger was well known at trading posts in West Palm Beach, Stuart, and Fort Pierce.

Tiger, known for his fluency in English, was also a leader in the Cow Creek band and a familiar figure throughout South Florida. The explorer Frederick Ober described him during an expedition at Lake Okeechobee: "He was over six feet in height, large and muscular. His eyes were black and fierce; his mouth firm, but not cruel, was shaded by a small black mustache. We soon made friends with him and found him gentle and pleasant voiced."

Tiger was credited with keeping the Cow Creek band together and establishing friendly trade relations with early settlers. But when one settler, Harmon Hull, refused to return Tiger's horse in 1899 after Tiger lent it to him, Tiger became the first Seminole to take an American to court.

left Chief Tallahassee, seen in this 1884 photo, led his band's movement in the 1880s from near Lake Wales to more easterly and southerly locations such as Lake Okeechobee, Hungryland, and Cow Creek. (Courtesy of State Archives of Florida, Florida Memory.) right Chief Tom Tiger, credited with keeping the Cow Creek band together, also helped establish trade relations with white people. (Courtesy of State Archives of Florida, Florida Memory.)

Harmon was later arrested and spent several months in the county jail. After the case was heard at the Brevard circuit court in Titusville, with witnesses for both sides testifying, Judge M. S. Jones directed the jury bring in a verdict of acquittal, which it did.

Tiger had been provided financial assistance to prosecute his case by Minnie Moore-Willson and her Friends of the Florida Seminoles. Moore-Willson would later write of Tiger as a "tall, magnificent looking savage" who presented to court spectators "the most imposing picture they had ever witnessed."

Shefveland says Moore-Willson's use of paternalistic language and the Friends' intervention in the Tom Tiger case fed into myths and fictionalizations of the Seminole: "Even as settler allies sought to assist Native

Floridians, they could not help but play a part in the romanticization of Native peoples, once again interconnecting themselves to a lasting narrative, Tom Tiger as the last of a noble people on the brink of extinction."

Tiger was killed by a lightning strike on August 28, 1899, while he was making a dugout canoe in Hungryland. A news item in the *Titusville Advocate* reporting his death described him as one of the "largest and finest Indians in the state of Florida." When he was buried, his best friend, medicine man Billie Smith, turned the canoe into a makeshift mausoleum and placed Tiger's body inside, interring him at Hungryland.

The disturbance of his grave several years later caused national outrage. John T. Flournoy of Johnstown, Pennsylvania, desecrated his grave during a visit in 1907, exhuming his bones with plans to sell his remains to the Smithsonian Institution. The episode nearly prompted threats of war by some Cow Creeks, but the controversy was calmed after Flournoy returned Tiger's remains to rest with the Seminoles.

Tiger was the father of DeSoto Tiger, who was killed in 1911 by outlaw John Ashley as he robbed DeSoto of valuable otter pelts on an Everglades canal leading out of Lake Okeechobee. He also was the father of Naha Tiger, who lived at Cow Creek with his wife, Lucy, daughter of Polly Parker.

The Tigers belonged to the Snake Clan, of which Tom Tiger's wife, Mary Tiger Tustenuggee, was matriarch. On the death of Mary, Ada Tiger, daughter of Mary and Tom Tiger, became matriarch of the clan. They lived at Indiantown, and by 1926 she was running a herd of 100 cattle on the open range. Ada was the mother of Betty Mae Jumper, who in 1962 was elected the first chairwoman of the Seminole Tribe of Florida.

Today, the Muskogee-speaking Cow Creek Seminoles and their descendants, concentrated mostly on the Brighton Reservation west of Lake Okeechobee, comprise a substantial part of the 4,000-member Seminole Tribe, though Mikasuki speakers and their descendants constitute the largest part.

From 1816 to 1858 and over three wars, the Seminoles were engaged in the longest continuous conflict by any Native American tribe against the US government. Avoiding complete removal from Florida, the Seminole Tribe asserts today that it is the only Native American tribe that never signed a formal peace treaty with the US government.

2

THE SETTLERS

A Family Is Born

Frank Raulerson was part of a prolific family of early settlers in South Carolina and Georgia, with several patriarchs fathering more than a dozen children who would make the Raulerson name ubiquitous in Florida. Their migration to Florida in the 1800s is a story of the accumulation of land and wealth through hard work but often at the expense of Seminole displacement.

The Raulersons were part of the waves of English and Scotch Irish, many of them livestock herders, who emigrated to the American colonies in the 1700s seeking better economic opportunities. They came down the Great Philadelphia Wagon Road, the main route for settling the Southern colonies, then down Virginia's Shenandoah Valley and into the North Carolina Piedmont region before reaching South Carolina in the mid-eighteenth century. The road began at the port of Philadelphia, the arrival point for many immigrants, and ended 800 miles away in Augusta, Georgia.

The Raulerson family's Southern history is traced to Benjamin Rawlinson (1727–1791), who was born in Kent County, Maryland, but later moved to South Carolina in what is now Richland County, home of the modern-day state capital of Columbia. He and his wife, Anne, were the parents of a daughter and six sons, five of whom served in the American Revolution: Benjamin, John, William, George and Richard. One son was killed, but four sons survived, including John (1749–1816), who was born in South Carolina and served as a private in the South Carolina Militia under Col. Lemuel Benton of Francis Marion's brigade.

Before the Revolution, John received a grant in 1770 from King George III for 100 acres of land at the fork of the Wateree and Congaree Rivers in Richland County. It was one of the first of many land grants that he and his descendants would be given, with the overwhelming number of them issued in Florida, where the name Raulerson would become synonymous with agriculture.

At his farm in Richland County, John Rawlinson raised sheep and hogs and grew cotton, corn, and hay. He also had a small herd of cattle. Feral cattle had been roaming in South Carolina even before the arrival of white settlers like John Rawlinson, originating from the remnants of Spanish herds in Florida. Like Florida, cattle in South Carolina at that time roamed mostly under free range and were periodically herded for branding, castration, and butchering, with enslaved people doing the work.

John Rawlinson married Avis Ann Fisher (1750–1815) in South Carolina in 1775. Building on his land ownership in South Carolina, in 1789 he was granted 200 acres of land in Effingham County, Georgia, one of the original eight counties established by the Georgia constitution of 1777. The land was given to John as a reward for his military service in the South Carolina militia during the Revolution.

Apparently keeping the farm in South Carolina, the family subsequently moved to Effingham, and John received two more grants, increasing his property to a total of 300 acres. His brother James also moved to Effingham but after a two-year stay returned to Richland County. John subsequently sold the land in Effingham County and moved farther south to Glynn County, now Wayne County, Georgia.

John and Avis had four sons and a daughter who would vastly increase the size of the family and both originate and propagate the Raulerson name: Jacob (1778–1857), William (1780–1856), and Noel (1782–1830), all of whom were born in South Carolina, and Nimrod (1795–1858) and Frances "Fanny" (1796–1841?), both of whom were born in Georgia.

Florida Introduction

The four brothers all served in the Creek War as part of the larger War of 1812. Because of their dark complexion and ability to blend in with the

Native American tribes they opposed, they were recruited as spies and served under Capt. Richard Walker's Wayne County Mounted Volunteers at nearby Fort Wayne.

Their skin apparently was so dark that in 1814 William, seeking the right to vote as a free white man, had Capt. William Cone file an affidavit on his behalf stating that he had known William's mother to be "a fair, white-skinned woman" and that he knew John Rollinson to be their father, a free citizen who voted.

The brothers' service in the war introduced them all to Florida, then a Spanish territory, where Peter McQueen's Red Stick Upper Creeks had sought refuge. Their service on the untamed peninsula would make a lasting impression, and in the ensuing years four of the five siblings would move there, three of them permanently.

The Raulerson name was first recorded on July 20, 1813, when Gov. David B. Mitchell issued a commission as lieutenant to oldest brother Jacob Rawlinson in the 335th District Militia in Wayne County and misspelled his name as Raulerson.

In an age when names were often spelled as heard or interpreted by whomever was writing the name down on a document, the family surname mostly had appeared previously as Rawlinson but also as Rollison and Rollinson. Family history does not record why, but after the war the four Rawlinson brothers and Fanny used the Raulerson spelling in legal documents. Henceforth, the Raulerson surname would be used, with descendants being able to trace their lineage back to either Jacob, William, Noel, Nimrod, or Fanny.

And there would be plenty of people who could claim the Raulerson lineage. The most prolific of the original five Raulersons was Jacob, who had seventeen children with three wives. His youngest child, Wade Hampton Raulerson, would become the father of Frank Raulerson. Noel Raulerson Sr., son of Noel Raulerson, had thirteen children, including Noel Jr., who in turn would father seventeen children.

The five original Raulersons valued their association with one another, as evidenced by Noel's tombstone at the Raulerson Cemetery near Trudie in present-day Pierce County, Georgia. The tombstone proclaims him as the brother of Jacob, William, Nimrod, and Fanny and spells his surname as Raulerson but notes that he is the "son of John Rawlinson." Noel's burial consecrated the cemetery, which was part of his brother Jacob's farm on the Little Still River.

The five original Raulersons remained in Georgia after their parents moved back to South Carolina sometime before 1810, when the Census showed Jacob and Avis living back in Richland County. Avis died in 1815, and John died in 1816.

After the War of 1812, Jacob remained in Wayne County in the pine region of southern Georgia, where he established a 500-acre plantation using slave labor and ran a country store. Census records show Jacob owned seventeen slaves in 1830 and nineteen in 1840. Some early settlers in Wayne had received land acquired from the Creeks through the 1802 Wilkinson Treaty, much of which was transferred to white settlers through Georgia's Land Lottery Act of 1805, which awarded 490-acre plots at four cents per acre.

Multiple Marriages, Children

Jacob married three times and had seventeen children. He married first wife, Nancy Biggs, back in Effingham County in 1798 before the move to Wayne County. She was sixteen and would bear twelve children through 1826. She died in 1828 at the age of forty-six.

Three months after Nancy's death, Jacob, fifty, married Courtney Keightly Stewart, a twenty-eight-year-old widow with four children. She and Jacob had five additional children. She died in September 1838, two months after the birth of Wade Hampton Raulerson, the father of Frank Raulerson. Jacob's third wife, Mary Ann Dennison, did not have any children and survived him, living to the age of ninety-three.

His tombstone at the Raulerson Cemetery at his farm in Patterson has the name of all three wives on it and is emblazoned with the capitalized words "Pioneer Settler."

Focus on Florida

For the other original Raulersons, their time in Florida during the War of 1812 clearly made a significant impact on them; they all would move there.

Perhaps they wrongly assumed that the hostilities with the Seminoles were over. Perhaps in Florida they saw raw wilderness that they, like their father and grandfather before them, could clear and turn into workable farmland.

The first brother to make the move, albeit briefly, was Noel. He was based in Appling County but was going back and forth to Florida to hunt and trade furs. At least one of his trips involved bringing a slave from Florida over the border into Georgia. He moved to East Florida around 1821, building a cabin on Lake DeSoto and becoming the first white settler in Alligator, located near the Seminoles' Alligator Village and established the same year as Noel's arrival. Today, the community is called Lake City. Noel returned to Georgia in 1822 and died in 1830, but his family's experience in Alligator had made an impression on his six children, who all eventually moved back to Florida.

That first move by Noel to what would become Columbia County created the Raulersons' Florida gateway, where family members would either stop and establish themselves or eventually take off to find their fortunes in other parts of the Florida frontier.

Noel's move also made the Raulersons among the first giants of Florida's cattle industry, whose names include Hendry, Hardee, and Carlton, to arrive in Florida. His arrival was only bested by the Summerlin family, whose patriarch, cattle king Jacob Summerlin, in 1820 was the first Euro-American settler born in Florida after Spain turned over the peninsula to the United States through the Adams-Onis Treaty of 1819.

Noel was the patriarch of the most prolific line of the original Raulerson family. His son, Noel Rabun Raulerson Sr., a soldier in the Seminole Wars, had thirteen children, seven boys and six girls, all of whom would live in Florida. Noel Sr., a cattleman, was an early settler in Plant City before moving on to Polk County, where he at one time ran 4,000 cattle. Noel Sr.'s son, Noel Jr., an early settler of Basinger, had seventeen children, including Peter Raulerson, the founder of Okeechobee.

William was the second brother of the original Raulersons to move to Florida, and he would make it his permanent home. William married Elizabeth Moore and from at least 1815 to 1825 was living in Ware County, Georgia. He later moved his family to Florida, settling on the St. Marys River on the edge of the Okeefenokee Swamp near the Florida–Georgia border.

Fanny, the scandalous sister, would soon follow William to Florida with her children. Fanny had grown up as the only girl in a family of boys and had developed an independent streak. In 1810, at about the age of fourteen, she gave birth to daughter Fanna out of wedlock. "Fanny was described as having a stubborn and independent streak that kept her family in trouble with their local church authority," historian Dr. Christopher M. Esing reported for a 2022 article in *Currents*, a magazine published by the *Lake City Reporter*.

Esing said Fanny and family followed William to what would become Columbia County around 1826. William and Fanny's sister-in-law Eleanor, wife of their brother Noel, joined them in Florida in 1830 soon after Noel's death that year. She would move with some of her children to Hillsborough County in 1844.

Nimrod Raulerson, a cattle farmer and the youngest of the original Raulerson brothers, would also move to Florida at St. Marys around Fort Moniac. He enlisted as a soldier in the Second Seminole War both from Georgia (1834–36) and Florida (1837–39). His first wife, Sarah, was killed during Native and white conflicts in August 1839.

Family of Soldiers

William and Nimrod were the only original Raulersons to serve as soldiers in the Second Seminole War; many other Raulersons from the second generation enlisted. One of the sons of Jacob Raulerson, Nichabod, had five sons who would serve in the Seminole Wars. They were Franklin, Jackson, Hardy, Moses, and Thorp Raulerson.

Like their ancestor John Rawlinson, who was given land for his service in the American Revolution, men in the Raulerson family were rewarded with grants of land for fighting the Seminoles or participating in other wars. The Military Bounty Land Acts of 1850, 1852, and 1855 granted warrants for service in all Indian wars from 1790 to the Civil War. The warrants entitled the holder to free government lands because of their service.

Some of the Raulersons who didn't qualify for the Military Bounty Lands Act received land for a nominal fee under the Land Act of 1820, which made public domain lands in the unsettled frontier available for purchase for $1.25 per acre, or about $32.50 in 2023 dollars. While the Land

Act helped settle the frontier, it led to increased confiscation of Native American lands, forcing the Seminoles onto less desirable lands.

Between 1854 and 1920 records from the US Department of Interior's Bureau of Land Management show that eighty-one Florida land grants were issued to people with the surname Raulerson. By contrast, Florida's other leading agricultural family, the Carltons, had seventy-five land grants issued during the same period.

The land grant counts include those awarded through the more commonly known Homestead Act of 1862. Passed during the Civil War, it allowed any adult citizen or intended citizen who had never taken arms against the US government to claim 160 acres of surveyed government land. Claimants had two options: The first was to live on the land and cultivate it, and after five years the property became the filer's free and clear for a small filing fee. The second enabled a filer to claim property for $1.25 per acre after only six months of residency and trivial improvements.

A move to Florida was appealing to the Raulersons because of the availability of cheap or free land through these grants. Much of the land in Georgia had already been sold cheaply in the state lottery system. During the period of the lotteries from 1805 to 1833, three-fourths of the state's land was sold to 100,000 families and individuals, who paid an average of seven cents per acre.

Since the inheritance of family farms usually went to the oldest son, the younger sons were left to find their own ways to make a living. With the first- and second-generation Raulersons sometimes having more than a dozen children, there were plenty of sons looking for new ways to make a living with little investment.

The Raulersons who participated in the Seminole Wars also benefited from the Armed Occupation Act of 1842, which gave 160 acres of land to any head of family or single man over eighteen who was able to bear arms. It was intended both to encourage white settlement and to reduce federal expenses and the need for more soldiers by creating an armed civilian population willing to defend their fellow citizens. Besides being armed, the settler was required to have a house, live on the land for five years, and cultivate at least 5 acres.

The availability of free wild cattle left by the Spanish in Florida must have also been an attraction for the Raulersons, a family familiar with raising cattle at least going back to the days of John Rawlinson, who had 18 head at his death. That held open the prospect of raising beef cattle in addition to planting crops.

With the attraction of grants for free or cheap land and free cattle on which to grow a herd, the Raulerson family migration to Florida exploded. From only a few families in the 1830s, the Raulerson family's presence in Florida had grown so that, by 1880, the number of Raulerson families living in Florida reached 197, representing 81 percent of all Raulersons in the United States.

3

FLORIDA MIGRATION

Wade Goes All In

Frank Raulerson's father, Wade Raulerson, arrived in Florida relatively late—nearly four decades after Noel Raulerson first built a cabin in what is now Lake City.

When Wade Raulerson's father, Jacob, the oldest of the original Raulerson siblings, died in 1857 in Georgia, he left an estate that consisted of enslaved people, property in Cherokee and Wayne Counties, and other personal property.

The estate inventory showed the land and slaves (he had sixteen in 1850) were valued at $8,223.74, while the notes on hand and perishables were valued at $3,235.83, for a total estate of $11,459.37, worth $400,000 in 2025.

He directed that the property be sold and the proceeds split among eight people. Five were his sons—Nichabod, James, David, Russell, and Wade—and three were his sons-in-law, Samuel M. Pearson, Abraham M. Knight, and Hillery Cason. If the property was sold based on the value of the estate, each of the eight heirs would get $1,432.42 or about $50,000 in 2025 dollars.

The will awarded only about half of his surviving children a significant part of his estate while the other half received nominal sums of $10 each. He left his wife, Mary Ann, a female slave and her four children.

Jacob's youngest heir and child, Wade, was nineteen at the time of his father's death. He remained in Georgia for just two more years. He married a woman named Agnes Elizabeth Norfleet, a seventeen-year-old native of Wayne County, in 1859. But the marriage was brief. The next year, twenty-two-year-old Wade headed to Florida and the prospect of cheap land, but he was not living with Agnes.

Wade curiously showed up as living in both Georgia and Florida during the 1860 Census, and in both instances no wife was listed. In the Georgia census, enumerated July 26, he was reported as living in Wayne County, with his occupation listed as a farmer. He was living at the home of Shadruck Anderson, forty-six, and his wife, Elizabeth, forty-five, and their eight children, ages six to twenty-one. At the time, Wade owned a twenty-four-year-old male slave and had Georgia real estate worth $2,500, and personal property worth $2,000.

The census taken in Florida, enumerated a month after the census in Georgia was taken, showed that Wade was living in Volusia County. On the same page, living in a separate dwelling, his older brother James, forty, was listed along with James's wife, Ruth, thirty-five, and their six children, ages two to eighteen. The occupation for both brothers was listed as farmer.

Wade reported owning no land in Florida in 1860 and having a personal estate of $500, about $18,000 in 2025 dollars. James apparently already had land in Florida, with the census showing he had real estate worth $2,000, and a personal estate worth $5,000, or about $185,000 in 2025 dollars.

Why Wade showed up in two censuses that year is unknown, but since the Florida census was taken after the Georgia census, it seems possible that his friends in Georgia may have listed him as still living there, even though he had already moved to Florida. Also unknown is what happened to his first wife, Agnes. No death records or divorce records could be found under her name.

Settling in Seville

The prospect of cheap land apparently brought Wade to Florida because four months after the census was taken, he became a Florida property owner. Bureau of Land Management records showed that on October 1, 1860, he received 120 acres of land in Seville, then part of Volusia County, under the Land Act of 1820, which allowed him to purchase the land for $1.20 per acre for a total of $144, or $5,300 in 2025 dollars.

The act was passed in response to a financial panic the year before, as settlers were faced with foreclosure because of their inability to repay loans from a previous act that allowed them to purchase public domain land on credit. The new act ended the extension of credit but reduced the minimum price per acre from $2.00 per acre to $1.25, and the minimum tract size from 160 acres to 80. Thus, the new law reduced land speculators operating on credit while also making the land more affordable for more settlers.

While it may have appeared that land grant recipients were getting a bargain, the endeavor wasn't for the work averse. Clearing land of thick woods and underbrush to make it suitable for farming or grazing would take place over years and, in the nineteenth century, was accomplished mostly with a hand ax and a few other tools made by a blacksmith.

After a tree was felled, branches were cut off and the trunk rolled aside. Then came the biggest challenge: attacking the stump. A grub ax was used to cut off small roots while a pick axe would cut off larger ones and also break up or remove rocks. If a horse, mule, or ox was available, it might be used to assist in pulling the stump. Brush, branches, and twigs would be piled around the stumps and burned. But sometimes in the rush to get crops planted, roots were left in the ground to deteriorate and planting was done around them. Cutting trees usually occurred during the winter, when farmwork slowed. Grubbing the stumps usually began in the spring, when the ground thawed. Sometimes, only a few additional acres were cleared each year before the farmer had to go back to focusing on planting and harvesting crops. Because of the work required to clear and cultivate the land, it wasn't unusual in the nineteenth century for homesteading families like the Raulersons to have multiple children, providing more hands to perform farm chores and clear land.

In purchasing his land at Seville, Wade departed from where most of the Raulersons had been locating within or around Columbia County in North Florida. Seville, located between Daytona Beach on the east coast and Ocala in Florida's interior, was about 100 miles from their Raulerson relatives in Columbia County.

A month after Wade received the land grants, he married a local girl, Catharine Frances Hart, on November 15, 1860. Catharine was the third of seven children of William B. Hart, forty-five, and Mary Ann Hart, forty-five, of Volusia County. William Hart's occupation was listed as planter in the 1860 Census and showed he owned six slaves. Hart was a master of the land grant. The name William B. Hart shows up thirteen times in Bureau of Land Management records for land grants in Florida received between 1847 and 1884 in Putnam, Sumter, Marion, and Volusia Counties for a total of 858 acres.

Wade and Catharine had their first child, Keightley Braxton Raulerson, on September 19, 1861. The boy was given Wade's late mother's surname, which was spelled differently as Keightly.

But as Wade was clearing land for his farm and settling down to his new life in Florida, the Civil War interrupted his plans. He fought for the Confederacy, mustering in May 6, 1862, serving as a private in the Seventh Infantry, and mustering out March 1, 1863. A separate record at the cemetery where he was buried shows he reenlisted in July 1863 in Volusia County. He was paroled in Waldo, Florida, on May 10, 1865, when his unit surrendered at Tallahassee.

While Wade was away at war, his second son, William Bartholomew, was born in 1864, and two years later, after Wade returned to Seville, he and Catharine had another boy, Claudius (Claude) Algernon Raulerson.

Move to Geneva

After Claude's birth in 1866, Wade and Catharine and their growing brood left Seville and moved 55 miles south to Harney Cove in Orange County. Today, the community is called Geneva and is part of Seminole County.

Wade apparently had kept his property in Seville—various family members lived there well into the next century—and in 1880 purchased another 80-acre tract in Harney Cove under the Land Act. Just three years later, Wade purchased another 160-acre tract nearby under the same act. Meanwhile, brother James and his family had moved to St. Augustine by 1870, land records show, and later moved to and remained in Espanola, near Bunnell in Flagler County, and were one of the first three white families to settle there.

Why did Wade Raulerson move his family to Harney Cove after settling in Seville? While no documentation could be found to verify what he was raising—census records consistently listed his occupation as farmer—it's likely that he was running cattle and even growing some of the state's early citrus, since the family had groves in the region through the early twentieth century.

Harney Cove/Geneva had been the site of some of the earliest groves in Florida until the Central Florida freezes of 1894 and 1895 moved the industry southward. Also, there was less competition in the south for cattle grazing in the open range than in the north as the population of Euro-American settlers slowly moved from north to south.

Harney Cove was located on Lake Harney, which connects to the St. Johns River, ending at the Atlantic Ocean in Jacksonville. After the Second Seminole War, settlers began inhabiting the region, and by the 1850s, the cattle industry arrived.

Adding to their first three children born in Seville, Wade and Catharine had six more children in their new home: Christopher Herschel in 1867; Ida Kate in 1870; Cyrus Franklin (Frank) in 1873; Lillian Courtney in 1877; Mary Sevenah in 1879; and Lucius Adolphus in 1886.

As more people arrived in Harney Cove, the community could offer more amenities for settler families like Wade and Catharine's. In 1874, a one-room schoolhouse was built out of logs followed by a replacement plank building in 1877. In 1875, the first store, Coefield's, opened on the northwest shore of Lake Geneva, with postal service established soon after. The burial ground that would become known as the Geneva Cemetery was consecrated with its first interment in 1878.

In 1880, the Geneva Dock was built at Lake Harney Landing. It was also that year that Harney Cove came to be called Geneva, a name apparently plucked from the hometown of a new arrival, Mrs. Van Brunt Wilcox of Geneva, New York. By 1887 the Orange County Business Directory reported a population of 300 for Geneva.

Catharine died in 1898 at the age of sixty. Two years later, the 1900 Census showed only three siblings remained at the family farm with Wade: Frank, twenty-seven; his sister Lillian, twenty-three; and Lucius, fourteen. The oldest son, Keightley, thirty-nine, had struck out on his own, leaving Wade's farm by 1885 and later running his own cattle and establishing his own citrus grove in Geneva and later in Fort Pierce. The second-oldest son, William, thirty-six, a farmer who would eventually become a carpenter, was living in Geneva with his wife, Ida, twenty-nine, and four children, ages three to twelve. The third-oldest son, Claude, thirty-four, was living in Geneva and would have his own citrus grove there. The fourth-oldest son, Herschel, thirty-three, was in Miami, where he would soon serve on the city council. The oldest daughter, Ida Kate, twenty-nine, was living in Madison, Florida, with her husband, Gibon Coffee, and their six children, ages one to nine. The youngest daughter, Mary, twenty-one, was living in Geneva with husband, Homer Nicholson, and a newborn child.

4

FORT PIERCE BECKONS

Keightley Seizes Opportunity

As the iron horse arrived on Florida's East Coast, Keightley Raulerson saw opportunity beyond the little community of Geneva where he grew up and began running his own cattle. The railroad arrived in Florida in the 1860s with the Florida Railroad line running across the state from Fernandina Beach to Cedar Key. But it was tycoon Henry Morrison Flagler's railway that would shape the Atlantic coast of Florida and promote the state as a tourist destination.

Flagler's Florida East Coast Railway expanded ever-southward as he built destination hotels. Flagler's railway reached Titusville in 1893, Fort Pierce in January 1894, West Palm Beach two months later, Miami in 1896, Homestead in 1904 and, finally, after seven years constructing the Overseas Railroad, Key West in 1912, just before Flagler's death in 1913.

Flagler didn't build a hotel in Fort Pierce, but a train depot was established there, making it a stop on his railway. Like other cities where the railway landed, Fort Pierce was transformed from a tiny frontier settlement into a small town almost overnight. Tourists visited and, seeing the region's promise, sometimes returned to stay for good. Hotels were opened, restaurants were established, downtowns created, municipalities and counties chartered, and newspapers began publishing.

It's easy to see why Keightley Raulerson, a cattleman and citrus grower, would be attracted to Fort Pierce, which originated as a US Army fort built in 1838 during the Second Seminole War and named for its commander, Lt. Col. Benjamin Pierce, brother of future US President Franklin Pierce.

After the Central Florida freezes of 1894 and 1895, Florida's nascent citrus industry moved south to places like Fort Pierce, which already had a thriving pineapple industry. With the arrival of the railway, citrus grown in the region, previously transported by steamer or a slow-moving oxen cart making barely more than 10 miles a day could be loaded into a train car and shipped to northern climes in a timelier manner. Keightley also saw opportunity for cattle to be more quickly delivered to market, as opposed to driving huge herds by horse hundreds of miles to a few select train depots or shipping ports.

Keightley arrived in Fort Pierce in 1896, just two years after the railway reached the community and put it on the map. Keightley's move was obviously a play meant to expand existing business interests, since he still had citrus groves in upper Brevard County and in Geneva. Census records from 1900 show Keightley still living in Fort Pierce, along with his wife, Elizabeth Randolph Raulerson, who was born in Missouri and had come to Fort Pierce from Wauchula. That same year, he won a seat in the Florida House of Representatives. A Democrat, he represented Brevard County, which then included what are now St. Lucie and Indian River Counties and parts of Martin and Okeechobee Counties. Fort Pierce's population grew to 500 by the turn of the century.

The Titusville-based *Florida Star*, which kept close tabs on the "Hon. K. B. Raulerson," reported his various comings and goings during his time as a legislator, including his visits to orange groves he owned in Seville and near the St. Johns River, as well as his business interests in Fort Pierce. Besides his legislative activities in the early days, he was a member of a committee that helped Fort Pierce incorporate in 1901. When St. Lucie County was created in 1905, after being carved out of Brevard County, Keightley became one of its first county commissioners. He served on the first grand jury in St. Lucie County and was active on the Board of Trade, the chamber of commerce of its time.

By 1905, Keightley's success reached a point at which he brought family members into the business, forming the Fort Pierce–based East Coast Cattle Co. with younger brothers Frank, still in Geneva, and Herschel, who could represent the company's interests in Miami, and friend J. T. Feaster, also of Miami.

Back in Geneva, Frank likely had been helping to oversee Keightley's cattle and citrus interests as well as his father's farm. But he wasn't all

Keightley Braxton (K. B.) Raulerson was on the first board of St. Lucie County Commissioners when the county was formed in 1905. The commissioners (*from the left*) are W. R. Hardee, J. F. Bell, K. B. Raulerson, Paul Kroegel, and R. D. Holmes. (Courtesy of Florida Photographic Concern/St. Lucie County Regional History Center.)

business. In 1901, Frank, twenty-eight, married Annie Louise Jacobs, twenty-two, of nearby Chuluota, just 7 miles south of Geneva. Annie Louise was the oldest daughter in a family of nine children—three boys and six girls—of farmer Joshua Jacobs and his wife, Mary. Joshua, born in Columbus County, North Carolina, had come to Florida as a child with his parents, William and Dorcas Jacobs, and Mary was born in Florida.

Wedding bells would also ring a few years later for Keightley and Frank's widowed father, who had moved to Fort Pierce. In April 1906, eight years after Catharine's death, Wade married Catharine's younger sister, Sevenah C. Trowel, sixty-two. Her first husband, Nathan Trowel, an early Florida citrus grower in Umatilla, died in 1894 at the age of sixty-four.

Wade and Sevenah's marital bliss wouldn't last long. Wade died the following August at Keightley's home in Fort Pierce after an extended illness. The *Miami Evening Record* observed his death with the headline "Prominent Man Dead."

"W. H. Raulerson, an old citizen of Orange County, but for the past year or two a resident of Fort Pierce, died yesterday, after a lingering illness," the dispatch read. "He was 68 years of age, and was a man of sterling worth. He will be buried at Geneva, his old home in Orange county." The burial in the Geneva Cemetery took place next to Catharine, Wade's first wife and the mother of his children.

Frank Joins Keightley

In 1907, a year after his father's death, Frank Raulerson moved to Fort Pierce from Geneva with Annie Louise. Also with them was their toddler son, Alfred Keightley, born in 1904. Frank looked up to Keightley, who was a dozen years older, as both mentor and business partner, so it seemed only natural that he honor him by giving his son the middle name Keightley.

By moving to Fort Pierce, Frank could work more closely with Keightley and their East Coast Cattle Co., which included a slaughterhouse, icehouse, and retail meat operations in Fort Pierce and at least a stockyard in Miami. The company's operations also included cattle raising and land buying. A sister company, Raulerson Grocery Company, was formed to handle retail grocery operations, and a grocery store was opened in Fort Pierce on Pine Street, now Second Street.

A 1906 article in the *Florida Agriculturalist* periodical provided a window into the East Coast Cattle Co. operations in the early days. In the article, Keightley gave a reporter a tour of the company's stock pen just south of Fort Pierce to see "a carload of cattle and pigs that had just been received for the Fort Pierce market. The shipment was composed of 30 head of beef cattle and 40 hogs."

The article quoted Keightley as saying that the company received a similar shipment every two weeks "for the market here and Miami," a reference to the company's stockyard in Miami. "This shows what can be accomplished in Florida, and no part of the state is better suited for the raising of beef cattle than the section west of Fort Pierce," the article concluded. A 1907 article in the *Florida Star* noted that Keightley had recently bought "all the beef and stock cattle" on Merritt Island and was going to place it on the range on the mainland near Titusville "as the range on the island has turned out very poor of late."

But all was not roses for the Raulerson extended family. Keightley and his wife, Elizabeth, quietly divorced around 1907. They had no children.

Elizabeth continued living in Fort Pierce and for thirty-five years operated the Rose Inn, a fourteen-room boardinghouse on Orange Avenue, until her death in 1945 at the age of eighty-two.

Keightley wasn't the only Raulerson brother with marital problems. A domestic scandal that caught headlines in 1907 involved brother and business partner Herschel Raulerson, who by then was a Miami city councilman after serving as Dade County treasurer. The scandal erupted when it was revealed that Herschel had left his wife, Annie, and was "living in adultery" with Mrs. Josephine Stewart, according to the *Miami Metropolis*. Herschel later resigned his post, left Miami, divorced Annie, and married Josephine. The couple lived in New York State and Arizona for nearly a decade before returning to Florida in 1916 and moving to Palm Beach County, where Herschel served as a county commissioner in the 1930s.

After the 1907 scandal, Herschel was never mentioned as being associated with East Coast Cattle Co. Keightley, or K.B., as he was referred to in print, continued to catch positive headlines from the *Fort Pierce News*, founded in 1903, and its rival upstart, the *St. Lucie County Tribune*, founded in 1905.

A 1909 article in the *St. Lucie County Tribune* duly reported an instance in which Keightley entered the newspaper's offices with "some of the finest specimens of Irish potatoes ever raised in this city." The article continued: "The East Coast Cattle Company have also decided to plant on their land next year an orange and grapefruit grove of twenty acres. Mr. Raulerson is elated with the success of his potato venture and predicts a rosy future for that infant industry in this section."

A New Wife

On the home front, forty-six-year-old Keightley in August 1908 married forty-one-year-old Effie Morgan Alderman, the divorced wife of his business associate (David) Lee Alderman, with whom he helped ship local cattle to Cuba.

Effie and Lee, who also served as a Fort Pierce city marshal, had a contentious divorce over property, mostly over their cattle and citrus homestead on what is now Adams Ranch west of Fort Pierce. Their divorce was finalized in 1906, but they had been feuding for years, with Effie in 1904 being granted a petition "to take charge of and manage her own estate and property as a married woman removed." That same year, she also obtained a restraining order preventing Lee from "interfering with the statutory property of complainant particularly the crop of oranges upon her grove" after alleging that he had been "depredating upon her said grove and removing fruit therefrom."

Married in 1883, Effie and Lee were the parents of five sons and two daughters, including Ruth, a piano prodigy who showcased her musical talents around Fort Pierce as a young girl.

Keightley's marriage to Effie united two of Florida's outstanding cattle- and citrus-raising families. Effie was the daughter of Eli O. Morgan, another cattle and citrus baron and early settler. Arriving in Basinger around 1885, where he set up the headquarters for his cattle operation, Morgan by 1899 owned more than 20,000 head of cattle. His first wife, Leacy, died in 1897, and he married Hetty Scharfschwerdt in 1903. Morgan later built a home and established citrus groves at Bluefield in St. Lucie County, and was shipping out an estimated 10,000 boxes of fruit the winter before his death. He died in 1914. Besides Effie, one of his surviving daughters was Emma, who married county judge Fred Fee.

By newspaper accounts, the K. B. Raulersons were enjoying a life of social, commercial, and political success in the second decade of the twentieth century. Keightley's various business trips were recorded in newspapers from Titusville to Miami, as were his wife's trips to visit relatives. They had become one of the region's earliest car owners, with the purchase of a Model T in 1911.

They had a farm far south of Fort Pierce, where Keightley was growing 40 acres of Irish potatoes and where he had also planted grapefruit, orange, and other citrus trees. The 1910 Census recorded five of Effie's children living with them that year.

In the political realm, Keightley was called back to the St. Lucie County Commission and was appointed in January 1913.

Keightley's only impediment appeared to be his health. He was plagued by illness, as newspapers recounted over the years. The *St. Lucie County Tribune* gave this account of his ultimate illness in its November 14, 1913, edition:

Six weeks ago Mr. Raulerson accompanied his wife to Atlanta for treatment by specialists. While in the city he consulted eminent specialists in regard to a minor ailment and submitted to a slight operation which was entirely successful. He was discharged from the hospital, where both he and his wife had been operated upon, and took a room in the Hotel Marion. At that time a sudden change in the weather occurred, frost and a light snow being upon the ground and in his weakened condition from the operation he contracted pneumonia, for four weeks he battled against his malady, and following seventeen days of unconsciousness he passed away Monday. When his condition became serious his brother Frank Raulerson and brother-in-law, Judge Fred Fee, were summoned and remained at his bedside until death.

Both Frank Raulerson and Fred Fee were signers of Keightley's will, which was written October 24 in Atlanta and filed and recorded on November 18, 1913. He bequeathed all his property and possessions to Effie with a provision that his stepson Morgan Alderman be given "the stock of cattle known as the John Jones cattle, consisting of about fifty head, and now in the range in St. Lucie County, Florida."

But the disposition of the assets of the fifty-two-year-old Keightley with the East Coast Cattle Co. was not amicable. In 1914, the *St. Lucie County Tribune* reported on a lawsuit in which Effie sued Frank Raulerson and the East Coast Cattle Co. In the days before Keightley's death, the prime property on which Raulerson Grocery was located in downtown Fort Pierce was transferred from K.B. and Effie to the East Coast Cattle Co.

The outcome of the case was never disclosed in the local newspapers, but Frank retained ultimate control of the East Coast Cattle Co. and Raulerson Grocery. Keightley's obituary in the *Tribune* detailed just how big an operation East Coast Cattle Co. had become: "The company [has been] buying cattle in all parts of Florida and Georgia and operating extensive slaughterhouses in Fort Pierce, supplying practically all the native beef used along the East Coast from New Smyrna to Key West, [with] shipments being made on practically every express train leaving this city. The company has also operated in the regular trade in many of the towns along the coast, and in Fort Pierce. Their meat and grocery business is known as the Raulerson Grocery Company."

Raulerson Families Multiply

Like the Seminoles who originally settled in North Florida, the Raulersons pushed south, where more land became available as the Seminoles retreated south and the lands they claimed dwindled. One, Noel Rabun Raulerson Sr., would largely be responsible for spreading the Raulerson name throughout Central and South Florida. Known as Rabun or Rabe, Noel Rabun Raulerson Sr. was the son of Noel Raulerson, one of the original five Raulerson siblings. Rabun was also Wade Hampton Raulerson's first cousin.

After first settling in North Florida near the other Raulersons, Rabun and wife, Tempa "Tempie" Whidden, moved to West Central Florida, with Rabun receiving 160 acres of bounty land in Hillsborough County. By 1856, he was living in Polk County on the southern edge of Lake Hancock.

Rabun served in both the Second and Third Seminole Wars. Despite his military commitments, he and Tempie created a large family, producing thirteen children—seven boys and six girls—between 1841 and 1865. By 1874, Rabun moved his cattle to the Kissimmee River Valley, settling at Basinger and purchasing land and a home from Henry L. Parker, who ran a trading post and had also moved to the region from Columbia County. Rabun was followed in 1876 by his grown son, Noel Rabun Raulerson Jr. Sons Peter, David, William, and Archibald also eventually made the move to Basinger.

Despite the migration of his sons to Basinger and the family's growing success in the cattle business, Rabun moved back to Bartow with Tempie in 1892. Tempie died there in 1904, and Rabun died in 1910 at the age of ninety-one, leaving more than one hundred direct descendants.

Rabun's fourth son, Noel Rabun Raulerson Jr., was even more prodigious and longer living. He and his wife, Elizabeth, had seventeen children, all of whom lived to adulthood. Most of the boys raised cattle or farmed, and many of the girls married husbands who worked in agriculture. When Noel died in 1952 at the age of 103, he left a total of 322 descendants: 13 children, 110 grandchildren, 165 great-grandchildren, and 34 great-great-grandchildren. A wire story carried throughout the country about his death

Peter and Louisiana Chandler Raulerson appear in a photo taken about 1902 with their son Cornelius, the first Euro-American child born in what would become Okeechobee. (Courtesy of the Okeechobee Historical Society.)

wondered whether he had set a record for most descendants. "Florida Resident, 103, Left 322 Descendants," said the headline on a story from the *News-Herald* of Marshfield, Wisconsin.

Okeechobee's Founding Father

Another of Noel Jr.'s brothers, Peter, nine years younger, would make a huge impact on the Kissimmee River Valley as the founding father of what would be known as Okeechobee.

In 1896, Peter (1857–1947), his wife, Louisiana Chandler (1861–1948), and their children loaded their belongings into an oxcart and horse-drawn buggy and moved from Basinger about 16 miles southeast to become the first Euro-American settlers of what would become known as Okeechobee. The section was then called The Bend, so named because the land was located in a bend between Taylor Creek and the Kissimmee River just a few miles north of Lake Okeechobee. Taylor Creek was named after US President Zachary Taylor, who as a US Army colonel was victorious over the Seminoles there in 1837. It was originally called the Onoshohatchee River.

The Raulersons arrived at The Bend with six children: Lewis (b. 1880), Adeline (b. 1882), Ada (b. 1888), Melville (b. 1890), Harmon (b. 1892), and Faith (b. 1895). Their oldest daughter, Mattie (b. 1878), had married and for the time being remained in Basinger. Their eighth and last child, Cornelius, was born in 1901, and became the first Euro-American born in what would become Okeechobee.

Peter and Louisiana Raulerson started the first school in the area. Peter Raulerson also started the first Star Route, a mail service on horseback. In 1902, with the help of Robert LaMartin of Basinger, Peter Raulerson in 1902 established a post office at The Bend and housed it in his home. The Bend was renamed Tantie, in honor of schoolteacher Tantie Huckabee, when the new post office was established. By 1911, the community became known as Okeechobee and was incorporated in 1915, with Peter Raulerson becoming its first mayor and his son-in-law W. L. Coats a councilman.

Peter died in 1947 at the age of ninety, and Louisiana died in 1948 at the age of eighty-seven leaving 83 survivors: 3 sons, 2 daughters, 22 grandchildren, 50 great-grandchildren, and 6 great-great-grandchildren. With his brother Noel's 322 survivors, the count of Raulerson heirs in the Okeechobee/Basinger region exceeded 400 by the early 1950s.

5

POLLY PARKER (EMATELOYE)

A Seminole Hero

In the Third Seminole War, a heroine emerged who would be closely associated with the Cow Creek waterway. She was Emateloye Estenletkvte, more widely known by her English name of Polly Parker. She was Muskogee, a member of the Bird Clan, and part of Chupco's band.

Perhaps no Seminole is more misunderstood or underrated. Because written US Army and newspaper accounts of the time focused on male warriors, there is little biographical information about Polly, who does not enjoy the celebrity of other Native American women such as Sacagawea. Yet her significance to her people is just as profound and her acts of daring perhaps even greater.

Assembling a biography of Polly is fraught with the typical challenges of researching Native Americans because of reliance on more plentiful but biased military records versus sparse information passed down through the Seminoles' oral tradition that is not generally public or recorded. Another challenge is the frequent use of similar English names adopted by Seminoles.

A Seminole woman referred to simply as "Polly" enters into the written record during the Second Seminole War, making Polly Parker a candidate as being the woman because she would have been of similar age and because so few Seminole women—including those named Polly—remained in Florida at the time of the writing.

This iconic photo of Polly Parker, also known as Emateloye, was taken in 1909 by Harry Hill at Florida Photographic Concern studio in Fort Pierce. Polly Parker was a frequent visitor to Fort Pierce from her camp at Cow Creek, 17 miles away. Hill displayed the photo on a wall at his studio that featured his best work. (Courtesy of Florida Photographic Concern/St. Lucie County Regional History Center.)

Author James W. Covington identifies Polly, a Seminole woman, and her husband, Chai, as guides for the Army during the Second Seminole War. He says Polly and Chai led patrols into the Everglades in efforts to eject Seminoles from Florida and send them to Indian Territory from 1835 to 1842. After the Second Seminole War, Polly and Chai apparently were outcasts from what remained of the tribe. Polly and Chai were relocated near Bradenton "for their own safety" and later, by 1845, were helping a storekeeper run a trading post for Seminoles at Fort Brooke in south Tampa.

With the outbreak of the Third Seminole War, Polly and Chai were asked once again to serve as scouts. "When the 1855–58 war broke out, Chai committed suicide rather than face the Seminoles again," Covington wrote.

Covington wrote that Polly accompanied Capt. Jacob E. Mickler during his patrols of Lake Okeechobee and the Kissimmee River in the summer of 1857. A woman named "Polly" also surfaces in the writings of Capt. Abner Doubleday, who would become better known as a Civil War general and the mythical inventor of baseball. Doubleday wrote that Polly, who married a Spaniard after her first husband's death, worked with him in 1857 to search for Seminoles on islands in Florida Bay. In Doubleday's view, Polly's true allegiance lay with the Seminoles as she never successfully located any members of the tribe: "I do not believe she ever found any indians for us or intended to find them. She kept out of their way & did what she could to prevent our troops from meeting them." Doubleday said Polly "presented quite a picturesque appearance straddling the bow of my boat with one foot on each side occasionally dipping in the water."

These stories have been woven into narratives about Polly in twenty-first-century newspapers. But do they reflect the life of the real Polly Parker? Willard Steele, former preservation officer for the Seminole Tribe, who once subscribed to the theory that the woman mentioned by Mickler and Doubleday was Polly Parker, said he no longer believes that because of evidence recently uncovered by another researcher. Steele said he was not at liberty to reveal the evidence.

If Polly Parker had ever worked for the government, that service apparently wasn't enough to prevent her from being rounded up with other Seminoles in the government's forced relocation of Seminoles to Oklahoma. In 1858, Polly was taken into custody by the US Army, southeast of modern-day Sebring.

According to historian Albert DeVane, Polly was one of thirty-nine Cow Creek Seminoles who had been rounded up along the lower Kissimmee River, Lake Istokpoga, Fish Eating Creek, and the cypress swamps and marshes along the East Coast in what are now St. Lucie and Martin Counties.

To achieve their goal of removing Seminoles from the peninsula, the US Army would target women and children. After their capture, the male warriors were told that their families were being sent west and that if they wanted to be with them, the men should surrender.

Gen. William S. Harney and his Florida volunteers, incentivized with rewards of $500 for the capture of Seminole men and $250 for women, seized Polly near Lake Istokpoga and loaded her and the other captives in oxcarts and transported them to Fort Brooke, now downtown Tampa. From Fort Brooke, Polly was taken 35 miles by boat south to Egmont Key, where she was imprisoned and held under armed guard. Because Egmont Key was a depot for the removal of the Seminoles from Florida, tribal members have referred to it as "The Dark Place," "Our Alcatraz," or simply as a concentration camp.

Polly was held in the stockade at Egmont Key until the arrival of the side-wheel steamer *Grey Cloud*, which was utilized to transport Seminoles up the Gulf of Mexico to New Orleans and up the Mississippi near the Arkansas River, where they would travel to Indian Territory. Also aboard the *Grey Cloud* as it lumbered into Egmont Key from Fort Myers on May 4, 1858, was another Seminole prisoner central to the tribe's history: Billy Bowlegs (Holata Micco) and a Miccosukee party of 125, who had surrendered and agreed to be moved west to Indian Territory in exchange for a monetary settlement.

This *Grey Cloud* voyage was its last during Seminole relocation, with the final substantive attempt to remove Seminoles from Florida occurring in February 1859. By the end of the Third Seminole War, military patrols and rewards to bounty hunters for the capture of Seminoles had reduced the population in the state to about 200, most of them men.

After leaving Egmont Key, the *Grey Cloud* followed the coast up the western side of the peninsula for a scheduled stop at St. Marks, south of Tallahassee, to pick up wood for refueling.

The public narrative of Polly's escape relies heavily on Euro-American accounts. DeVane, founder of the Peace River Historical Society, had spent decades interviewing the Cow Creek Seminoles at the Brighton Reservation and said he developed his narrative of Polly's journey based on records and interviews with elders, including her daughter, Lucy Tiger (Fee-Gaa Pee). Writes DeVane of Polly's escape:

> The ship being quite heavily loaded and her boilers being fired with cord wood, it was necessary to skirt the coast, taking on wood at St. Marks and Mobile before arrival in New Orleans, where transfer was made to river steamers to transport them up to the Mississippi River to Arkansas.
>
> While wood was being loaded for fuel for the boilers at St. Marks Polly asked for permission through an interpreter for some of her band to go ashore into the woods along the St. Marks River to gather some roots and herbs to make medicine, as some of her band were quite sick. The permission was granted by the officer in charge. . . . When quite a distance away from the boat and at a prearranged signal, they all ran in different directions.

DeVane said a group of five Cow Creek Seminoles reunited at night, using owl calls as a prearranged signal, and began their trek southward. The Seminole Tribe says Polly was accompanied by six other women.

Based on an interview with Lucy Tiger at Brighton in 1968, *Miami Herald* reporter Nixon Smiley said the women included Polly's mother and sister and another Seminole named Pahee. Smiley wrote that a male warrior also escaped from the *Grey Cloud*.

While some accounts say Polly and the others returned to Fish Eating Creek or the Everglades, both DeVane and the Seminole Tribe put her return at Lake Okeechobee, near Cow Creek territory, a trip that would have been a 335-mile walk. Wrote DeVane: "At last they arrived at the northeast side of Lake Okeechobee, their old hunting grounds. They recovered a cook pot from the charred ruins of their former camp. A canoe was found hidden in the sawgrass in which they slowly made their way south to the Everglades—to their people."

The escape made Polly a folk hero among both Seminoles and white people, establishing her place in history as a symbol of Seminole independence, courage, defiance, and love of homeland. Because of her daring escape, she is often referred to as the Evangeline of the Seminoles, a reference to the fictional character in the Longfellow poem who led the Acadians out of their homeland in Canada to Louisiana.

Little is known about Polly's years as a fugitive or where she lived. The federal government's attention to the Seminoles and their relocation waned as the Civil War got under way, and certainly by that time the desire to capture a noncombatant runaway Native American had all but been forgotten. With national sympathy for Native Americans increasing, Polly's flight became legend, and she grew to become known among both Seminoles and white people as Old Polly Parker and Aunt Polly.

When Clay MacCauley in his 1881 survey located the Cow Creek settlement, he did not specifically mention Polly, who around that time was married to a Seminole named Henry Parker, said to have taken his name from the settler Henry Parker, who ran a trading post at Fort Drum.

Later in the 1880s, the woman who became known as Polly Parker was frequently seen in Fort Pierce on the east coast, some 17 miles from Cow Creek. The community had the Hogg and later Cobb trading posts, which commonly traded with the Seminoles. While visiting the posts, the Seminoles would camp along Moore's Creek, the tiny waterway that flows into the Indian River where the Manatee Observation and Education Center is today.

Hogg's trading post was in a group of eight houses in a section called Edgartown, where a "dead-line fence beyond which Indians might not pass still stood," according to a Historical Records & State Archives survey. "At that time the country was in its wild state and only a few fishermen and the Indians patronized the one store."

The fence was just a few blocks west of the Indian River, with most of the Euro-American settlements staying close to the coast and distances beyond perceived as perilous. Year by year, the boundaries were extended as settlements grew.

Pioneer Emily Lagow Bell wrote about her encounters with Polly Parker in a memoir about her early years in St. Lucie from 1876 to 1898. She wrote that she first met Polly in 1882, when she and other Seminoles, including her daughter Lucy Tiger, three children, and a Black woman named Nance, who was Tuscanuga's wife, were in Fort Pierce. Bell said she was making syrup cookies at her home on the Indian River and gave them to Polly.

Mary Summerlin, who reported her interactions with the Cow Creek

Seminoles in a series published in the local *News-Tribune* in 1936, recalled first encountering Polly in 1895 while Summerlin was a teacher in St. Lucie, now known as St. Lucie Village, just north of Fort Pierce. She described Polly's arrival:

> on a lean pony, bareback, astride with only a saddlebag of croker sacks slung across the pony's back. She dismounted at Ned Summerlin's gate and was welcomed very cordially by the whole family, invited to sit at our table and was led to talk by Mr. Summerlin, who was liked and trusted by the Seminoles. She told us her people were camped just over the hills, back of St. Lucie for a little while, and invited us to visit them, so in a few days the horse was hitched to the wagon and we returned her visit—my first and last to an Indian camp for almost 30 years.

Summerlin did not say precisely where Polly's camp was: "I don't remember details, except that they had a deerskin stretched under the trees about five or six feet from the ground, not yet cured and in it strips of venison were drying along with the skin. Aunt Polly very happily gave us bundles of dry skins to sit on and very patiently taught me many Indian words. I wrote them down as they sounded and had quite a vocabulary."

Polly had become well enough known in Fort Pierce that in 1909 photographer Harry Hill had her sit for a portrait at his Florida Photographic Concern studio on Pine Street, now Second Street. The photo is the only one of Polly known to exist. Hill founded his photographic studio in 1900, and in 2025 the tiny building was still standing, converted into a cider bar.

The photo shoot of Polly appears as photo No. 839 in Hill's logbook as "Aunt Polly." Hill considered the photo one of his best, displaying it on a wall in his studio with other examples of his greatest work.

Cow Creek is about 5 miles closer to Okeechobee than Fort Pierce, and Polly also was a frequent visitor to what became downtown Okeechobee and Meserve Hardware owned by Faith Meserve, daughter of Peter Raulerson, and her husband, Ellis. Faith Meserve liked Polly so much that she hung Hill's portrait of her in the store, where it was displayed for decades. "Meserve always enjoyed the old woman's presence in the store, and even though she spoke no English, she was always smiling and nodding," historian Harry Kersey wrote.

In 1899, the Friends of the Florida Seminoles organization took up her cause, buying an 80-acre tract in what is now St. Lucie County, according to Kersey. But the land, referred to as Polly's Camp, was lost in 1926 for failure to pay property taxes when pioneer J. G. Coats brought suit to quiet title after paying the delinquent taxes.

Polly was in the limelight in her final months of life as the center of a festival in the spring of 1922 in West Palm Beach. The celebration, called the Sun Dance Festival, was intended to promote tourism by showcasing Seminole culture.

The *Miami Metropolis*, quoting promoter A. V. Brown, reported in announcing the visit that Polly "has promised to come in from Cow Creek to take part in the Seminole Sun Dance" and would lead the Seminoles in a parade. In the days before the festival, the *Tampa Morning Tribune* reported that a festival official was in the Everglades encouraging members of the Cow Creek and Big Cypress's bands to attend.

The *Tampa Morning Tribune* reported that Polly had indeed attended the festival: "Aunt Polly Parker, reputed to be 100 years of age, and the oldest Seminole living, is here and posed freely today for her picture." The notice was carried by the wires, without photo, and appeared in newspapers throughout the country.

Polly died in in the summer of 1922, just four months after her appearance at the Sun Dance. According to historian Kersey, she was buried in a traditional log pen grave between Okeechobee and the Brighton Reservation. The *Sebring White Way* was one of the few newspapers that reported her death that summer, saying that word has been passed along by Mose Lanier of Basinger. "Up to a few days of her death she was said to be very bright and her memory exceedingly keen, and she used to tell of things that happened almost from the beginning of the United States," the Sebring newspaper reported. "Until a few years ago she was a most active woman, and after passing her century mark was doing the work around camp that the women do with as much ease as a woman of half her age."

Accounts vary widely about Polly's age at the time of her death. The 1920 US Census put her birth year as 1828, which would have made her about ninety-four when she died. A 1914 Seminole census put her birth year as 1826, which would have made her about ninety-six at death. Newspaper accounts added far more years. The Sebring newspaper quoted Lanier as saying that Polly was "said to be 130 years of age." The *Tampa Tribune* said her age was estimated to be "all the way from 112 to 119 years."

Even the date of Polly's death was shrouded in confusion. The Sebring newspaper first reported her death, which presumably had occurred a few days earlier, in its August 3 issue. But a wire news brief about her death, which often was accompanied by the Hill photo of her, didn't go out until November.

Nobody knows exactly where Polly's camp was at Cow Creek. The late Alto "Bud" Adams Jr., owner of neighboring Adams Ranch, remembered his family bringing food to an elderly Seminole woman shortly after his father, the late Alto Adams Sr., established Adams Ranch in 1937, fifteen years after Polly's death. The woman could not have been Polly, and it is unknown whether she was related, but the hammock has always been known at the ranch as Polly's Hammock.

Archaeologist Robert Carr excavated the site and several others at the ranch in the early 2000s and confirmed that the site known as Polly's Hammock is a former Seminole camp. Carr said he found remnants of chickee posts and historical trade items such as a coffee grinder that would have been purchased in a store.

When Polly's daughter Lucy Tiger died in 1976 at the age of 106, it was reported that there were more than two hundred descendants of Polly Parker in the Seminole Tribe of Florida. Tiger had a daughter, Lena Morgan, whose descendants included former tribal chairman Howard Tommie, former tribal president Richard Bowers, and many other notable leaders.

Sally Rene Tommie, a former tribal official and head of the national Redline Media Group advertising agency, paid tribute to her ancestor on her agency's website:

> Polly Parker was my great-grandmother. A true Seminole, and a true American as well. An amazing woman who single-handedly helped write—and indeed create—the story of today's Seminole Tribe of Florida. She refused anything less than a life of liberation, and I'm so very proud that her unconquered spirit lives on in me and in my Seminole brothers and sisters. I believe her story can serve as a beacon for those who face and overcome adversity—especially women. Polly Parker showed us it is possible to achieve the impossible.

Former tribal chairman James E. Billie paid tribute to Polly in a column he published about her in 2013, the same year he helped organize a commemoration of her escape. "Emateloye's destiny was to start the Seminole Tribe as it is today," he wrote. "Eventually her children and their descendants would play monumental roles in our modern tribe. I wonder: What would have happened if Polly had never escaped and returned home?"

6

FRANK AT THE FORE

Vision for the Future

After his brother Keightley's death in 1914, Frank Raulerson took front and center in business and politics in Fort Pierce all while continuing to expand the East Coast Cattle Co., despite having just an eighth-grade education.

A 1915 article in the *Fort Pierce News* shored up the East Coast Cattle Co. with Frank as its head. The article, which appeared to be sourced by Frank, mentioned the company's purchase of 700 acres two miles west of Fort Pierce several years earlier and said that "since that time the company has added to its holdings somewhat, realizing that the time was coming when the country would be settled up and the range would no longer be available and ranches would be the order of the time." That prophetic statement was made thirty-four years before Florida's fence law was enacted.

The article also mentioned that East Coast Cattle Co. had transitioned in the last two or three years to feeding its stock in large enclosures for several weeks before slaughtering, and "as a result the St. Lucie county beef has been considered as fine as noted of the vaunted Western beef." "Fields of para grass, better weed and crab grass have been raised and the stock has been fed with that and grain and the market has been supplied along the east coast at the rate of about one hundred beeves a week."

At the time, Miami was one of the chief markets for the East Coast Cattle Co.'s live cattle, but Dade County had implemented a requirement that any cows shipped into the county be dipped for tick eradication before shipping. As a result, East Coast Cattle Co. hired a local contractor to build a concrete vat with a shed over it. The article explained how the cattle were dipped in arsenic and what precautions were taken:

> The vat is six feet deep and about four feet wide and has a slide at one end and a runway at the other end. The cattle are driven into a pen and chased up to the vat, which is filled within eight inches of the top with the solution. There is a steel incline of about three feet and when the cattle strike this with their front feet they slide quickly into the vat, sink to the bottom, rise and start to swim out. As soon as their front feet strike the runway at the other end they make their exit up the cleated incline and enter the dripping shed, where they are kept for some little time to allow the solution to run off them and dry, as it might be injurious if they were turned loose at once and it dripped onto the grass, as it contains arsenic.

The *St. Lucie County Tribune* in 1915 also shared East Coast Cattle Co.'s accomplishments, calling it the biggest meat-shipping concern on the East Coast. The newspaper also reported on improvements the company had made to its butchering plant on Angle Road west of Fort Pierce and at its cooling, freezing, and loading plant at the St. Lucie Ice Company, where beef carcasses were off-loaded onto train cars with freezer compartments: "The cooling and freezing rooms will each have a capacity of about a carload of meat, while the cooling room at the butchering plant will accommodate about 30 beeves and 25 or 30 hogs. The automatic loading machinery at the ice plant is capable of loading a car in thirty minutes."

The article explained how the butchering system worked. Cattle for butchering were taken to a pen on Angle Road and then dipped for ticks and fed in stalls in their last weeks before being butchered. The meat was butchered at the Angle Road plant and then conveyed into a cooling room by an overhead track system, where it remained for three to six hours to dry out. It was then loaded onto a truck and driven two miles to the cooling and freezing rooms of the icehouse, adjacent to the downtown railway tracks.

The carcasses were then loaded into a special refrigerator car East Coast Cattle rented for service between Fort Pierce and Miami. Once in Miami, the meat was delivered by truck throughout the city and as far north as Fort Lauderdale and as far south as Homestead. About 70 beeves were delivered weekly into Miami.

The article reported that the East Coast Cattle Co. had 10,000 head on the open range, along with 885 acres of land, with 30 acres devoted to citrus trees and 50 acres in para grass.

The growth of East Coast Cattle Co. continued to the end of the decade. In 1919, as president of the East Coast Cattle Co., Frank built a $25,000 cold storage plant in Miami and a $100,000 slaughterhouse in Fort Pierce, according to a *Miami Herald* article.

The article also noted that the company had an existing cold storage facility in Fort Pierce and quoted Frank as saying that the company's standards are so high that only four out of five cows are selected to be butchered "as proper food for the public."

A 1920 article in the *Okeechobee Call* newspaper also remarked on the scope of East Coast Cattle Co.'s operations:

> C. F. Raulerson has been loading 27 cars of beef cattle that will be shipped to Texas. The shipment will make a solid trainload and will be carried to their destination by a special train. The sale of these cattle calls for the delivery of one thousand head and will bring the magnificent sum of $37,000 [about $583,000 in 2025 dollars], which is believed to be a record shipment of purely beef cattle from any one place in Florida. The cattle have been raised here in Okeechobee County and are the product of the excellent range and pasture land of this county.

Frank's standing in the industry was also in the state's forefront. When a state cattlemen's association was formed in 1916 "for the purpose of encouraging better breeding of cattle, better range conditions and better marketing," Frank was one of its earliest members.

As the 1920s approached, Frank tossed his hat into the political arena, following the footsteps of his older brother. In 1918, he was elected as an alderman to the Fort Pierce City Council, as it was then known, running unopposed. He served as the chair of the Laws and Ordinances Committee. That same year, with no apparent prohibition against holding two

Frank and Annie Louise Raulerson built their 1922 home in the Mediterranean Revival style popular at the time in South Florida. The house featured an arched porch, barrel-tile roof, and rough stucco walls. (Courtesy of the Sloan family.)

offices, he also won election to the St. Lucie County Commission, where he remained until 1928. He continued serving as a city alderman until 1922.

Florida Boom of the 1920s

Frank got ahead of the Florida land and building boom of the 1920s, beginning land purchases and construction projects before the boom's peak about 1926. The boom was sparked in part by Carl Fisher, who launched a nationwide advertising campaign touting the profits to be made on Miami Beach real estate. Promotions for other Florida communities followed suit, real estate prices began rising, and large numbers of people began moving to Florida. The state's population increased from 958,470 in 1920 to 1,263,540 in 1925. Unlike the earlier arrivals, who came by train for limited visits and stayed in resorts and hotels, the new arrivals wanted to stay for good, attracted by easy credit, improved roads, and increased access to automobiles for the middle class.

The otherwise financially cautious Frank, flush from his success in the

Frank Raulerson completed the Raulerson Building, a downtown Fort Pierce landmark, in 1924. Pride for the building ran so deep that a postcard was created using this photo. The building still stands.

cattle and grocery business, in 1922 completed his family's spacious new home at 1033 Orange Avenue in Fort Pierce. The house was designed in the Mediterranean Revival style, evoking an Old World image with a barrel-tile roof, arched porch, and rough stucco walls. Previously, the family had been living at 1015 Orange Avenue, on the same block in a home just east of the new one.

The Mediterranean Revival style became popular in South Florida during the 1920s as the old, boxy cracker-style houses made of wood in late nineteenth and early twentieth-century Spain and other countries. The movement was influenced chiefly by Palm Beach architect Addison Mizner, who said he sought to "make a building look traditional and as though it had fought its way from a small, unimportant structure to a great rambling house that took centuries of different needs and ups and downs of wealth to accomplish." In addition to Palm Beach and Fort Pierce, other cities heavily influenced by the Mediterranean Revival style in the 1920s were Miami, Coral Gables, Boca Raton, and Sarasota, to name just a few.

Besides its design, the Raulerson home was also unusual in another respect. It was built with a hideaway under the main staircase, apparently to conceal liquor during Prohibition. Under the Volstead Act, passed in 1919 and which went into effect in 1920, purchase or possession of liquor was illegal in Florida, as in other states, until its repeal in 1933.

With his new home completed, Frank in June 1923 announced plans to erect a "modern business and office building of two or more stories" to cover an entire block at the southwest corner of Pine and Palmetto, now known as Second Street and Avenue A in Fort Pierce.

While Frank used the Mediterranean Revival style for his home, he also utilized the architectural style for the landmark Raulerson Building he completed and opened in 1924. The building was finished just a year after the opening of the only grander structure in Fort Pierce, the Sunrise Theatre, also designed in the Mediterranean Revival style.

The Raulerson Building, constructed of reinforced concrete, tile, and stucco and replacing the wooden building of previous decades, was a massive L-shaped structure with storefronts on the first floor and offices on the second floor. Its estimated cost of construction was $100,000, about $1.85 million in 2025 dollars. It was built by the John B. Orr Company of Miami, hailed as one of Florida's largest builders and which had also constructed hotels in Miami, West Palm Beach, St. Petersburg, and Orlando and the Scottish Rite Cathedral in Miami, among other projects.

The Raulerson Building's opening in May 1924 was heralded in an eight-page "Raulerson Building" section in the *Fort Pierce News-Tribune*. The lead headline in the May 20 edition screamed, in all capital letters: "Magnificent Raulerson Building Is Complete."

The building featured eight spaces on the first floor and twenty-five offices on the second floor. The anchor tenant was Raulerson Grocery, located on the first floor of the building's south side. The previous Raulerson Grocery had been housed in a frame building on the same site. The new grocery space featured a "modern ammonia self-refrigerating plant that gives perfect dry refrigeration to three compartments—a vegetable room, a meat cooling room and a meat freezing room."

Other tenants included Pioneer Drug Store, which for its grand opening offered "free cigars to the men, free candy to the ladies, and free balloons to the kiddies"; the St. Lucie Abstract and Title Insurance Company, "a new business established in Fort Pierce"; Edenfield Jewelry, "a high class jewelry business"; Powder Puff Beauty Shoppe, where "special attention is given to hair bobbing"; and Rieta's Gown Shop, "one of the shops of most interest to the ladies of the county."

The Raulerson Building, which still stands today and remains one of downtown's signature buildings, was designed by architect William Hatcher, who had been working with developer C. E. Cahow of Fort Pierce and the firm Harvey & Clarke of West Palm Beach.

Hatcher had come to Florida from Alabama, where he had worked as architect for the State of Alabama. Shortly after the Raulerson Building's completion, Hatcher took up one of its offices to open his own firm and work full-time in Fort Pierce, bringing in partner Lawrence S. Funk. Hatcher's architectural firm remained in the Raulerson Building for several decades, and the building was a showcase for one of his greatest works.

Other Hatcher projects in Fort Pierce included Fort Pierce City Hall, the First United Methodist Church, White City Elementary School, a city power plant building, the Gates Building, a pastorium for the First Baptist Church, an annex for Fort Pierce Memorial Hospital, the Fort Pierce Golf and Country Club, an addition to St. Lucie High School, and various residences. He also designed other buildings in the region, including Okeechobee City Hall, Okeechobee High School, and Sebastian Elementary School.

Near Hatcher's office, Frank established his own corporate office upstairs in the Raulerson Building, which featured a massive safe with the name Cow Creek emblazoned across it. Not content to confine himself to the cattle and grocery business, Frank in 1926 headed a syndicate that purchased the local *News-Tribune* newspaper, created from a 1920 merger of the *Fort Pierce News* and the *St. Lucie County Tribune*. He and the syndicate ran the newspaper until selling it to Kansans W. H. Halbe and brothers Paul and Nick Enns in 1929.

In 1927, Frank headed a group that formed the St. Lucie County Cattlemen's Association consisting of about a dozen ranchers, becoming its first president in 1930. Also during this period, he continued his work on the state Livestock Sanitary Board, which issued requirements for how cattle are to be treated in order to stop the spread of diseases such as tick fever and brucellosis. Since all selling and buying of livestock was regulated by the board, Frank got to know many of the cattlemen around the state and learned about their cattle-raising practices. He also had early insight into who was selling their ranches and why.

Frank gave up his seat on the Livestock Sanitary Board in 1931 when he was elected to the state Senate, where he served until 1935, resigning before his second term ended. No explanation was given for the resignation, although it was announced with the same news as his reappointment to the Livestock Sanitary Board—an indication that the proceedings of the livestock board were far more important to him than those of the Florida Senate. He served on the sanitary board for the next decade.

Making a move to focus more on cattle, Frank got out of the grocery business at the end of the 1920s, leasing the space to a tenant but allowing the continued use of the Raulerson name. The store was closed in May 1933 after the owner was served with a "distressed for rent" warrant for $2,779, or sixteen months of rent. Sheriff B. A. Brown held a sale of the store's entire stock of goods the following month.

Creating More Ranches

Frank's time on the county commission, the Livestock Sanitary Board, and Florida Senate gave him the insight needed to execute his next business play: purchasing large land tracts on which to graze cattle.

In the first quarter of the twentieth century and earlier, land in interior Florida was not seen as valuable. Before the creation of drainage districts, which dug canals and built dikes that made swampland usable for grazing, much of interior South Florida was either marsh or run over with scrub. In those days, cattle roamed freely, grazing wherever they chose without fences, with branding and marking being the means by which a cattleman could identify his livestock. During the days of the open range, a single steer could command far more money than a single acre. In 1931, for example, cattle had a value of forty-one dollars per head, whereas agricultural lands, as Raulerson's purchases would prove, could be had for as little as a few dollars per acre or less.

In the 1930s and even into the 1940s, Florida was still in the time of the open range. But all that changed as fences began to go up. After train tracks were laid and roads created for motor vehicles, free-ranging cattle would cause train or motor vehicle accidents or overrun agricultural crops. As a result, states began to enact laws requiring the fencing of cattle and other livestock. Florida was the last state in the nation to do so, with the Legislature passing the Fence Act in 1949 and Gov. Fuller Warren signing it into law. Cattle owners who did not comply faced fines and potential liability for damages caused by wandering cattle.

During the days of the open range, much of the land on which the cattle grazed was owned by the state or absentee landowners, and few raised issues about using their property for range purposes. Cattle were rounded up by the owners of the various herds once or twice a year to take some to market and to separate calves and brand them, returning them to the herd not going to market. This system enabled men of more modest means to get into the cattle business without the need to own large tracts of land. Some of these cattlemen saw the erection of fences as a threat to their livelihood and furtively snipped the fences as they went up.

While cattle roamed freely on the open range, small fences using barbed wire were typically erected around a homestead to keep a milk cow and other small livestock from wandering. The wire, which has sharp points along the strand, had been invented in 1867 and became a quicker and easier way than building wooden fences to keep livestock contained.

Fences became more prevalent in 1923, when the Florida Legislature enacted a tick eradication program that required cattle to be dipped in vats of arsenic every fourteen days until they were tick-free. This required the use of fences for quarantining.

The ticks attached themselves to cattle and gorged on blood and in the process transmitted a protozoan pathogen that invaded the cow's bloodstream and destroyed red blood cells. This caused a raging fever, and the cow often died, though scrub cattle had a high immunity. Nevertheless, the only way to eliminate the ticks within a given area was to routinely dip the cattle in vats of arsenic.

The eradication program succeeded in making parts of Florida tick-free, and fencing requirements soon were abandoned. The industry enjoyed a resurgence in the 1930s as cattlemen focused efforts on improving breeds and better grazing.

While it would take several decades before the 1949 Fence Act for many Florida cattlemen to realize the open range was ending, Frank Raulerson was executing a strategy of buying up as much land as he could get. His purchases of land began in the 1910s, and by 1916 the *Fort Pierce News* made its first reference to his Cow Creek Ranch. In 1923, Frank purchased an additional 600 acres, where he would establish his ranch headquarters and build his weekend home in 1930. In the 1930s, using a company he formed in 1925 known as the Raulerson Cattle Co., he began purchasing large tracts of land to add to his Cow Creek Ranch.

One of the largest purchases was announced in a May 1937 article in the *Miami News*, which noted that Frank had acquired 6,390 acres at the dividing line between St. Lucie and Okeechobee Counties for $13,000, or $2.03 per acre. The newspaper reported that the purchase brought his land holdings to 8,550 acres, adding, "He will use the acreage for pasturage of thoroughbred cattle."

In August that same year, the *Miami News* also reported that Frank had bought another 8,600-acre tract in St. Lucie and Okeechobee Counties, for $17,000, or $1.98 per acre, "to further increase his already extensive pasturage." The acquisition would bring his total ownership on the tract to 16,689 acres.

Both purchases were made from the Consolidated Naval Stores Company. Founded in 1902, the company mined longleaf pines on the property for crude turpentine. Once distilled, the turpentine could be used for lamp oil and the making of medicine, paint, and rubber goods. Rosin was also created from the distilling process. Smelting pine logs made tar and pitch. The tar could be used to protect the rope rigging of sailing ships, to grease axles, and to make tar paper. Rope soaked in pitch was wedged between the planks of ships to make them watertight. Pitch was also used to coat hulls for protection. Because of their association with ships, the turpentine, rosin, tar, and pitch that was yielded from the pines became known as naval stores.

Buying Other Ranches

Frank eventually would buy enough land to create a 23,000–acre ranch at Cow Creek, about the size of a township but not technically one. The ranch extended from Okeechobee Road, State Road 70, to Orange Avenue, State Road 68.

Under the Public Land Survey System to measure lands acquired from the British following the American Revolution, grids were drawn creating individual townships. Each township was square, measuring 6 miles by 6 miles, and within each township were 36 sections, with one section containing 640 acres. Thus, a township equaled 23,040 acres.

Frank also made similar purchases farther west in Okeechobee County, buying land that became the Dixie Ranch and the Taylor Creek Ranch, both about 23,000 acres, about the same size as Cow Creek. Besides the three larger ranches, Frank also purchased another ranch, Fellsmere Farms in Indian River County, of about 6,000 acres.

The old book that records Okeechobee County real estate transactions is full of Frank Raulerson transactions, indicating that he assembled his ranches over several decades, with many of the purchases appearing to be smaller plots owned by homesteaders. Certainly his two decades on the Livestock Sanitary Board made him intimately familiar with the cattle owners across the state, as well as landowners who might be looking for a quick sale.

7

THE OPEN RANGE

Working Cattle

When Frank Raulerson began creating his Cow Creek Ranch, the first thing he would have constructed would be cow pens and a small shack where cowboys could stay overnight. The pens might have even existed before his purchase of the property, one of several for common use that cattlemen would utilize in the days of the open range.

Together on horseback, the owners and their hands and their dogs would round up their cattle and drive them to market. Once the cattle were rounded up, they were sorted to determine which to send off for eventual butchering and which would stay on the range to reproduce and build the herd for ensuing years. The sorting required the use of cow pens, which were built at various spots in the open range.

In the first half of the century, some cattlemen tried to import new breeds. But their efforts were thwarted by diseases such as tick fever. The new breeds simply were more sensitive to tick fever than the native cracker cattle.

Hardee County cowboy J. P. Platt championed additional attributes of the lowly scrub cow in the days of the open range in an interview with author John S. Ott: "Scrub cattle were small, cows weighed about 400 pounds, steers 500 pounds, and bulls 600 pounds. Most of them had long horns. The advantage they offered was that they could survive on sparse forage in the winter, retreating in hammocks to protect themselves from the wind and browsing for acorns or Spanish moss, while purebreds often required food supplements."

Nathan "Teet" Holmes, a partner with Raulerson in the cattle business during the 1930s and 1940s, described the use and locations of pens during the open range in an interview with author Joseph Ackerman: "Frank Raulerson, Arch Henry, Kyle Hilliard and 'Teet' Alderman and others of us would pen cattle in a regular set of pens that were scattered over the country. We gave 'em names such as 7 Mile Pen, Padgett Island Pens, Cowbone Island Pen, Eagle Island Pen, Dad's Pen, Oak Creek Pens, etc."

Since the Cow Creek swamp was a landmark in the days of the open range, Frank Raulerson likely knew about or used the property for grazing cattle soon after his arrival in Fort Pierce in 1907. The swamp, barely a mile from the headquarters Frank would build for his ranch, certainly had an appeal for a cattleman who intended to eventually fence his property, since it guaranteed a constant supply of water for his herd.

In the days of the open range, various cattle owners once or twice a year would round up cattle over miles and miles, hunting them down in hammocks and by rivers and streams. Thus, long before the word "cowboy" became popular, these equestrians were known as cow hunters. The biggest roundups were held in the fall, after the cattle had gained their most weight grazing on the green spring and summer grasses and could demand a higher price at market.

In contrast to Western cattlemen who primarily relied on the lariat to round up cattle, Florida cattlemen used 10- to 12-foot-long whips, usually of braided leather or buckskin. At the end of whip is a thin piece of deerskin about a foot long called a cracker. It is this part of the whip that creates a cracking sound, a small sonic boom that happens as the section of the whip moves faster than the speed of sound.

The whips weren't used to strike the animals but to control their movement. Thus, the term "cracker" originated as a nickname for Florida cowboys because of the sound their whips made cracking in the air. Over the years, the term has grown as a reference for everything from horses and cows to multigenerational Floridians.

The Florida Cur

Like modern cattle ranchers, the early ranchers also used dogs—most frequently the Florida cur—to round up cattle, since the bovines perceive the dogs as predators, forcing them to instinctively herd together. If a cow strayed from the herd, the dog was trained to bring it back. A good dog could do the work of three cowboys while herding.

The cur's short, smooth coat, stamina, and ability to withstand Florida's challenging terrain make it an outstanding working cattle dog. Besides herding ability, the curs during the open range also protected livestock against boars, bears, and wildcats. The dog's origins are traced back to Hernando de Soto, who brought the first dogs to tend cattle in Florida in 1539; today's dogs are descendants of those first canines as well as of mixtures of other dogs, with each rancher developing his own strain based on the dog's ability to perform certain tasks.

A good Florida cur, also called a Florida cracker cur, might be hunter, herder, guardian, and companion. The dog could hunt stray cattle and bring them back to the herd and then ring, or circle, the herd and keep the cattle together. When the owner is off the horse, the dog might track game such as deer. Some are specifically used for hog hunting, with teams of two working a hog, one encircling it while howling, called a bay dog, and one called a catch dog that moves in to hold the hog, usually by the ear, until the hunter arrives. On the road, the dog guards the back of a truck and its contents while the owner might run into a store. And back at home, the dog, if not penned, may roam free around the homestead, guarding owner and family.

Many owners breed their cracker curs to continue outstanding traits, with some lines going on for generations. One of the best-known and most coveted lines of Florida curs is the Partin cur, attributed to the prominent Partin ranching family of Osceola County, which also brought the first quarter horse to Florida in 1934 and established the Brahman cattle breed in Florida.

On drives, cattle would be rounded up in bunches and held by dogs circling them. On a cow hunt, for example, four men might go out hunting cattle with their dogs while another four men and their dogs would be responsible for holding up the cattle that had been gathered so far until they could be herded to the pens. Usually they chose a shady spot or somewhere near a water source. As the use of fences became more common, small fenced areas called traps were created to hold the cattle until all were gathered and could be taken to the pens.

Once at the pens, the cattle were processed for a variety of reasons. Unimpressive young bulls were castrated to become steers and marked and branded.

Branding was done with a hot iron that seared a cattleman's brand onto the flesh of the animal. The mark was created by cutting flesh from the ear to identify sex and the owner. Because cows have a tendency to look forward, cowboys could see the marks from much farther away than the brand, which was susceptible to hair growing over it in the winter. The types of marks have names like crop, underbit, underslope, sharp, fishhook, and swallowfork. Often a combination of several of these is used to create a unique mark.

At the cow pens, as veterinary medicine advanced, cattle might be dewormed or vaccinated and, with the arrival of arsenic vats, dipped.

In the days of the open range, steers of three or four years old and old cows and bulls would be identified to be taken to market. This group would be driven to market while the others would be released back into the open range. This all was decided at what was called the parting gate. Standing on a platform where he could see over the pens, the owner or foreman would signal which gate the cow should be directed to either with a hand signal or a call.

Some of the calls might be "cull," meaning the cow might be defective in some way, perhaps a bad eye or hip, and should go to market; "cut back," meaning it should be kept in the herd; "wet," meaning it's nursing a calf; "bred," meaning it is pregnant; and "open" or "dry," meaning the cow didn't breed. Sometimes the open cows are sent directly to market, and sometimes they are given another chance to breed and expand the herd.

Historian Kyle Van Landingham, a descendant from a long line of cattlemen, wrote about South Florida cattle drives during the open range in his *South Florida Pioneers:*

> Often cooperative roundups were held by neighboring cattlemen. The cows were marked and branded, then driven to the west coast where they were shipped to Cuba and other ports. Pioneer cattleman Teet Alderman, son of William Alderman, often recalled the many horseback jaunts he would take, often to be gone for several weeks at a time. They were equipped with saddlebags of biscuits and potatoes and other "grub," and wallets of corn for the horses. He also remembered that at

one time a crew was building a set of cow pens at Indian Town Hammock, when they killed 37 rattlesnakes during the work period.

Alfred Norman, who grew up in the 1940s just as the days of the open range were ending, recalled that Raulerson's outfit drove cattle to Tampa, where they were shipped to Cuba. But more often, he said, they were simply driven to Raulerson's slaughterhouse on Angle Road in Fort Pierce, where they were butchered for the local markets.

Before that, many South Florida herds were driven to Punta Rassa southwest of Fort Myers for shipment to Cuba, which had a population three times the size of Florida's by 1900—1.6 million compared to 528,542. The drive to Punta Rassa was celebrated in Patrick Smith's popular 1984 novel *A Land Remembered*.

James E. Ingraham, president of the South Florida Railroad, reported in his 1892 expedition across the Everglades from Fort Myers on the west coast to Miami on the east coast that Punta Rassa was "from where most of the cattle raised in South Florida are shipped, and where the Cuban and Key West cable comes ashore."

Jacob Summerlin, "Florida's cattle king," had begun shipping cattle to Cuba from Punta Rassa in the late 1850s, establishing it as a principal port. Summerlin, one of the state's wealthiest men and once hailed as the world's largest cattle raiser, also owned a wharf at Punta Rassa.

The trade with Cuba increased in the early 1860s. During the early part of the Civil War, Florida became a chief supplier of beef and leather for the Confederate armies. Cattle were driven to places like Savannah, Georgia, where they could be shipped by boat to northern Confederate states such as South Carolina, North Carolina, or Virginia. Some were also shipped out of Florida ports such as Charlotte Harbor. When the Confederacy no longer paid in gold, Florida cattlemen turned to the Cuban market.

Regardless of where the cattle were going, the drives could last weeks. Said Teet Holmes in his interview with Joseph Ackerman:

> When we were cow hunting or driving cattle we might be gone three weeks, so we used to just take what we could carry in our saddlebags. We cooked our coffee in tin cans, but we had a special way of fixing salt pork that made it taste real good. First, someone would cut some

palmetto stems. Then we would put strips of pork on them and hold 'em over the fire. When it got hot, we poured cold water over it, washing the pork. Next we would turn the pork strips over, cooking the other side. It was mighty good once it was browned up and crispy.

Holmes said cattle were rarely killed as food on drives. Since owners would band together to drive cattle to market and then separate them, a variety of owners and their hands would drive the cattle. Wives would cook up hams and sausage and smoked beef. There also was plenty of syrup for biscuits and to sweeten coffee. Holmes's wife, Mary Louise, recalled baking as many as three hundred biscuits before roundups.

Holmes, who was born in Fort Drum in 1891, began working cattle at the age of seven and started his first herd when his father, Henry Alan Holmes, gave him a few cattle and a brand, as he had done for all of his twelve children, a custom common in Florida cattle-raising families of the time. When Teet Holmes turned sixteen, he moved to Fort Pierce with his younger brother, Minor. In 1916, he married Mary Louise, a member of the Stracke family from Nebraska that had moved to the Kissimmee River Valley.

Holmes began partnering with Frank Raulerson in the 1920s, and in 1928 joined the Raulerson Cattle Co., purchasing 7,000 head of cattle from the Miller Bros. 101 Ranch in Okeechobee County. At the same time, Raulerson continued his East Coast Cattle Co., apparently as sole owner.

Holmes was known for his ability to mammy up cows. Calves are often separated from their mother during branding and marking, castration, or vaccination. When the cows aren't interested in reuniting with their calves, the cowboy's expertise is needed to get them back together. Holmes said mammying up takes years of practice and a special technique. "He was one of the best I knew," St. Lucie County rancher Bill Roy Hutchinson said upon Holmes's death in 1983 at the age of ninety-two.

Sometimes mammying up is an ability to spot similar coloring or marking or simply reading a cow and calf's actions, intentions, and natural communications. "Usually there was one man that was better at it than anybody else," cowboy J. P. Platt said. "He would just call them in the pen. He'd call them out, 'This calf belongs to so-and-so cow!' [He identified] them from the markings of the mama and the color markings on the calf."

John Norman was foreman of Cow Creek Ranch, perhaps as early as 1923, until his retirement in 1952. Among his many contributions as foreman in the ranch's early years, he transformed thick Florida scrubland and marshes into grazing pastures for cows. (Courtesy of the Norman family.)

8

THE FOREMAN

John Norman's Early Years

John Norman served as Frank Raulerson's cattle foreman for more than three decades, helping him build his cattle empire. One of seven children, Norman was born in Narcoossee, in Osceola County near Orlando in 1892. The family moved to Fort Drum in 1898, and Norman left home at the age of fourteen to work as a ranch hand.

He had other jobs in those early years. He worked on the rail line from Holopaw in Osceola County to Sherman in Okeechobee County. He hunted raccoon, otter, and alligator in the winter. One of his odd jobs was transporting John Ashley's mother to get groceries in the days before Ashley was a wanted outlaw. One of John Norman's early jobs was hauling fruit from Basinger to Fort Pierce for Henry Holmes, who had a packinghouse in Fort Pierce and was an early settler of Fort Drum. Norman also began working cattle with Henry's son, Teet Holmes.

Though his education was brief, Norman learned to "cipher" and speak Muskogee, the language of the Cow Creek Seminoles, family members said.

In 1912, Norman married Julia Roberts of White City, a community just south of Fort Pierce. He was twenty; she was sixteen. They had five children: Margaret, Rachel, Lewis, Jack, and Vernon. Julia died in 1925 of what family members say were complications of childbirth. John later married Anzie Morgan, and they had six more children: Ephraim, George, Stella, Bertice, Anzie Josephine, and Alfred.

Besides Teet Holmes, Norman also worked cattle for Frank Raulerson, and after establishing his ranch headquarters in 1923, Raulerson tapped

Norman to become his foreman, a job Norman would hold for nearly three decades.

The job kept him busy. Census records showed he was working more than sixty hours per week in the 1940s. Besides Cow Creek, Norman also oversaw Frank Raulerson's other ranches, Dixie Ranch, Taylor Creek Ranch, and Fellsmere Farms. "At one time I heard my daddy say that Uncle Frank paid taxes on 72,000 acres in Indian River County, St. Lucie County and Okeechobee County," said Norman's daughter Bertice Harper.

Bertice and brother Alfred and sister Anzie in 2023 interviews recalled life on Cow Creek back in the early days. The family first lived in Fort Drum and then moved to Fort Pierce around 1938 and moved to Okeechobee in the early 1940s. They said their father would leave at 3:00 a.m. Mondays for Cow Creek from their home in Fort Pierce and later Okeechobee and return on Saturdays.

All of Norman's sons worked at the ranch at various times. Alfred and Ephraim dropped out of school early—Alfred in fourth grade—to work full-time at Cow Creek. The pay was one dollar per day. It's no coincidence that all of Norman's sons turned out to be cowboys. "Back then in Okeechobee, you were either a cowboy or you fished," Bertice said.

Taking Cattle to Market

In his earliest days working cattle at Cow Creek, Alfred said the cattle were driven from Cow Creek mostly along modern-day State Road 70 and then north to Raulerson's cow pens at his slaughterhouse on Angle Road in Fort Pierce.

Alfred said cattle were also sometimes driven to Raulerson's smaller ranch in Fellsmere, where the steers were fattened up. His sisters recalled stories from their father of running cattle from Fellsmere and then to the Kissimmee River, which they would have to swim across, and then bringing the herd through downtown Bartow before reaching Tampa.

The trail used from Fort Pierce to Okeechobee was what is today State Road 70, also called Okeechobee Road. But there was another trail to Basinger, with the turnoff being where the entrance to the old Cow Creek Ranch was, now part of the Wynne Ranch. The trail, called the Old

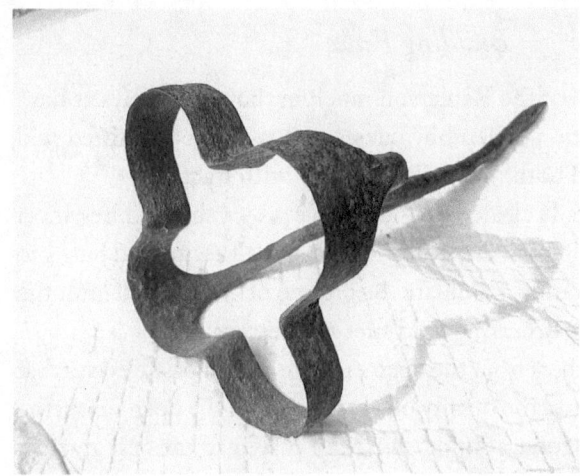

The Cow Creek branding iron, used for identifying cattle ownership, was shaped somewhat like a cloverleaf. (Photo by Gregory Enns.)

Basinger Road, went west right through Cow Creek headquarters and cow pens and then through Dark Hammock Ranch and Dixie Ranch to Basinger. It may explain why today the Cow Creek headquarters appear to be in the middle of the ranch, with headquarters at other ranches being closer to the main roads. Since various trails were used by different groups over time, it's possible that the Old Basinger Road trail was used by the army to get from Fort Pierce to Basinger during the Seminole Wars. Paleo-Indians might also have used it millennia before.

Deroy Arnold, who grew up at Cow Creek and is also Alfred Norman's son-in-law, recalled his step-grandfather, Harley Raulerson, who once cowboyed at Cow Creek, talking about the route. Arnold said Harley Raulerson lived in Basinger with his family during weekends but would ride his horse Sunday afternoon along a trail that went from Basinger through Dixie Ranch and Dark Hammock Ranch to Cow Creek, a distance of about 20 miles.

Alfred Norman's earliest memories are of Cow Creek Ranch, which had sections with names like Dog Slough, Cypress Creek, Blue Mountain, JB Pasture, Wagon Wheel, Joe Byers Strand, and Son Arnold Gulley. "I've been over every foot of it," said Alfred, who was born in 1936. He said Raulerson used a "club brand" for his cattle. The brand is elliptical and appears to be based on a four-leaf clover.

Building Fence

Alfred described much of the Raulerson ranch in those early days as hard scrub, or heavy vegetation of scrubby oaks and saw palmetto. Alfred said the scrub was removed both manually and later with tractors.

Land was also naturally cleared of undesirable growth by wildfires, most often caused by lightning strikes. Later, ranchers used controlled burns to reduce unwanted vegetation, stimulate the growth of grasses, and limit the fuel on which naturally occurring wild fires could spread.

One change for ranchers from the open range to fenced pastures was that it enabled them to control the quality of a cow's diet. In the open range, the cattle had to forage for food, going to whatever place had the best grazing.

Cow Creek had been in the open range until a barbed wire fence was erected around the 23,000-acre ranch. It's not known exactly when Raulerson erected the perimeter fence, but Alfred said it was up during his earliest memories, which would have been the early 1940s and well before the 1949 fence law.

Alfred said in those days it was customary to have only the perimeter fence, with cattle grazing over the entire ranch instead of being rotated among smaller fenced pastures of a few hundred acres. He said individual pastures weren't created until years after the perimeter pasture was up. That meant that to round up cattle the cowboys would have to hunt the entire ranch.

Because of the expanse of the ranch and the lack of small pastures, rounding up cattle was an intensive process. "Things were different back then," Alfred said. "There weren't any fences. The cattle were pretty easy. They wasn't real bad cattle to handle. But people didn't have no small places. There weren't no damn fences then. You drove the cattle and held them up."

Alfred said dead cypress were harvested from Cow Creek swamp and then cut into posts to build the fence. The barbed wire was purchased and came wound in large spools.

"I toted many a post out of that swamp," Alfred said. "Back then you didn't buy fence posts. You cut them. In the dry time is when you'd cut the dead cypress. You didn't cut green cypress."

Repairing and extending fences typically was done in the off time of working cattle. The fences were constructed with barbed wire, an 1867 invention that also helped tame the American West. In the 1940s, barbs were about a foot apart, with just two points on each barb. Today, the barbs are closer to six inches apart with four points on each barb.

Today, a ranch might use five strands of barbed wire on a perimeter fence and four strands on interior fences. Posts might be 10 to 12 feet apart.

In the early days, U-shaped nails were pounded by hammer over the wire into the posts, and holes for the posts were dug manually with post-hole diggers. Today, heavy-duty staple guns are used to fasten the wire and motorized augers to dig the post holes.

Rather than pastures of hundreds or thousands of acres during the days of transition from the open range, pasture sizes today are considerably smaller, with a common pasture size being about 40 acres.

"The outside fence we kept up," Alfred said. "There weren't any small fenced places. You didn't rotate cattle like you do now. You turned them out and that was it."

In those early days of the ranch, much of the work focused on clearing land, improving pastures, and putting up fence, Alfred said. Cow Creek had a sawmill, which was used to cut cypress from the swamp, among other places. "I remember when it wasn't nothin' but rough woods," he said.

When long-lasting cypress wasn't available for fence posts, ranchers used lighter pine, so named because its heavy resin made it highly flammable and easy to light. But the heavy resin also makes the wood more durable and resistant to insects.

Raulerson also had a herd of sheep, and parts of the ranch were leased out to tomato farmers, Alfred said.

Like other ranches in the region, Cow Creek benefited in the early days from tomato farmers, who would lease land for the crops but also clear it. In the process, ditches often had to be dug around the tomato fields to drain the swampy marshland. Trunks from sabal palmettos were stacked in ditches to make a crossing onto the tomato field.

To keep cattle out of the tomatoes, fences around the tomato field were erected inside the ranch's perimeter fence. When the tomato farmer's lease on the property ran out, the rancher was left with an improved pasture that was fenced and required little more than grass seed to make it suitable for grazing cattle.

The early years required planting of new grasses to improve pastures

In a photo taken in the early 1940s, Alfred Norman, son of Cow Creek foreman John Norman, drives a tractor cutting torpedo grass, some of the first pasture grass planted at Cow Creek. Alfred dropped out of school in fourth grade to work full-time at Cow Creek. (Courtesy of the Norman family.)

and make cattle more competitive at market. Carpet grass, a warm-season perennial, and common Bermuda were the existing grasses at the ranch. Alfred said his father in the 1930s planted the first pastures in torpedo grass, a high-growing perennial with lateral shoots. The torpedo grass was eclipsed in the 1950s by Pan-gola, a higher-quality grass for grazing that thrives in the tropical climate. Alfred said the grasses were fertilized by hand.

Besides his business savvy, Frank Raulerson had another quality for which he is still remembered: He was frugal. His only extravagance was the Cadillac he drove. "He was tight with his money," Alfred recalled. "He was a businessman. He didn't throw no money away. If he spent a dollar he expected to make 50 cents back."

Alfred said that when an old fence was repaired, Raulerson would have the cowboys remove the old staples and straighten them so they could be used again: "He wouldn't buy no fence posts. He'd cut 'em out of the [cypress] swamp."

Alfred also recollected the well-circulated story about the time cowboys who worked for Raulerson got their money together to buy ingredients to have the cook bake them a pie, an extravagance not on Raulerson's budget-conscious menu at the ranch. When the pie was done and the cowboys were eating it, they offered a piece to Raulerson. But Raulerson demurred, saying it was a luxury they couldn't have every night. When the cowboys told Raulerson they had pooled their own money to buy the ingredients, Raulerson offered that he'd have a piece after all.

Cow Creek at the time of Frank Raulerson raised cattle to sell for beef, instead of today's Florida cattle ranches, which are typically cow/calf operations. Up until the 1960s, Alfred said, area ranchers focused on feeder beef, raising steers and selling them when they had reached maximum weight at three or four years old. Older bulls and cows would be sold, too. "Back then you didn't sell any calves," Alfred said.

In cow/calf operations, the rancher keeps a select permanent herd to produce calves for later sale. The calves are sold at the Florida ranches and shipped to feed lots, typically in the Western states, where they are fattened before being slaughtered.

Alfred said the cattle in the early days were worked with what he called scrub horses, also commonly called cracker horses. The horses are the descendants of the Andalusians that escaped from the Spanish. "They were small, but back then we had smaller cattle, too. We had scrub cows." Later, around 1950, larger quarter horses came into use and gradually replaced the cracker horses, though some remain around today.

Game was abundant at Cow Creek, with the most common quarry being deer, turkey, and hogs. Alfred said some ranchers actually kept herds of wild hogs and marked their ears to identify their ownership. "People back then hunted for stuff to eat, not to have fun," he said. Much of the deer hunting then was done at night, he said, a practice that is illegal today.

By the 1940s, the days of rounding up cattle and driving them to market by horseback had ended, with tractor trailers arriving at the ranch to pick up steers. Alfred said the cattle were moved out in straight job trucks with large sides. These haulers are more like oversized pickups with giant ventilated compartments that could hold ten or twelve cows. Later, semi-tractor trailers came into use.

Uncle Frank and Aunt Lou

Alfred's sisters, Bertice Harper and Josephine Glenn, remember going to the ranch on weekends and seeing Frank and Annie Louise, whom they called Uncle Frank and Aunt Lou. Frank was a tall man who smoked Tampa Nugget cigars. Annie Louise always wore a hat and often had a peppermint to give out to the children. "She was very proper, always dressed very well," Bertice said.

For Christmas, Frank and Annie Louise would always host a party for the cowmen and their families. "I always looked forward to their Christmas party," Josephine said. "They'd have a big gathering for everybody working for them. I remember Mama saying the only time she'd have a drink was at Uncle Frank's Christmas party. He always had peach brandy."

The Norman girls loved seeing Jo Ann coming out to the ranch on weekends. Jo Ann grew close to their brother Ephraim, with whom she would ride horses and go squirrel hunting. Jo Ann also would recruit Alfred to

Cow Creek foreman John Norman's son Ephraim (*left*) and son-in-law Stanley Waldron appear at Dixie Ranch in Okeechobee County in 1949. (Courtesy of the Norman family.)

Frank Raulerson (*left*) after a successful bird hunt with dogs in about 1920. His wife, Annie Louise, is standing, and his son, Alfred, is in the far right. The man second from left is Jim, a cow skinner at the ranch and trusted employee for Raulerson. (Courtesy of the Sloan family.)

go hunting with her. "She was a good-looking girl," Alfred said. "I used to go squirrel hunting with her down in that old grove. She could shoot and could kill a squirrel. I had a brother Jo Ann was crazy about at one time. She used to come out and they'd ride horses and she'd hang out with him at the cow pens and stuff."

When on business, Frank Raulerson often arrived at the ranch with an African American man named Jim, whose last name the Normans or others interviewed could not recall. Jim was an almost constant companion of Frank Raulerson, driving with him on visits to Cow Creek or hunting missions. He also was known as Frank Raulerson's best cow skinner.

Cow Creek Honeymoon

Bertice lived at Cow Creek after she married ranch hand Stanley Waldron on December 31, 1949, New Year's Eve. Stanley was eighteen, and Bertice was sixteen.

"I remember Aunt Lou and Uncle Frank's house—we called it the big

Stanley Waldron worked in the late 1940s and early 1950s as a cowboy at Cow Creek, where this photo was taken. He and his wife, Bertice, lived at the ranch, and they spent their honeymoon there. (Courtesy of the Norman family.)

house. Whenever they were out there, that's where they stayed. There was another house where the cook lived and cooked for the cowboys, and I remember the horse stables. And there was a barracks, where the cowboys would sleep."

Until a small, wooden one-bedroom was built for them, they lived for two months in the bunkhouse, a barracks with a rubber floor that apparently had been World War II surplus. Bertice and Stanley spent their honeymoon in the barracks. "I had to set up house in that barracks for my husband and me. It was one room, and I had my kitchen set up at one end of it."

Bertice said at the time there was no electricity to the ranch—service would have had to be run several miles just to reach the headquarters. Oil-burning lamps were used at night. There was no indoor plumbing, just an outhouse.

The couple brought an icebox from Okeechobee for their kitchen and borrowed four hundred dollars from the bank to buy a stove, table, four chairs, and a rocker. They repaid the bank five dollars per week out of their twenty-eight-dollar weekly check—after taxes—that Stanley earned as a cowboy. Money was tight.

"I remember one Friday night we went to a drive-in movie and we had just enough money to go to the movie and buy some popcorn and something to drink. We had one dime left. We needed ice, and a block of ice was a dime, and my husband said, 'I'm not going to be broke. I'm not going to spend this dime to buy ice.' When we went home we got stuck and had to walk to get a tractor to come and pull us out. Stanley said, 'I sure am glad we didn't spend the dime on that ice.'" Luckily, payday was on Saturdays, so they could build on the dime the next day.

Bertice said her husband would work at the other ranches, Taylor Creek and Dixie, owned by Raulerson. The ranch at Taylor Creek had cow pens and a cookhouse, where Frank's youngest brother, Lucius, was cook. "I remember going there whenever Stanley was working cows, and we'd go and eat dinner with them sometimes. Loosh was a good cook. It was mostly beans and rice and some meat. There were also a lot of biscuits."

The Normans said their father, whose top pay as foreman was $150 monthly, was able to save money despite his large family. "My dad was a hardworking man," Alfred said. "He didn't spend nary a dollar unless he had to."

John Norman retired as foreman of Cow Creek in 1952, when he was sixty, and was replaced by Floyd Thomas, a distant relative of ranch hand Will'um Thomas. Retirement from Cow Creek didn't mean John Norman was leaving the cattle business. He had saved enough money to buy six sections of land, 3,840 acres, from Frank in Basinger. Bertice Harper said he paid the balance of the mortgage on the land by 1955.

In John Norman's final years, the Florida Cracker Trail Association riders would often stop by to salute him as they passed by his house on their annual ride on horseback from Bradenton to Fort Pierce. Norman died in 1993 at the age of 101. Stanley Waldron died in 1980 at age forty-eight.

9

SEMINOLES LEAVE COW CREEK

The Last Days

As the 1940s approached, the Seminoles' days of living along the creeks and streams east of Lake Okeechobee were numbered. More ranches would be established, fences would go up, and a reservation would be opened nearby.

The population of Seminoles living in chickees near Cow Creek actually increased in the 1920s until a precipitous fall in the 1930s. In 1920, 24 Seminoles were recorded in eight separate camps or dwellings on the St. Lucie County side of Cow Creek compared to 1930, when 48 Seminoles were reported living at seven separate camps. A notation on the page of the 1930 Census with the Seminole names carried this handwritten declaration: "Seminole Indians permanently living in St. Lucie County Streams and lakes. All American (Florida) born." But by the 1950 Census, no Seminoles would be reported living along Cow Creek, with many of them leaving over this period to move to the Brighton Reservation that opened in 1938.

Mary Summerlin unknowingly recorded the last decades of the Seminoles living near Cow Creek in her 1936 series for the *News-Tribune*. Mary and Frank Raulerson undoubtedly knew each other, since they both came from Geneva and were just a year apart. Mary was the daughter of Progar Debogory, a Russian émigré who settled in Geneva in the early 1870s. Debogory donated the land for Geneva's schoolhouse, built in 1874 and which Frank and his siblings attended. Debogory also donated the land for the Geneva Cemetery, where twenty Raulerson family members, including Frank's father and mother, Wade and Catharine, are buried. In 1883, Debogory received 160 acres in what is now called Seminole County under the 1862 Homestead Act.

In the first installment of her newspaper series, entitled *My Life Among the Cow Creek Indian Tribe,* Summerlin disclosed her relationship to the Seminoles. Her husband, Clarence, began a citrus grove in 1922. When she and Clarence moved to the grove west of Fort Pierce in 1925, her husband began employing several Seminoles to clear the land and plant and cultivate trees. Their property was on the south side of what is now State Road 70, where a street named Summerlin Road peels off the highway.

"After I moved out and we started truck farming on a rather large scale, we have always had them near us," Summerlin wrote. "We found them willing and conscientious workers. We paid the current wages and they never questioned anything the 'Old Man' did. They all trusted him and still do. If an Indian gets in jail or is in any other trouble from snake bite to pellagra, they come see the 'Old Man' and know he will never refuse to help them if he can."

Summerlin said that her husband employed as many as fifty Seminoles at a time, paying them weekly. She noted that the family kept a commissary from which the Seminoles could buy on credit. Summerlin described the women and children helping during harvest and said they were expert at picking beans, squashes, and tomatoes.

Seminole Families near Cow Creek

In her 1936 series, Summerlin gave a summary of each of the Cow Creek Seminole families she knew living near Cow Creek at the time:

- The Joe Bowers family, who "make their home nearer Cow Creek than any others" in their tribe. Joe was killed in 1935 while traveling through Georgia. "His widow, Lena, (granddaughter of Old Polly) has seven grandchildren, of whom Andrew Jackson is the oldest, two daughters, who were children when we first knew them, and four young boys." Summerlin said the women and girls did wash for her. "Almost all the squaws I know have used my sewing machine, making their own dresses and sheets for the men, and they have helped do my sewing and mending."

- The Naha Tiger family, who lived not far from Cow Creek. Tiger married Lucy, the daughter of Polly Parker. Naha was the son of Cow Creek chief Tom Tiger and brother of DeSoto Tiger, the Seminole trapper killed by the outlaw John Ashley.
- The family of Willy Billy, a grandson of Polly Parker. "Willy Billy married Courtenay Parker, a cousin, having Aunt Polly for a grandmother. They have a daughter, Julie, married to 'one of the Smiths' with two children, and a son George." Summerlin wrote that Courtenay had left Willy Billy and has a three-year-old girl.
- The Jack Tommie family. Jack, from Miami, married Sally, sister to Willy Billy and granddaughter of Polly Parker. They had eight children, with the oldest, Rosalie, and youngest, a girl, and six boys. Summerlin said the family included Jack's brother Sam Tommie, who is married to Joe Bowers's daughter, Melie, and their two children. "Both the [Tommies] live here as by tribal law they can't take their Cow Creek Indian wives away, so they become Cow Creeks too."
- Jake Morgan's family of sisters and cousins, including Jake, who is unmarried, his widowed sister, Shelie, who was married to Hilliard Johns, and her two grown children, including Mamie, "who now has a little girl," cousin Melie, and "maybe another cousin or two." "They go wherever they can find work, or else on hunting trips. They own a few hogs and when camping any length of time they acquire a few chickens."
- The Willy Johns family, who lived at Parker's Branch, about 15 or 20 miles southwest from Bluefield. Johns had died several years earlier, leaving his wife with eight daughters and three sons. The oldest daughter, Edie, also had died, and left a six-year-old child, Laura. "All of these children from Edie down have worked and camped here. Even the little girls five and seven years old helped pick beans."
- The family of medicine man Billy Smith, "who before dying, they say he asked the tribe to accept his son-in-law, Sam Jones, as chief in his place. Sam Jones married his daughter, Mussie, and they have 11 children. The old squaw (Billy Smith's widow) looks to be one hundred, but I don't suppose she is near that. She lives with her old maid daughter, Collie, who is perfectly devoted to the old mother and waits on her hand and foot." Summerlin said Smith's widow didn't approve of women working for white men, but she let Collie work for the

Summerlins. "The three Smith sons are Dick, who married Jake Morgan's sister, who had recently died, with two sons and a daughter, all grown; Morgan Smith, who married Courtenay's daughter, Julie, and left her with three babies, of which one has died since; and Tom, who lives farther north."

- Dan Parker, a widower who had recently remarried, and his brother Argie, both brothers of Courtenay and Melie, all of whom are Polly Parker's grandchildren.

Of these Seminoles choosing to live near Cow Creek, Summerlin wrote: "These Indians could all have had more [services] by going to the Reservation at Dania, but when they go they return in a few weeks, homesick for their Cow Creek Country."

Drastic Measures

The Dania Reservation, now known as the Hollywood Reservation, had opened in 1926, and Indian Commissioner Lucien Spencer tried to get the Seminoles living along Cow Creek to move there, apparently thinking they would do so to be closer to school and medical facilities. When the Cow Creek Seminoles refused, led by the Tiger family in Indiantown, Spencer resorted to drastic and inhumane measures.

"The Indian Town Camp which I was preparing to move here refused to come on account of the above interference, and I promptly cut off their ration supply," Spencer wrote. "At the end of three weeks of starvation they moved here and placed their children in the school."

Special Indian agent Roy Nash later documented the lives of the Seminoles living near Cow Creek in 1930, writing that eight or ten Seminoles "live in an old house on the farm of a friendly white man, Mr. Clarence Summerlin; they come and go, working for him when he has work for them, hunting and berrying as the mood strikes them, distinctly a transition type. . . . Dan Parker houses his family in an old barn and makes a precarious living as a casual laborer."

The 1930 Census listed the occupations of the older boys and adult males as hunters. At the time, many Seminole families in camps subsisted primarily on garfish, gopher turtles, and swamp cabbage, with a few of them raising hogs for their meat. Those who could began to work as day laborers picking fruit and vegetables. Some followed the crops. Wrote Nash:

> Most did not have crops planted because they maintained temporary camps along canal banks or on land they did not own. Some well-known Seminoles of this region were numbered among the hard-core unemployed. For example, Dan Parker was now out of work after living for nine years on the Summerlin farm. Jack Tommie had recently worked for three months in the CWA project at Dania but had no job at the time of the survey. Sam Tommie, too, had earned some money at the CWA project but was also unemployed. Naha Tiger and a group of twenty-three persons from the Cow Creek band were temporarily camped on the prairie west of Okeechobee; it was huckleberry season, and they could get sixty cents a gallon from the local storekeepers. On the other hand, there was relative prosperity in the camps of Morgan Smith, Johnny Josh, Ely Morgan, and the medicine man Sam Jones; all had been employed for about six months working railway crossties out of a nearby stand of timber.

Alexander Spoehr, an anthropologist with the Field Museum in Chicago who later served as president of the American Anthropological Association, reported in 1941 that the Cow Creek Seminoles appeared to be the last living in individual camps instead of on a reservation or in towns.

Spoehr wrote a book specifically about the Cow Creeks called *Klan Camps of the Cow Creek Seminole Indians*. Spoehr put the number of Cow Creek Seminoles in 1941 at 175, and by that time the term "Cow Creek" had come to represent a geographic area east of Lake Okeechobee over to the Brighton Reservation, up to Southern Indian River County and down into Martin and Palm Beach Counties.

Outside the Brighton Reservation, Spoehr identified five clan camps in the Cow Creek region, including two at the St. Lucie–Okeechobee line, three in Okeechobee County, one in Indian River County in Vero Beach, and one in Palm Beach County. Spoehr identified four of the clans—Panther, Deer, Bird, and Snake—as being totemic, meaning that clan members have a spiritual connection with their ancestors, who become their totem animals after death. The fifth clan, which was nontotemic, was called Tallahassee. The Panther Clan today is the largest in the Seminole Tribe. The other clans within the entire Seminole Tribe today are Bear, Wind, Bigtown, and Otter. The tribe says that when the last female of a clan passes on, the clan is considered extinct, and this happened with the Alligator Clan.

Many of the Cow Creek Seminoles became Baptist after Creek Baptist missionaries from Oklahoma came to the region in the early 1900s.

Seminole Camp Life

Synthesizing the insights of field surveys from 1880 to the 1940s provides a window into Seminole camps and camp life before many of Florida's Seminoles moved to the reservations.

Seminole camp housing consisted of open-sided chickees that were supported by cypress or palmetto posts and had roofs made of thatched palmetto fronds. One theory about the origins of this design was that it was developed for life on the run during the Seminole Wars, because chickees could be put up quickly, unlike the sturdier cabins that the Creeks and other early Seminoles had been using. But countering that theory were observations from explorer and chronicler William Bartram, who in 1789 had noted that the Creeks used a spacious open hut during the summer.

Wrote Clay MacCauley of the chickees of the 1880s:

> The thatching of the roof is quite a work of art: inside, the regularity and compactness of the laying of the leaves display much skill and taste on the part of the builder; outside—with the outer layers there seems to have been less care taken than with those within—the mass of leaves of which the roof is composed is held in place and made firm by heavy logs, which, bound together in pairs, are laid upon it astride the ridge. The covering is, I was informed, water tight and durable and will resist even a violent wind.

The site chosen for the camp usually was high flatwoods or tree island hammocks, where oaks and sabal palmettos would provide shade cover. During the years Seminoles were being hunted down for deportation to Indian Territory, the location in or near the hammocks also helped conceal them because the chickees blended in with the hammocks. Camps near creeks or other bodies of water were situated at the highest elevation to make them less prone to flooding.

Each chickee was designated for a certain use, with different ones for sleeping quarters, storage, and cooking. The cooking chickee was located in the center of the camp, with all the other structures surrounding it. The camps typically housed a clan of four or five families, with each family having at least one chickee.

"A Seminole family can erect a shelter in three days that will last him 30 years with an occasional renewal of thatch," anthropologist Nash wrote during his 1930 survey. "The Seminole lives in an open house because he likes an open house."

Matrilineal Hierarchy

The camps were matrilineal, with each camp being under the clan of a matriarch. Seminoles could not marry within their own clan, and marriages between certain clans were also restricted. After marriage, the man lived in the camp of his wife's clan. Unmarried men stayed in the camps of their mother and provided coaching. They often had more influence on children and training in the ways of the clan than the fathers, because the unmarried uncles came from the mother's clan, while the father was new to it.

Moving to the Reservation

In the mid-twentieth century, Seminole life in chickee camps outside reservations was nearing an end. The guarantee of land at Brighton, where they were not subject to a landowner's whim or required to obtain permission to live on property, was a big attraction to joining the reservation. By the 1950 Census, all of the Cow Creek families had dispersed, with members of the Bowers, Morgan, Johns, and Smith families living at the Brighton Reservation.

The Bowers family's move from Cow Creek occurred amid heartbreak after the tragic death in 1935 of family patriarch Joe Bowers, whose Seminole name was Tushlanee. Bowers and his wife, Lena, were living at Cow Creek with seven of their eight children, ages three through twenty, when the 1930 Census was taken. As the daughter of Lucy Tiger and granddaughter of Polly Parker, Lena held exalted status among the Cow Creek Seminoles.

At 6 feet, 2 inches tall and weighing 280 pounds, Joe Bowers was an imposing presence. During a visit to Miami in 1904, he was described in a *Miami Metropolis* news brief as "a noticeable pedestrian on our streets today."

He had taken his English name from Joe Bowers, a white settler friendly to the Seminoles who ran a trading post and lived in a chickee camp in Indiantown. Based at Cow Creek, Seminole Joe Bowers helped Frank Raulerson and partner Teet Holmes work cattle, and Holmes remembered Bowers's outstanding abilities as a cattleman. At least one and possibly two areas of Raulerson's Cow Creek Ranch were named for the Seminole: Joe Bowers Strand and JB Pasture.

"Some Indians seemed to have a way with cantankerous cattle," Holmes told author Joe Ackerman. "One of the best I rode with was an Indian named Joe Bowers. He knew every trail and every road in the woods and like most Indians he was completely honest."

Bowers had become part of a show with other Native Americans in Lake Ariel, Pennsylvania. Bowers and nineteen other Native Americans had been traveling back from Pennsylvania on August 17, 1935, when Bowers, fifty, was found in the middle of a road near Hardeeville, South Carolina, after having been struck by a hit-and run truck driver. He suffered a crushed chest and other injuries and died at a local hospital.

Sadly, instead of being returned to Florida, Bowers was buried in the Laurel Grove Cemetery North in Savannah, Georgia. The cemetery confirmed in 2023 that Bowers is buried there, but the location of his unmarked grave cannot be determined because a fire destroyed many of the cemetery's records.

"Bowers was well known in Fort Pierce," an article in the *News-Tribune* that recorded his death said. "He was a resident of the Cow Creek section, but frequently visited town and also did considerable grove work."

Besides the opening of the Brighton Reservation in 1936, the enactment of Florida's fence law of 1949 certainly contributed to the diaspora of the Seminoles along Cow Creek. Cattle owners who didn't have fences on their property were now required to keep their livestock fenced. And much of the exodus of the Seminoles at Cow Creek may have come down to subsistence. Although at the turn of the twentieth century, they were able to supplement their income through trading in animal hides, the erection of fences had greatly reduced their access to hunting grounds.

Alfred Raulerson was the heir to Frank Raulerson's fortune, but he died in 1938 in a boating accident. (Courtesy of the Sloan family.)

10

A NEW HEIR

Alfred

In his final years, Frank Raulerson continued to build and grow Cow Creek but sold off his Taylor Creek and Dixie Ranches, preparing his estate for an easy transition to his granddaughter and sole heir, Jo Ann Raulerson.

He sold both ranches to the J. R. Edwards Cattle Co., which subsequently flipped them. Edwards sold the Dixie Ranch to a number of people, including J. C. Pearce; Wiley Reynolds; Paul Helsel; Robert Reichter; John Norman, Frank's old foreman; and Oscar Bass. Edwards sold the Taylor Creek Ranch, located in the north section of Okeechobee between State Road 441 and Basinger, to Harry Hood Bassett of Miami.

"By the time he got elderly, he looked at what he had, and he had three ranches the size of Cow Creek," Raulerson's great-granddaughter Debra Sloan said in a 2022 interview. "He decided to sell two of the ranches because he didn't think a woman could handle all that property, and then he put it into a trust until Mother was thirty or so."

Frank Raulerson's attention to his estate might not have been so detailed if not for the death of his only child, Alfred. Although Alfred would follow his father's footsteps into the cattle business, Alfred's mind was elsewhere in his youth.

Published accounts, many of them apparently inspired by contact with newspapers by Annie Louise, detailed the delightful youth Alfred enjoyed in the 1910s. He went on various motoring trips with his parents, including Hot Springs, Arkansas, their favorite vacation spot, and New York

City, where they would visit Annie Louise's sister, Ida, who was married to Gerald Underhill Macy, a New York stage, radio, and television actor.

Alfred was academically gifted, appearing on the school honor rolls, and athletic, playing football and running track. But he was also accident-prone, and injuries caused him several setbacks. Near-tragedy struck at the age of thirteen, when he was accidentally shot by his friend Ruddy Alderman while the two were hunting with their fathers in the woods.

The *Fort Pierce News* gave this account of the 1917 incident:

> The two boys had carried along their trusted fowling pieces in the expectation of bagging some big game, and like the big hunters for big game that they had read about, they separated and began to stalk for the game. By and by Ruddy saw something moving along stealthily in the bushes not far away. Raising his ever ready shot gun he placed it to his shoulder, took aim and fired, but instead of bringing down the big game anticipated, he brought forth a yell from Alfred, his companion, whom he shot in the leg.

The wound was considered "not necessarily serious," but it kept Alfred out of school for more than a month.

The following fall, Alfred was dispatched to the Georgia Military Academy in Atlanta, which he attended for two years. By the spring of 1919, he was back in Fort Pierce, enrolled in a high school program called "commercial department," with the *Tribune* in April reporting that he was injured while pole vaulting in a lightning storm at the school grounds.

"When he struck the ground his ankle turned slightly and in giving way to that he fell in such a way that he came very near breaking his leg at the knee joint," the *Tribune* account said. "As it is he will be 'out of the game' for some time and suffer considerable pain before he recovers."

Later in that fall of 1919, he headed for Stetson University in DeLand, apparently enrolled in a college prep program. He departed in early September after hosting a "straw ride" for his friends. "A good time is anticipated by all those who are fortunate enough to be invited," the *St. Lucie County Tribune* reported.

Alfred joined the football team at Stetson but soon broke a rib and fractured two others during practice. While recovering but still bandaged, he returned to practice days later and broke his collar bone while tackling a dummy.

Again, the *St. Lucie County Tribune* reported details of the latest accident: "He was called on by the coach to demonstrate the correct method of tackling and it was while giving this demonstration that the accident occurred. He will remain home until the bone is well knit, when he will return to Stetson to resume his studies."

Alfred returned to Stetson later in the semester and was reported arriving home for Christmas break. Before leaving for Stetson for the spring 1920 semester, he "gave a delightful dance party for Miss Beulah Allen and Morgan Alderman" at the home of his parents. He was back in Fort Pierce in February, having "delightfully entertained" several out-of-town visitors at the home of his parents with refreshments, cards, dancing, and music furnished by the Frey Sisters. A list of those attending the party was included in the notice. Invitations to the party apparently were so prized that a follow-up notice was published in the newspaper expressing the disappointment of the Misses Addie, Ruth, and Hazel Holmes, who, shopping and visiting relatives in Palm Beach one Saturday, "return[ed] too late to attend the delightful party given by Alfred Raulerson."

News of Alfred's comings and goings ceased for the rest of 1920 after that notice, and it wasn't until March 18 that his name reappeared in the newspaper with the news that he had married Thelma Alderman, daughter of Okeechobee cattleman Robert Alderman and the late Laura Alderman, who had died in 1908. He was just seventeen, and she was eighteen.

The notice, appearing in the recently merged *Fort Pierce News-Tribune*, said the two were married at the groom's home in a ceremony attended by only the bridal party, with Frank Raulerson giving the bride away. The Rev. Stephen F. Reade, rector of St. Andrew's Episcopal Church in Fort Pierce, officiated.

The newspaper described the wedding as "quite informal, though beautiful," with the bridal party as the only attendees. The bride wore a dark-blue suit coat and small blue hat and black pumps. The room where the ceremony was performed was decorated in pink roses and streamers. A wedding dinner followed in the dining room decorated with yellow roses. A large wedding cake bore a bouquet of white roses in the center.

The article also noted that the bride had recently spent the winter in

Jo Ann Raulerson, about age three, with her father, Alfred Keightley Raulerson, in about 1933. (Courtesy of the Sloan family.)

Daytona Beach, just about 20 miles from Stetson. Joining Alfred and Thelma for a wedding trip to Bartow and Tampa were Frank and Annie Louise and another visiting relative.

But the handsome playboy's marriage didn't last. Alfred apparently divorced Thelma, and in April 1923, at the age of nineteen, married twenty-year-old Willie Mae Ford in Hot Springs, Arkansas. Debra Sloan says it's likely that Alfred met Willie Mae during a vacation in Arkansas, a favored vacation spot for Frank and Annie Louise.

The marriage to Willie Mae didn't last, either. Records show Alfred, then twenty-three, married a third woman, twenty-two-year-old Mae Pearce of Okeechobee, on June 15, 1927, in Indian River County. That marriage enjoyed more permanence, and the couple produced two daughters: Kathryn Louise, who was born September 25, 1928, but died just four months later; and Jo Ann, who was born July 22, 1930, and would become the sole inheritor of Frank's estate and the keeper of the Raulerson tradition.

"He spoiled her," Kathy Sloan Blanton, Jo Ann's oldest daughter, said in a 2022 interview. "He doted on her. Nobody could dote on her more. She was just the apple of his eye."

With a daughter and his marital inclinations stabilized, Alfred joined his father in the cattle business, with the 1931 city directory listing his occupation as cattle raiser.

Newspaper editor Charles S. Miley wrote that Alfred Raulerson started out with one black calf that later produced six bulls in a row. "It was only after his father gave him a cow and a heifer calf that he had the nucleus of a small herd," Miley wrote. "In time, his cattle roamed over Indian River, Brevard and Osceola counties."

Poor Little Rich Girl?

Despite the fact that they were held in the grips of the Depression, many of Jo Ann's early birthdays were celebrated in grand style with her extended family.

A 1937 newspaper item reported that "Jo Ann Raulerson, daughter of Mr. And Mrs. Alfred Raulerson, was feted with an afternoon party Tuesday at the home of her grandparents, Mr. and Mrs. C. F. Raulerson, the occasion celebrating her seventh birthday anniversary."

Alfred would spend only one more birthday with his daughter. He was killed on Labor Day weekend 1938 when a boat he was piloting at night carrying his wife, Mae, and fellow boatman Hansel Smith struck a channel marker and then a dredge pipeline pontoon in the Fort Pierce Inlet near its intersection with the Indian River.

Newspaper accounts reported that Alfred, thirty-four, was thrown from the boat and suffered a gash to the head. His body, also hit by the boat propeller, was recovered the next day. Mae and Smith escaped without serious injuries.

With Alfred's sudden death, Annie Louise and Frank immediately

Jo Ann Raulerson, appearing here about the age of six in 1936, learned the exacting standards of being a lady from her grandmother. (Courtesy of the Sloan family.)

moved to take custody of eight-year-old Jo Ann. The Raulersons, apparently without the need for court action, persuaded Mae that they could better raise her daughter. "They had the money and they thought it was better," daughter Kathy said.

Although the custody agreement didn't involve a divisive court action, it faintly echoed the national case that played out just four years earlier of "poor little rich girl" Gloria Vanderbilt, who, after the death of her father, was entrusted to her aunt over her mother, who was declared unfit. And like the Vanderbilt case, the Raulerson succession would involve a large trust fund.

"Alfred drank a lot," Debra said. "Mother never said a thing about Mae being a drinker. I believe that Frank and [Annie Louise] had the means to take better care of Mother."

Joyce Palmer McCall, who grew up on Orange Avenue a few houses from the Raulersons until moving in the fourth grade, said the Raulersons were caring for Jo Ann even before her father's death. "She always lived with her grandparents when I knew her from first to fourth grade," McCall said in a 2022 interview.

"Jo Ann and I spent the night with her mother one night. She was living in a small house behind the big one. I remember because she put us to bed with wet hair after our hair had been washed." McCall said that her own mother had never put her to bed with wet hair.

McCall remembered that she and Jo Ann on Saturdays would often ask her grandfather for a dime each to go to the movies at the Sunrise Theatre in downtown Fort Pierce. "Her grandfather would pay because my parents didn't have any money," she said. When Alfred Raulerson was killed, McCall recalled seeing Jo Ann soon after. "We were out on the sidewalk, and Jo Ann said, 'My Daddy won't be home anymore.'"

A year after Alfred's death, Mae married Floyd Davis of Duval County. Her daughters said Jo Ann saw her mother occasionally as a child and reconnected in her college years, though Mae died of cancer in 1955, when Jo Ann was twenty-four. "She never talked much about her mom, especially growing up," Kathy said. "I'd literally have to pry anything out of her. I'd ask, 'Did you all get along?' She just never had a lot to say."

According to Debra, "When Mother grew up in the 1930s, she didn't experience much of what other people felt, the lack of food, money, or pretty much anything. I think Mother never lacked for anything except love."

Jo Ann was an obedient ward, never complaining or talking about anything unpleasant. The overbearing Mother Lou was exacting about the social expectations she had for Jo Ann and, perhaps sensing that she and Frank had been too lenient with Alfred, made sure she kept Jo Ann on a tight tether. "There wasn't a lot of physical love back and forth," Kathy said. "She had a very formal upbringing. Mother Lou made sure she could have tea with the queen or dinner with the president."

The tragic death of Jo Ann's father and the separation of her mother at the same time instilled in Jo Ann an ability to shield her emotions, a trait she would carry into adulthood. With little or no power to influence events around her, the only option was to accept the things the way they were. Above all, her upbringing reinforced the notion that she shouldn't share or voice her feelings, no matter how bad things got. She simply soldiered on.

Influence of Elders

Much of Jo Ann's childhood was spent around relatives two generations older. Not only was there Mother Lou, but she also had a great-aunt, Grace Lee, who lived in a house behind the Raulersons, with her husband, Pete, to hover over her. "You have to understand the generation gap," Kathy said. "She was very spoiled, but as far as affection goes, they didn't show a lot. She didn't have a whole lot of other kids to play with, but she was around the adults and she would learn to do the things adults could do."

Kathy said the worst thing her mother told her she ever did as a youngster was to buy a comic book, a purchase of which Granddad disapproved. "She told me she didn't say 'damn' until she was twenty-four." While Mother Lou taught Jo Ann the nuances of entering formal society, Granddad schooled his only heir in the cattle business.

Being raised by a cattleman, Jo Ann learned to ride, shoot a rifle, rope a calf, and crack a whip at an early age. "She knew how to rope cattle, and she could crack a whip louder than anyone else," said Kathy, who recalled her mother telling her that she would go on roundups with her grandfather. "Granddad taught her to do everything the cowboys could do," Debra said.

Weekdays were spent going to school, and weekends were often spent at the ranch, where Jo Ann could pursue her passion of squirrel hunting. Debra and Kathy said it was a skill she brought with her to adulthood, often enlisting Kathy and Debra to carry her quarry for her.

"She hunted with a .22 long rifle and she would shoot 99 percent of those squirrels in the head," Debra recalled. "Most people shoot squirrels with a .410 shotgun. She'd say, 'Why would you want to use that? You could spoil all the meat.'"

Perhaps Jo Ann also gained some of her cooking skills in those early days. As an adult, she'd share recipes on cooking delicacies such as such as squirrel, swamp cabbage, rutabaga, and greens, including collards, which she cooked without water. She sometimes even used softshell turtle eggs for cake baking.

She also was precocious in another respect. At about the age of twelve, she began driving Mother Lou and Granddad on yearly trips to one of their favorite vacation spots, Hot Springs, Arkansas. Kathy and Debra said Frank apparently used his political influence as a former state senator and county commissioner to get Jo Ann an early driver's license. "Granddad Frank probably went to some judge and said, 'Jo Ann needs a driver's license,' so at twelve she drove them out to Hot Springs," Debra said.

School Days

At Fort Pierce High School, Jo Ann didn't spend a lot of time with students outside of school. Few students knew about her abilities as a young cattlewoman. A classical beauty with alabaster skin, jet-black hair, and a lithe form, she was never too far away from Mother Lou and Granddad. "They were really strict with her," recalled Elinor Phillips Blum, a member of the Class of 1948 with Jo Ann.

Though Jo Ann was known to be wealthier than the other kids, she wasn't snobby, Blum said. "None of us had any money back then, so she probably was the wealthiest kid in our class. I can just remember her being a really nice, sweet girl. She didn't flaunt that they had a little more money than anyone else."

Nevertheless, like she did with her son, Mother Lou made sure that the local newspapers shared what she perceived as Jo Ann's wonderful life. Newspaper accounts record that she spent her eleventh birthday at an all-day celebration at the ranch; her Sweet 16 birthday, recorded with a photograph in the *Miami News,* featured a formal dance at the Indian Hills Country Club; and her eighteenth birthday was "a gay celebration by a group of her friends" at the Pleasant View Inn.

In high school, Jo Ann belonged to the Glee Club and participated in a theatrical production called Stunt Night. She also appeared in the junior play and was on the yearbook staff. Classmates voted her wittiest, an attribute that would stay with her through life. "She is always bright and witty; her you'll never have to pity," her yearbook said.

Jo Ann Raulerson attended Rollins College in Winter Park. Her grandparents hoped she would meet a boy who could help her run Cow Creek Ranch. She appeared close to getting her degree but never graduated after meeting Tommy Sloan. (Courtesy of the Sloan family.)

Thomas Kindred Sr., another member of the Class of 1948, remembered that in their senior year Jo Ann dated Joe Baggett, son of W. C. Baggett, who would become the clerk of courts for St. Lucie County. Joe Baggett was captain of the school band and a member of De Molay, a student fraternal organization. Classmates voted him most talented.

Despite the relationship with Joe, Jo Ann maintained her old friendship with Ephraim from Cow Creek. "They stayed in touch as friends as they got older," said Ephraim's sister Bertice Harper. "I know Jo Ann came to visit him and his wife at their home."

One potential young suitor who didn't work out was Alto "Bud" Adams Jr., whose parents, Florida Supreme Court Judge Alto Adams Sr. and

Jo Ann Raulerson, twenty, helps her grandfather Frank, seventy-eight, and grandmother Mother Lou, seventy, celebrate their fiftieth anniversary in March 1951 at the parlor of their home in Fort Pierce. (Courtesy of the Sloan family.)

Carra Adams, owned the neighboring Adams Ranch. "My dad told me my grandmother would make fried chicken on Sunday to bring over to Frank Raulerson," said Robbie Adams, Bud's youngest son. "They were trying to pair up Dad with Jo Ann."

After graduation, Jo Ann attended Rollins College, a small private coed liberal arts school in Winter Park. The college yearbook listed her as attending in 1949, 1950, and 1951. Debra said that Mother Lou and Granddad were hoping that by sending her to nearby Rollins, also in the heart of Florida citrus and cattle country, Jo Ann might find a mate who could help run the ranch after they were gone. "Mother didn't really want to go to Rollins," Debra said. "That was Mother Lou's deal. I think Mother probably wanted to go farther away from home and have a little more freedom."

During a college break, Kindred recalled Jo Ann telling him that she and Baggett were no longer dating. Baggett attended the University of Florida for two and a half years before enlisting in the US Air Force in 1951. He was from a family of six boys and one girl, with all of the boys serving in the military. He flew fifty-four firefighter bomber missions in Korea and was killed during a combat mission in Vietnam in 1965. "I think Joe Baggett probably did love her but for whatever reason they didn't hang on together," Debra said. "In her later years, Mother always spoke very fondly of Joe."

Though Jo Ann appeared close to getting her degree, she never graduated from Rollins. The year leading up to what would have been her graduation was hectic. In March 1951, Mother Lou and Granddad celebrated their fiftieth anniversary, an event noted in newspapers from Miami to Tampa. But Mother Lou, in declining health, died nine months later at the age of seventy-one.

Frank felt his loss so profoundly that, as a memorial, he paid for a speaker system to be installed at the Fort Pierce Cemetery that gently chimed music during funerals regardless of the denomination. A tablet in stone at a traffic circle in the cemetery dedicated the system to the memory of Annie Louise.

11

ENTER TOMMY

A Humble Beginning

During Mother Lou's last months, Jo Ann met a handsome, self-assured clothing and shoe salesman named Tommy Sloan while she was shopping at I. M. Waters menswear store in downtown Fort Pierce.

"He kind of swooned her," Debra said. What was even better was that he had the approval of Mother Lou and Granddad. "They wanted her to have somebody who could help run the ranch," Debra said. "Mother Lou loved him because he brought her booze."

Thomas Leighton Sloan, who would also become known as TL, was born October 17, 1932, in Barrows, Georgia, outside Atlanta, the son of railway inspector Aubrey Sloan and his wife, Catherine, who became universally known as Honey.

"I think they were pretty poor because when he would talk about growing up in Georgia, he'd say that they had all those tobacco houses," said Darren Robertson, who would consider Tommy a father. "When he was a kid, he said they made him catch rats coming into the tobacco houses. He hated rats. I think him being poor he always wanted more. That's just the kind of guy he was. He always wanted to be out front."

The family eventually moved to Melbourne and then to Fort Pierce in 1948 while Tommy was in high school, living hard by the railway tracks in a modest section of town at 211 Avenue E. Aubrey had become disabled, and Honey worked as a theater cashier and later was a longtime motor carrier for the *News-Tribune*.

Jo Ann's daughters said Honey spoiled their father growing up and

Tommy Sloan's photo and bio as it appeared in his senior-year yearbook in 1950. (Courtesy of the Sloan family.)

THOMAS SLOAN
"Tommy"
"I'm like a powder puff for the ladies."
Class Treas., 3; Annual Bus. Mgr.; Biggest Flirt, 4; Lettermen's Club 3, Sec-Treas., 4; Most Popular Boy, 4; Football, 3, 4; Basketball, 3; Baseball, 3; Fire Fighter's Club, Pres., 3.

instilled in him a sense that he could get whatever he wanted. One of his greatest strengths was getting people to see things his way. "He could sell ice to Eskimos," Kathy said.

Aubrey and Tommy's relationship was strained, the daughters said, and Tommy considered himself a better man than his father and was embarrassed by him, apparently feeling that Aubrey hadn't achieved enough in life. "He wasn't respectful to his father," Kathy said.

The differences in social stature and wealth between Jo Ann and Tommy were widely known, with Tommy always having to overcome the notion that he was after Jo Ann for her money. There was also a slight difference in age. Tommy was two years younger than Jo Ann.

Tommy's high school yearbook revealed that his charming ways came early. As a senior, he was class secretary-treasurer and was voted most popular boy in school, quite an achievement since he had been at the school for just two years, and most of his classmates had known each other since first grade. The high school was attached to the elementary school, and both took up an entire city block on Delaware Avenue. Students would enter first grade on the east side of campus and move each year until reaching the west end in twelfth grade. A bell tower separated the elementary and high school, and when the bell was struck in the morning and the US flag raised, motorists on Delaware would stop their cars, get out, and salute the flag. Known as the yellow brick school because of its distinctive exterior, the building was Mission style, constructed in 1914 with additions in 1924 and 1926 that made it appear as one uniform structure.

Tommy also was voted biggest flirt by his fellow seniors in the Class of

1950. On the gridiron, he played flanker and was known as Choo Choo.

"He was a charmer," Debra said of her father. "He had a way of coming across to people in a real kind of slick 'I'm all good, I'm in charge' attitude. Obviously you can see that from how he was represented in the yearbook."

The romance between Tommy and Jo Ann was a whirlwind. On April 12, 1952, just four months after Mother Lou's death and not long after she withdrew from college, Jo Ann married Tommy in a ceremony at Indian River Presbyterian Church, followed by a reception at her grandfather's house. She was twenty-one. He was nineteen.

Their newlywed years were interrupted by Tommy's service in the US Army. Sixteen months after their marriage, with the draft still in effect and President Eisenhower having ended the paternity deferment for married men just two months earlier, Tommy enlisted in the army, serving stateside for two years beginning in August 1953.

Bruce Center, who rode the bus to Miami with Tommy for induction and their assignment to military duty, remembered that Tommy made friends quickly by passing out one-dollar cigars, expensive for the time, to his fellow recruits in Fort Pierce and then offering them up to officers when he was in Miami.

Handing out cigars became Tommy's trademark. He'd always have a few at the ready in his pocket or in a box to give out to a prospect or old friend. Later, he consumed and gave out cigars that had a custom band with his name or initials on them.

Darren Robertson recalled some of Tommy's stories of his days in the army, which seemed more like a Beetle Bailey tale.

Darren said that Tommy finagled himself out of having to go through boot camp. He had ridden a troop train, apparently to Washington state, which made various stops along the way.

> He said he went along and got off at the last stop. Officers called out the names of everybody, and everybody's name was called out except his. Everybody was gone, so he sat down on his [duffel] bag, lit up a cigar and sat there. Pretty soon a guy came along and said, "Why are you here?" And he said, "They never called my name." They were trying to figure out what to do with him, and they asked what he did and he told him he was a businessman and this and that. And the guy said, "Man,

I could use a clerk," so they made him one. He claimed he never had to do calisthenics or basic training or anything like that. He was just a clerk all the time.

Generational Shift

As Tommy left for the army, Jo Ann was five months pregnant with their first child. On November 30, 1953, Jo Ann gave birth to Kathryn Louise, named after the older sister she never met, and Mother Lou. The *News-Tribune* recorded Tommy's absence: "Mr. Sloan, on duty with the Army at Tacoma, Washington, was expected to arrive here by plane Tuesday afternoon."

As one generation arrived, another departed. Four months after Kathy's birth, Frank Raulerson, in declining health for months, died at home two days before his eighty-first birthday. Except for a fifty-dollar monthly allowance given to his brother, Lucius, the old ranch cook, Frank left his

Jo Ann Sloan inherited Cow Creek Ranch after the death of her grandfather in 1954. She married Tommy Sloan in 1952, and he began running the ranch after service in the army. Though he had no experience raising cattle, he slowly learned the ropes and by the late 1960s was depicted nationwide as a model rancher. (Courtesy of the Sloan family.)

entire estate, worth at least $5 million in 2025 dollars, to a trust in Jo Ann's name.

The trust was overseen by Frank's longtime bookkeeper, O. G. Nanney; L. O. Stephens, a lawyer in the Raulerson Building; and Grace Lee, Jo Ann's great-aunt. Under the terms of the trust, Jo Ann would not have direct access to her inheritance until past her thirtieth birthday.

Jo Ann and baby Kathy would visit Tommy at Fort Lewis in Tacoma in June 1954. Tommy graduated from the Forty-Fourth Infantry Division's School of Standards. A newspaper item that August said he was a radio operator in the Repair and Maintenance Company of the division's Sixteenth Signal Battalion. He was stationed later that year at Fort Huachuca in Arizona.

While Tommy was away in the army, their second child, Debra Anne, was born December 13, 1954.

Darren said that Tommy learned to fly while in the army. He also had a car during part of his service. "He just did his time and learned how to fly. At some point he had a car and he would give his buddies rides into Mexico. I think he charged them for it."

Despite Tommy's absence, Jo Ann was surrounded by help. She still had her great-aunt Grace Lee living behind her home. "Aunt Grace was an RN who had Woolworth's red-dye hair," Debra said. "She couldn't cook, but she apparently was a good nurse. She was right there when Mother gave birth to Kathy and me. Let me tell you she was opinionated, and her opinion was what she wanted to happen."

Jo Ann also had help from Rosetta "Rogie" Wright, who was just eighteen when she was hired to work as a housekeeper for the Raulersons on the day Jo Ann came home from the hospital in 1930. Rosetta, born in Georgia, would remain Jo Ann's housekeeper for forty-five years, working with five generations of the family.

Married to Ben and the mother of four daughters, Christine, Jervene, Rose Ann, and Evelyn, Rosetta was active in the Mount Olive Missionary Baptist Church in Fort Pierce. She worked for the Sloans until retiring in the mid-1970s. She died in 2001 at the age of eighty-nine after an active retirement.

"She was always very kind and very caring and very supportive," Debra said. "If we were carrying a secret, she'd protect the secret. She was a great caregiver of us. It was amazing that she stayed around for five generations of the family."

Jo Ann also had help from her in-laws, Aubrey and Honey. The couple had moved from their modest home on Avenue E to a roomier and more impressive home on Rosedale Avenue and began a tradition of hosting the girls for overnight stays on Fridays.

It was during one of those weekends, apparently when Aubrey and Honey were shopping for a new home, that Catherine was given the nickname Honey. With the girls riding in the back seat, Aubrey would ask Catherine, "Honey, what house do you want to see today?" Taking that cue, the girls then began calling their grandmother Honey, a name everyone else embraced as well.

Becoming a Cattleman

After returning from the army in June 1955, Tommy began focusing on the ranch. The new generation of the Raulerson family rode on horseback in the first Cattlemen's Day Parade in 1956. A picture of them appeared in the paper, with Jo Ann riding with erect posture and Tommy slouching with two-year-old Kathy on his saddle.

The parade, which would become an annual tradition for decades and would be held as part of the city's annual Sandy Shoes Festival, featured more than two hundred people from area ranches on horses. That first parade was a tribute to five early cattle families: the Raulersons, the Carltons, the Clevelands, the Aldermans, and the Holmeses.

Said the *News-Tribune:*

> All of the area ranches were represented by cow-punchers on horseback carrying the banners of the ranch brands. Civic organizations and commercial houses entered floats; the Dan McCarty High and Lincoln Park Academy bands, complete with mascots and majorettes, rhythmed the steps; county and city officials trucked along in hay-bale style; a bull-rider showed his prowess; cow-girls from the Okeechobee Rodeo high-stepped their horses; and all were headed by Sheriff John Norvell, as marshal, flanked by two be-feathered pseudo-Indians.

Meanwhile, back at the ranch, Alfred Norman recalled that Tommy had a steep learning curve. "He didn't know what he was doing," Alfred said. And yet, he acknowledged that Tommy slowly learned how to be a rancher, eventually taking control of Cow Creek, though in Alfred's mind Tommy was always suspect.

"I never did think a helluva lot of Tommy Sloan, to tell you the truth," Alfred said. "Not one bit. Tommy, he was a big-timer, had his name wrote on his cigars and all that kind of shit."

Deroy Arnold, son of early Cow Creek ranch hand Curtis Arnold and nephew of hand Will'um Thomas, said Tommy even had to learn how to ride a horse.

"I remember my daddy and Will'um talking that when Tommy went there, he didn't even know how to saddle a horse or ride a horse, but it wasn't long after that he caught on," Deroy said. "Then he started having all these handmade saddles and his name on his cigars."

Deroy said Tommy would always have a box of cigars in his vehicle and three or four in his pocket. His initials appeared on the cigar band, which Darren Robertson said he always twisted before throwing away.

Besides his ranch duties, Tommy immersed himself in the community. By 1958, the twenty-six-year-old Tommy became head of the St. Lucie County Cattlemen's Association, the youngest person ever to head the organization. He also was named disaster chairman of the American Red Cross and a director of the Junior Chamber of Commerce.

He captured headlines in 1959 when a blown tire caused him to crash in a ditch while driving on a dirt road at the ranch. With the car underwater, Tommy escaped through a back window and managed to crawl to Okeechobee Road, where a passing motorist took him to the hospital. Newspaper accounts reported that his leg was shattered and emergency surgery was required.

Meanwhile, as the 1950s came to a close, Jo Ann received multiple notices for her work with the Poinciana Garden Circle and the Presbyterian church. She literally took Fort Pierce's center stage when she was tapped for the leading role of Nora in Ada Coats Williams's *Along These Waters*, a somewhat annual production about early Fort Pierce settlers performed at the Fort Pierce Amphitheater.

"Mother really enjoyed acting, and she was very good," Debra said. "I had fond memories of that. I just remember her getting all wrapped up in it, and Honey would take us to some of the productions. It was a lot of fun. She was really good. Everything she did, she did with perfection. I think that was ingrained in her on a cellular level."

12

COW CREEK IN THE 1960S

The Cowboys

Jo Ann and Tommy Sloan were fortunate to be able to rely on a core group of cowboys to help run Cow Creek, some of them going back to Jo Ann's grandfather's ownership.

In the late 1950s and throughout the 1960s, the couple found much of their guidance in the form of brothers Aubrey and Curtis Arnold, who were raised in Sherman, southeast of Okeechobee. Both had worked at Cow Creek under ranch foreman John Norman in the early 1950s, served tours in the army, and returned to Okeechobee, eventually working full-time at Cow Creek. Aubrey would become the ranch's foreman.

They were the sons of a state road department foreman and were adept at working heavy equipment. Curtis, a quiet man with bright-blue eyes, also was instrumental in starting the ranch's citrus groves. Aubrey's wife, Ethel, whom Aubrey married in 1958, eventually would become the full-time cook at the ranch. They lived and reared their children in one of the small houses on the ranch.

Ethel said in a 2022 interview that the ranch was an ideal place to raise children. They could ride horses, play with the pet pig Spots or the tame deer Moses, or swim in Cow Creek. "That was their swimming hole when it rained," said Ethel, who divorced Aubrey in 1974 and remarried and became known as Ethel Durden. "They always had something to do. It wasn't like kids nowadays, sitting on the phone."

above The crossing at Cow Creek was a popular swimming hole for ranch families and visitors. (Courtesy of the Arnold family.)

right Aubrey and Ethel and children Steve and Patty stand near the ranch-hand houses at Cow Creek in 1965. (Courtesy of the Arnold family.)

Ranch life was challenging. Ethel said she'd start making the cowboys breakfast at 5:00 a.m., drive her kids 4 miles through the ranch to the bus stop, come back to feed the bulls molasses, and clean the kitchen before beginning to prepare lunch and then serve it.

When the ranch was short-staffed, in between meals, she'd be called upon to saddle up and help with cattle roundups or work the parting gate separating cattle to be sold from cattle that will be kept. She even learned to work heavy equipment, a skill that would later become useful in the longtime job she held running bulldozers and front-end loaders for Osceola County.

Ethel and Aubrey's son, Steve, recalled that Tommy was so closely involved in managing the ranch in the late 1960s that he even oversaw how workers would interact with each other. When two of the summer ranch hands got in a fight and nearly drowned each other while putting up fence, Tommy made them actually kiss and make up. "They either had to do that or pack their bags," he said.

Steve recalled the kindness of Jo Ann, grabbing him to go squirrel hunting at the ranch with her or sometimes shuttling him around Fort Pierce, where he attended school. "You couldn't ask for no better lady than what Jo Ann was," said Steve, who followed the cowboy life and has worked for Perry Smith and Sons farms of Okeechobee for four decades.

Also working at the ranch was Curtis's brother-in-law, Will'um Thomas, a highly skilled horseman who also worked at Cow Creek in the Raulerson years. Will'um could find—and inject—humor into any almost any situation. Born in Avon Park without a father who would acknowledge him, he referred to himself as "an old woods colt."

Will'um was the next-best thing to being a brother to Curtis and Aubrey. Will'um had married Arizona "Punk" Raulerson in 1943. When Curtis married Punk's younger sister, Vena "Vee" Raulerson, a decade later, the two became lifelong best friends.

Punk and Vee were the daughters of Arabell Carter Raulerson and Walter Raulerson, the son of Noel Rabun Raulerson Jr. Walter died in 1954 at the age of seventy-four, and Arabell, at the age of fifty-eight, married Walter's much younger brother, Harley, sixty-five, in 1961. Thus, Punk and Vee were distant cousins of Jo Ann.

Punk was a cook at the ranch in the late 1950s, and Will'um often took

Cow Creek cowboys Will'um Thomas and brothers Aubrey and Curtis Arnold (*left to right*) at a party at TL and Jo Ann Sloan's home in the 1960s. (Courtesy of the Pickering family.)

over the duties when Punk couldn't. "I've known a lot of ranches, and the one thing about Cow Creek is they always had a cook," said Deroy Arnold. "They had breakfast, lunch, and dinner."

Curtis and Will'um stayed in the ranch's bunkhouse during the week and would return to their homes in Okeechobee over the weekends or, more often, camp with their wives and Deroy on the north side of the ranch where they first had a small trailer and then a cabin.

The four were almost inseparable and together raised Deroy. "It was like having two sets of parents," Deroy said. "If one wouldn't give me what I wanted, I'd go to the other one."

Another fixture in the 1960s was cowboy and strongman Earl Story. He and wife, Joan, and their children, Little Earl, Mordy, and Nancy, also lived in one of the ranch houses.

"Earl worked the cow pens in the catch and squeeze shoot," said Kent Mills, whose father, the legendary cowboy George Harrison "Junior" Mills, and mother, cook Betty Mills, worked and raised their family at Cow Creek from 1970 to 1977. "It required a pretty stout fellow to do that, and Earl had some pretty strong cannons and was exactly what was needed for that job."

Earl's pride for Cow Creek ran deep. Besides his cowboy duties, one of his favorite chores was making sure the grass was meticulously mowed around ranch headquarters.

William Washington, an African American who had the nickname Old Folks, also drove the ranch tractors and worked on maintenance. Washington was a native of Brunswick, Georgia, who had moved to Fort Pierce in the 1920s. On his Sundays off, he'd frequently return to the ranch with friends and family to cane-pole fish in the ranch's many canals.

At a time when many ranches used day cowboys—men hired by the day for certain jobs such as roundups or working cow pens—having a core of cowboys who lived at the ranch over several decades was unusual. Kent Mills said his parents had worked at several ranches over the years before landing at Cow Creek.

"Their pay was probably upward of what they had earned from any other place," he said. Besides the free meals at the bunkhouse or on-site, the

left Cow Creek cowboy Curtis Arnold cuts strips for making a cow whip, used for herding cattle. The popping sound from a whip prompts the animals to move but is not applied to them. (Photo by Michael Enns.)

Sloans also gave the full-time cowboys a house to live in and all liberties in the use of the ranch, including hunting rights. Some of the cowboys were even allowed to raise their own small herds on Cow Creek.

"It was like one big family out there," said Darren Robertson, who lived for several years at the ranch as a young boy and worked there during the summers as a teen.

Sport Pickering, who grew up at Cow Creek from 1960 to 1965 when his father worked there as a cowboy, said Tommy had tight reins over the ranch in the early years. "I can remember going with my dad to the old bunkhouse for breakfast," said Pickering, who also would later work as a cowboy at Cow Creek and later as a detective for the Okeechobee County Sheriff's Office. "Everybody would be sitting at the table and Tommy would be at the head dishing out what everybody needed to do that day." He also remembered Tommy's generosity. "Every year for Christmas he would buy me a hat or something," he said. "He was just always a nice guy."

Pickering's roots at Cow Creek run deep. His maternal grandfather, Sherrod Evers, operated a sawmill at Son Arnold Gulley, south of the ranch's headquarters, and then moved it to the north side of Cow Creek. "There's a lot of history at that ranch," he said.

Pickering shared the following memories of growing up at Cow Creek in the 1960s:

> All I wanted to do when I was growing up was work for Cow Creek someday. When we first moved to Cow Creek, I was only a few weeks old, and we lived in an old wooden house for a little while before moving into one of the block houses. I think three of those old wooden houses were on the west side of the cow pens and were used for storage. The mineral was kept in one of the old houses. I remember the old wooden bunkhouse before the new one was built.
>
> I was told that cowboys were playing cards late one night and were flipping cigarettes out of a hole in the screen door, and it caught fire and burned down. I remember eating in that old bunkhouse. I remember Earl and Joan Story living in one of the old wooden houses. As a small child, I remember seeing my father ride to the horse barn on his horse, ole Buck, and I would run to him from the house so I could ride Buck before he unsaddled him.

I remember swimming in the Cow Creek crossing as a child and going with my father and Aubrey Arnold rabbit hunting at night. I remember riding with Aubrey in the cow truck, backing it down into a ditch, jumping the horses into it, and bringing the cowboys and their horses back home from the Steer Pasture on the north side of the Cow Creek crossing.

I remember playing with Aubrey's son, Steve, and Earl Story's children. I remember riding in an old Jeep with my father putting out minerals, stopping at the old Seminole grove, picking oranges, tangerines, and grapefruit, and eating them while putting out minerals. When I got older, I did the same thing with Will'um.

Will'um would drive the Jeep, pull up to the mineral boxes, and tell you how many bags of minerals to put into each box. He was a card. He taught me when I was a child how to cuss, and more than once, I got into trouble with my mother for cussing, and Will'um would laugh.

There used to be an old domestic sow hog turned loose on the ranch, and she always hung around the houses. I can remember getting on her back and riding her. My mother has pictures of me riding her.

There was a deer, a buck, that they raised on the ranch called Moses. They castrated the deer when he was young, so when he started growing horns, he never lost them. He always stayed in velvet, and his horns were covered in ticks. They had a bell around his neck, and you could hear him walking around the woods. When you heard his bell, if you started calling his name, he would come to you looking for something to eat. My father would feed him a cigarette or two. He loved tobacco.

The first time I flew in a plane, Tommy took my father and me flying. Jimmy Percy once flew me from the ranch to the Okeechobee County airport to meet with my father. I remember cow hunting on an old gray horse named Matthews. I remember the Blue Mountain range, Dog Slough, Indian Slough, Wagon Wheel, Steer Pasture, Big Island, JB Pasture, as well as the small field pastures riding alongside people like Jimmy Percy, Will'um Thomas, Deroy Arnold, Earl Story, Junior Mills, Larry Kesner, Bucky Walters (Bucky worked for the St. Lucie County Sheriff's Office, but he passed away a few years ago. He and Jimmy were the best of friends), to name just a few. I remember staying in the new bunkhouse with Will'um and Curtis. They would go to bed by seven or seven thirty, and if you did not go before them, you did not get much sleep because they snored severely.

The Sloan family in the 1960s near their home on Orange Avenue. Jo Ann and TL are in the middle. Kathy is on the left, and Debra on the right. (Courtesy of the Pickering family.)

Beyond the cowboys who could hunt at the ranch, Tommy and Jo Ann had a small circle of seemingly strategically selected people who could hunt at the ranch. Two bankers, Bob Terry Sr., president of St. Lucie County Bank, and Howard Jernigan, president of First National Bank of Fort Pierce, had hunting camps at the ranch. Bobby Enns, the editor of the *News-Tribune*, helped work cattle at the ranch on Mondays, one of his days off at the newspaper, and camped and hunted at the ranch with his family. Vinnie Gorham, owner of Gorham Construction, a Fort Pierce–based road construction company that excavated shell and marl at the ranch, also hunted at Cow Creek.

Tommy and Jo Ann also became friends with Riviera Beach psychiatrist

Dr. Jack Wright and his wife, Sally, and allowed them to build a small house next to theirs at the ranch's homeplace. Jack Wright, an avid hunter, had become friends with Tommy through the orthopedist who treated Tommy for his leg injuries, and Sally and Jo Ann also grew to be close friends.

Extra Help

Kathy and Debra also became involved at the ranch at a young age, learning to ride horses almost as soon as they could walk. Debra remembered working with the cowboys when she was five. "I asked to go work with the cowboys, and my father said, 'Well, I don't want to hear "I want a drink of water." I don't want to hear anything,'" she said. "And so they always put me at the tail end of the cows driving them up."

Debra began driving the ranch Jeeps at the age of seven, and one of her favorite things to do was to run the mineral Jeep and deliver mineral blocks to various pastures around the ranch. "I would go out with Will'um . . . and I loved that because he knew all the cool places to go," she said.

Kathy, a year older than Debra, said that during school they'd mostly spend weekends at the ranch. "During spring and fall roundup, we'd stay out there, and Debra and I would take the bus from the ranch to school. A lot of summers we'd go out there and spend all summer."

Family on Parade

During the 1960s, the Sloan family was one of the most prominent in what had become Fort Pierce's biggest event: the Cattlemen's Day Parade, the climax of the annual Sandy Shoes Festival. Riding on their horses as part of the Cow Creek Ranch unit, the Sloans won "best family unit" in 1963 and 1965, the same year Jo Ann also won the award for "best horsewoman."

Held on a Saturday during the peak of tourist season, the parade featured dozens of ranch units and often more than one hundred horse-riding cattlemen and cattlewomen. From the spectators' points of view, sitting on the curb or standing on the sidewalk, it was a grand display of the town's agricultural roots and seemed almost as if the cattlemen and cattlewomen were riding off their ranches into downtown for the afternoon.

For many years the parade passed right by the Sloans' home on Orange

Tommy Sloan led the Cow Creek Ranch unit during the annual Cattlemen's Day Parade. (Courtesy of the Sloan family.)

Avenue and Eleventh Street, with the Cow Creek Ranch unit tying up their horses behind the house to attend a big parade after party each year. "The Sandy Shoes parade was the only time of year I wore boots and a hat," Kathy said. "I usually liked to ride in shorts and barefoot."

In the early years, Tommy's mother, Honey, and Jo Ann would sew shirts for those riding in the unit before buying the matching attire from the Farm Supply Western store. "We'd all have matching shirts riding in the parade," said Debra.

Memories of the Cattlemen's Parade are cemented in the collective minds of the cowboys' families: bourbon pints not so well hidden in saddles; the year that a parade-watcher who happened to be a horse trainer helped calm a colicky horse that Junior Mills was riding; and, best remembered of all, the year Jack Crain's Model T broke down and Will'um towed it in the parade with his horse, Jack, showcasing Will'um's cowboy ingenuity and creating a scene that made the next day's newspaper.

He's the Boss

Though Jo Ann was the inheritor of the ranch, it was Tommy who exercised chief control over it and the other assets, including the Raulerson Building, which provided steady commercial rental income. Only a men's clothing salesman when he met Jo Ann, Tommy worked his way into becoming part of the power elite of Fort Pierce. Despite his having grown up with modest means, Tommy's civic involvement in organizations such as Red Cross, the Jaycees, and the Elks, in addition to his leadership of the Florida Cattlemen's Association, created a wide network of influential friends. He never lost his boyhood self-assurance and married one of the largest landowners in the county. With a cigar clenched in his mouth, he began to exude a sense of money and power to those around him. People and the press began to take note.

In 1960, he gained local press notices for his ranch work. In a column titled "Hammock Country," the *News-Tribune* reported that "Sloan is responsible for the daily health of his stock, for the maintenance of 36 sections of pasture and for seeing that the herd increases through careful breeding."

The profile also noted that he was raising "Herefords, Brahmans and selected cross-strains of cattle for sale to all parts of the U.S." It described facilities at the ranch as "machinery for land clearing and planting, homes for the three families who live there year-round, a bunkhouse for the hands, barns and maintenance sheds."

Okeechobee property records show that three houses, two of 960 square feet and one of 1,217 square feet, were built on the property in 1960. The original ranch house built by Frank Raulerson in 1930, where the Sloans spent weekends, remained the biggest house on the property.

The article detailed Tommy's typical work day as leaving Fort Pierce at 5:00 a.m. for the 17-mile drive to the ranch, "breakfast at 6 and then 12 more hours overseeing the work of seven employees. Much of the time is spent on horseback checking stock or moving herds from one pasture to another." The article also noted that Tommy was trying to improve 500 acres of the ranch each year, "acting on the theory that where 20 acres of raw land is needed to support one animal, one acre of improved pasture will do the job."

A 1962 article in the *News-Tribune* credited him with creating a doctoring chute that holds cattle still during the administration of antibiotics and a drenching syringe that would stay loaded with stomach worm and liver-fluke medicine through pressure hoses instead of having to reload the syringe after each usage.

Tommy's work was so hands-on that in 1963 he was charged by a bull and broke his leg while attempting to drive it to another pasture. It was the same leg that had been injured in the 1959 automobile accident on the ranch. The latest break left him with a slight limp for the rest of his life.

The injury didn't stop his rise in the cattle industry. That same year he became head of the Florida Beef Council, an arm of the Florida Cattlemen's Association aimed at increasing the consumption of beef. The Sloans also attended the National Cattlemen's Association convention in Las Vegas that year.

Perhaps feeling overconfident in his establishment support, Tommy in 1966 made an impressive but unsuccessful run for a seat in the Florida House of Representatives on the Democratic ticket against longtime incumbent representative Frank H. Fee. In his concession speech, Tommy said, "Let me assure you that my interest in obtaining good clean government for our area is only strengthened and I will continue to work in every way possible for the advancement of our four counties."

Tommy's work with the Beef Council and his ranch garnered further statewide recognition. In 1967, the Alachua Lions Club honored Tommy as the man contributing the most to the Florida cattle industry in the past year. The club cited Tommy's work as president of the Florida Beef Council. In the five years Tommy served as president, the council's contributions increased from $6,000 to $50,000 annually.

Ranch Improvements

Since taking over the ranch after the death of Frank Raulerson in 1954, Tommy had mechanized many of the functions, such as vaccinating and dipping cattle against diseases. He wisely leased many of his pastures to tomato farmers, who rotate their crops to avoid disease and in the process clear and improve irrigation at little cost to the ranch.

A sign of the ranch's success under Tommy's leadership was the construction in 1968 of a modern concrete bunkhouse to replace the wooden one. The new bunkhouse was outfitted with central air conditioning, a television, a large bathroom with two showers, a kitchen equipped with a dishwasher, an ice maker, two ranges, a refrigerator freezer, and a walk-in cooler for hanging beef, deer, and hog carcasses.

The new bunkhouse was decorated with paintings from wildlife artist Robert Butler and cowboy artist E. L. "Buster" Kenton, both of whom have been inducted into the Florida Artists Hall of Fame. The bunkhouse's most prominent feature was a large round table—capable of seating a dozen or more people—created from the bottom of the ranch's old cistern.

During the 1960s, Tommy also increased his geographic reach around the state. He bought a Cessna airplane and later a Helio Courier, a plane that can take off and land on a short runway and that can maintain control at speeds as low as 27 mph without stalling, perfect for ranching. He was so smitten with flying that in 1969 he created a grass runway behind the main ranch headquarters.

Tommy's flying passion also led him to another one: owning German shepherds. He met a dog trainer at an airport one day who had a shepherd and asked her whether it was for sale. She declined to sell it but told him about other dogs she had. The discussion led to Tommy's purchase of Gunner for Jo Ann, the first of many German shepherds the family would

From left: Darren Robertson, Deroy Arnold, Steve Arnold, and Donnie Robertson astride their horses about 1969 in front of Tommy Sloan's Helio Courier at the runway behind the Cow Creek Ranch headquarters. (Courtesy of the Robertson family.)

have over the years. The family's shepherd brood sometimes numbered as many as five.

Jo Ann in the Limelight, Too

While Tommy was gaining local and state prominence in the 1960s, so was Jo Ann. She continued playing the role of Nora in Ada Coats Williams's *Along These Waters* and, along with Kathy and Debra, also appeared in another play, *24 Carat*, produced by the Fort Pierce Woman's Club. Jo Ann also played Mrs. Clyde Platts in a production of *Doctor of the River Ridge*, a pageant at the Fort Pierce Amphitheater that "continues its historical account of the pioneers who saw the future of a new country and how they met the problems and forged a thriving area out of wilderness."

A talented floral arranger and gardener, Jo Ann also became president of the Poinciana Garden Circle and was heavily involved with the St. Lucie County Fair, where she was chairwoman of the Booth Committee.

Playing to her strengths as a cattlewoman, she helped form the St. Lucie County CowBelles, the local chapter of the auxiliary of the Florida Cattlemen's Association, often hosting meetings in her home. In 1964, she was elected president of the St. Lucie County CowBelles, a position she would hold for three years before becoming president in 1968 of the statewide organization, now known as Florida Cattle Women Inc.

The CowBelles were founded in 1939 by ranching women living in Cochise County, Arizona, "to promote friendly and social relations among cattle people and to cooperate for the best interests of our industry, our community." The first statewide organization was established in Wyoming in 1940. Florida formed a statewide chapter in 1961, and by 1964, more than three hundred women had joined the Florida CowBelles, with the *News-Tribune* describing the St. Lucie County CowBelles as being "one of the most active chapters in the state."

When Jo Ann began her county presidency of the CowBelles in 1964, she oversaw a Beef Institute cooking school that area homemakers were invited

Kathy and Debra Sloan appeared in a 1963 production of *Li'l Abner* with their pet pig Spots, a wild hog they tamed as a pet. The sow raised generations of piglets around the ranch headquarters. (Courtesy of the Sloan family.)

to attend free. The school, held at the Fort Pierce Armory, featured tutorials on cooking beef by a home economist for Swift & Company. Jo Ann also was involved in planning for the Florida State Cattlemen and CowBelles convention held in June in Port St. Lucie, just south of Fort Pierce.

Another activity sponsored by the CowBelles was a "Beef Round-Up" program that "was a brainchild of the Florida Beef Council under Tommy Sloan of Fort Pierce," the *Fort Pierce News-Tribune* reported. Under the program, whose overall goal was to increase beef sales, the CowBelles arranged with local supermarkets to promote the Beef Round-Up, offering special sales on beef. The CowBelles supplied the stores with banners and window streamers and set up information tables in the stores. The *News-Tribune* reported that the women, "all decked out in cowboy (or cowgirl) garb, will be on hand in the stores to answer housewives' questions that are expected to range from 'How to prepare inexpensive cuts' to 'How many calories in sirloin steak.' They also distributed literature published by the Florida Beef Council that includes beef charts, cooking times for different cuts, calorie charts and recipe booklets." The *News-Tribune* also reported that CowBelles at the Fort Pierce Publix had passed out beef balls in steak and mushroom sauce during one of their Beef Round-Ups.

During one event later that year, Jo Ann presented a king-sized steak to Fort Pierce Mayor L. A. O'Laughlin Jr. to promote beef as a great gift for Father's Day, with the mayor announcing that he would issue a proclamation calling on Fort Pierce residents to do more "beefing." In 1965, Jo Ann led a Cattlemen's "Steer Project," which raised money for a new St. Lucie County Agriculture Building.

Jo Ann was elected president of the Florida CowBelles in 1968. Serving on the board with her as corresponding secretary-treasurer of the three-hundred-person organization was Diane Robertson, wife of a new ranch hand hired at Cow Creek.

One of the activities the Florida CowBelles produced in 1968 was the annual Beef Cookoff, in which high school girls would submit original recipes for dishes using beef. The three girls submitting the best recipes—Shoulder Round Pot Roast, Hamburger Stroganoff, and Peppered Stripped Chuck Steak—were declared the first-, second-, and third-place winners. The association also prepared beef recipes in 1968 for the Festival of Florida Foods supermarket showcase held in Orlando.

13

RANCH IMPROVEMENTS

Developing a Better Herd

In the two decades that Tommy and Jo Ann Sloan had taken over the reins of running Cow Creek, the ranch had come a long way from the open-range and scrub cow days of Frank Raulerson. Tommy had modernized the vaccination and dipping of cattle while also transitioning the scrub cattle herd that Frank Raulerson had raised mostly on the open range.

The ability to improve the herd had mostly come along with the change from grazing cattle in the open range to keeping them within fences. With enclosed pastures, ranchers could improve their herd through selective breeding and improved nutrition. They could identify the bull yearlings with the best physical attributes and adaptability to the Florida environment and use them as sires for the herd. The rest of the young bulls would become feeder steers that could be fattened. In some cases, bulls from the outside were purchased from breeders. They could also better identify cows that didn't give birth, culling them from the herd and sending them to market.

With enclosed pastures, they would put bulls and cows in separate pastures, mixing the bulls with the cows to time the birthing of most calves to happen in early spring. Living in a grass-fed operation, cows thrive best in the spring, the time of year when grass begins to grow its thickest, providing more nutrition for the cows, which then pass it on to their young through nursing. Like humans, cows have a nine-month gestation period.

Timing births enabled the ranchers to work cattle at a similar time and to take them to market in similar groups. For example, young bull calves that weren't going to be used as sires could be castrated at about the same age, with a preference for castrating them as early as possible to reduce stress-related weight loss or illness. The castrated young bulls would become steers, the primary beef cattle sold at market.

Like many other Florida operations, the ability to time births had transitioned Cow Creek from a feeder beef operation that supplied grown scrub cattle for butchering to mostly local markets into a cow/calf operation that focused on the reproduction of calves that, after reaching 300 pounds, could be sold and shipped to be fattened in richer pastures and feed lots in the American West.

With Florida's growing season lasting up to two hundred days longer than that in other parts of the country, agriculture has long been one of the state's most dominant industries. In 2022, agriculture was the sixth-largest industry in Florida, after tourism, international trade, life sciences, financial services, and aerospace. Nearly half of Florida agricultural land is involved in cattle production.

Alfred Norman, the cowboy who worked at Cow Creek going back to the 1940s, said Frank Raulerson predominantly ran Florida scrub cattle until the late 1940s, when he introduced Hereford bulls to the herd. The cross with Herefords helped the beef grade out better, but the Herefords didn't hold up well in the Florida heat. The Herefords are a British breed, with a bull and two females imported by the politician Henry Clay of Kentucky in 1817. Herefords today are predominantly white-faced with a red coat.

After the Herefords, Alfred said, the ranch introduced Brahman bulls, native to India and far more heat tolerant than the Herefords. The Brahmans are easily identified by the hump above their shoulders and their folds of loose skin. They have a short coat and can be dark gray and various shades of red or black.

One of the earliest introductions of Brahmans in the United States came in 1854 with two bulls that were given as a gift from Great Britain to a Louisiana farmer who had assisted the British government in teaching about cotton and sugarcane production in India, according to the American Brahman Breeders Association. The American Brahman, touted as the first beef breed developed in the United States, is a quick weight gainer, has a long lifespan, and is more resistant to pests, disease, and temperature fluctuations.

The introduction of new breeds and the arrival of fences marked the beginning of the end for Florida's lowly scrub or cracker cattle, which had been Florida's foundation for nearly five hundred years.

Descended from the Andalusian cattle brought by the Spanish in the 1500s, the cattle developed through natural selection in Florida's hostile environment. Like similar herds developed elsewhere by the Spanish in North and South America, these cattle became known as Criollo, meaning that they originated in Spain but were developed in the New World.

Scrub cattle are related to the more familiar Texas longhorns, also escapees from the Spanish as they moved up from Mexico, with the main difference that, whereas the horns of the Texas cattle grow long and out, the horns of Florida cracker cattle were shorter, perhaps due to poorer nutrition, and turned up, likely an adaptation to having to forage in scrub instead of wide plains.

The strengths of the scrub cattle were that they developed tolerance to heat, resistance to parasites and diseases, and were able to forage in swamps and thick brush before the creation of improved pastures. The main drawbacks were that they were scrawny and hard to market outside Florida because they competed with higher-quality purebred beef from the West.

To counter this, Florida cattlemen like Frank Raulerson crossed the scrub cattle with other breeds until they nearly eliminated scrub cattle from the state. Today, scrub cattle are rarely found in Florida. A few herds are maintained in state parks and forests. A group called the Florida Cracker Cattle Association, supported by the Florida Department of Agriculture, was established in 1988 to ensure the breed's continuation.

The Brahman and Hereford crosses that Raulerson and other ranchers were producing became a hearty cattle called Braford. "The Herefords grade out better for meat, but they aren't as heat tolerant," said Deroy Arnold. "That's why they crossed the Brahman with the Hereford to make a Braford because they could tolerate this Florida heat better."

Neighboring Cow Creek rancher Bud Adams is credited with developing the foundation herd of these red cattle, which are five-eighths Hereford and three-eighths Brahman. In 1947, Adams began with a base herd of Brahman cattle bred by Edgar Hudgins, one of the biggest influencers on the Brahman breed, and Henry O. Partin, considered the father of the Brahman breed in Florida and a founder of the Florida Cattlemen's Association.

In 1936, Partin brought in a herd of 131 purebred Brahmans to Florida from a ranch in Texas, and by about 1941 a young bull that Partin had bred, Emperor, won grand champion honors at the state fair in Tampa. Emperor was soon used as a sire by other Florida cattlemen, and his descendants won 108 blue ribbons around the nation in a two-year period. Partin and Emperor were credited with establishing the Brahman breed in Florida.

Adams had been breeding Herefords and found success with the resulting steer and heifer calves, but he discovered that the bulls had problems with feet, eyes, and adapting to Florida's conditions. He then began experimenting with Brahman-Hereford crossbred bulls to achieve the right percentage to meet the needs of his ranch and market demands. In the process, he established the foundation herd of the Braford breed in the United States.

Over the years, Adams continued improving the herd, selecting bulls for reproduction based on weaning and yearling rates, and using natural selection to eliminate calving issues. Soon other Florida and Texas ranchers were taking note. The International Braford Association was established in 1969 in Fort Pierce, and a second organization, the American Braford Registry, was established under the American Hereford Association in 1985. Because of demand for his bulls, Adams began auctioning his registered Brafords in 1979, an annual tradition that continues today under his sons. Adams died in 2017 at the age of ninety-one.

With 40,000 acres in St. Lucie, Okeechobee, Osceola, and Madison Counties, Adams Ranch Inc. is the fourth-largest ranch operation in Florida, behind No. 1 Lykes Ranch, with more than 600,000 acres in South Central Florida; No. 2 Deseret Ranches, owned by the Mormon Church, with 312,00 acres; and No. 3 Bluehead Ranch, near Lake Okeechobee, with 66,000 acres.

Though not as scientific in his approach as Bud Adams, Tommy was also developing his own crosses of Brahman and Hereford cattle. At Blue Mountain, he put Brahman bulls on Hereford cows. Then at pastures near State Road 68, north of the Cow Creek swamp, he put Hereford bulls on Brahman cows. At the JB Pasture on the south side of the ranch he put Braford bulls on Braford cows.

The other breeds of cattle in Florida today besides Hereford, Brahman, and Braford are Angus, a Scottish breed with a black hide and muscular body; Charolais, a French breed typically white with a pink muzzle and pale hooves; Limousin, another French breed with a gold hide, a small head, and a short neck; Brangus, a cross between Angus and Brahman; and Beefmaster, a composite breed developed in Texas that's about half Brahman and a fourth each of Hereford and Shorthorn, a dual-purpose breed that can be used for beef or milk production.

Besides quality of beef, the breeds are chosen for ease of calving. Some breeds are also developed to eliminate horns, and these are called polled breeds. The horns, used in nature to defend the animal from predators such as coyotes, can injure handlers and other cattle, make shipping difficult, and are an obstacle to modern skinning techniques. Horned cattle also can command less at market. Two of the more popular polled breeds in Florida are Angus and Hereford. Some ranches that run horned cattle add dehorning to their workups before the cattle are sold.

Switch to Cow/Calf Operation

Besides providing the ability to improve breeds and control reproduction, fences also helped Cow Creek transition from a feeder beef ranch that supplied beef to local and regional markets to a cow/calf operation.

Cow/calf operations typically have two birth seasons, the fall season, which covers the last months of the year, and the spring season, from about February to May. In a cow/calf operation, ranchers try to time most of their calf birthing for the spring, when grasses grow the fastest and provide more forage for cows, which in turn pass on the nutrition to their nursing young, enabling them to gain weight more quickly.

During their first few months, calves are rounded up and taken to pens to be worked up. During one workup, calves receive shots for viruses and bacteria and are wormed, either by injection or oral drenching, delivering the medication into the mouth.

Unlike the old Western movies that depict high-energy chases, much of the focus in handling cattle is on keeping them calm and reducing stress, which causes the animals to eat less and grow more slowly.

Young bulls that aren't selected for breeding are castrated and become steers, which grow faster, reach heavier weights, and command more money at market than heifers, young female cows that have not yet given birth.

At about 400 to 500 pounds and about six to ten months of age, the steer and heifer calves are weaned, meaning they are permanently separated from their mothers. If the calves aren't weaned, they typically continue nursing from their mother even after the mother gives birth to a new calf, causing stress on the mother and providing less nutrition for the younger calf.

Ranchers typically retain most of their heifer calves to expand their herd. Once calves are designated to be removed from the herd, they are sold and shipped to the West to feed on richer pastures there, or the owner can retain them and have them graze on his pasture. These are known as stocker cattle. At about 800 pounds, the stocker cattle are taken to feed lots to bulk up on grain until reaching about 1,250 to 1,500 pounds, when they are slaughtered. The calves that are kept in the herd are given marks in their ears, which identify their sex and the ranch. Heifer calves are always branded because they will stay in the herd.

With the calves and stocker cattle sold, the focus is kept on herd reproduction, ensuring that the adult cows and bulls are reproducing at optimal levels. Cows that don't give birth and bulls that don't have a high fertility rate are typically culled from the herd, meaning they are taken to market and sold, most often for slaughtering.

Bull to cow ratio can vary, but a common range is 1:20 or 1:30 for experienced older bulls and 1:10 for younger bulls. Bulls are typically introduced into a pasture of cows for a period of three months to time the fall and spring birthing seasons and then rested. They can lose as much as 200 pounds during breeding season. Bulls are in their prime between the ages of two and five, after which their chances of being culled increase.

Heifers have their first calves at two to three years and produce about seven calves over their lifetime. They are typically culled at about ten years of age, as their reproduction success declines.

Florida was the No. 9 beef cow state in the country in 2024, with nearly 900,000 head, a decline of about 16 percent since 2017. Nearly half of Florida's agricultural lands are used for cattle grazing, and two-thirds of the state's cattle are found in South Florida. Most Florida ranches today are cow/calf operations, and in 2023 Florida was shipping out some 450,000 calves yearly.

In the days of Frank Raulerson, each cow required 10 to 15 acres of native range. Today, each cow requires 3 to 4 acres of improved pasture.

To supplement their grass diets during the slow-growing winter months, many ranchers supplement cattle diets with molasses, which is transported by tanker trucks to tanks that can be filled on a ranch. Mineral blocks, delivered to small sheds placed strategically in pastures, also provide supplements.

Then as now, unless a widespread disease is detected, cattle at Cow Creek generally do not receive individualized veterinary care. Many ranches like Cow Creek allow nature to take its course in the belief that natural selection will improve the herd.

At ranches like Cow Creek, most veterinary care is focused on the horses, the real workers of a ranch. Today, quarter horses have replaced the old cracker horses at many ranches. They can be used at two years old, reach their peak at five, and can still work through about fifteen years.

When they end their useful life, the horses are typically turned out to pasture to live out their remaining years. Buddy Mills retired Spur, the last horse owned by his dad, Cow Creek cowboy Junior Mills, at a pasture behind his home in Basinger in 2014, and the horse lived there until his death in July 2022 at the age of thirty-seven, an unusually long lifespan for a working horse. Mills said that in his experience most ranch horses live twenty-five to twenty-eight years.

Diversifying to Citrus

Many South Florida ranches, like Cow Creek, had developed citrus operations in addition to cattle to diversify and counterbalance times when cattle prices were flagging.

In the late 1960s, Tommy tapped Curtis Arnold, who had been cowboying at the ranch since the early 1950s, as grove manager and tasked him with creating a citrus grove on the north side of the ranch. It was a smart business decision. Cow Creek was located in the heart of the world-famous Indian River citrus belt, and the ranch could market its citrus as Indian River, which commands a higher price at the market.

Citrus is not indigenous to Florida and is another gift the Spaniards left to the peninsula. Indian River citrus traces its history to the early 1800s, when Douglas Dummett (1784–1857) planted a grove at his homestead on the Indian River at Merritt Island, about 80 miles north of Fort Pierce and

55 miles east of Orlando. Dummett, born in Barbados and the son of an English planter, during travels to Connecticut had encountered something foreign to him: the sweet fragrance of orange blossoms. He traced the smell of the blossoms to a wild grove along the east bank of the Indian River and later established his own grove at Merritt Island, near the present-day Kennedy Space Center.

While cultivating his groves, he developed a method called top-working, in which he grafted sweet orange trees to sour trees such as rough lemon, and the first fruit from the region was commercially shipped in 1828. Top-working resulted in a base tree of sour stock that was more resistant to disease, and the top produced sweet fruit from the sweet orange grafts. Perhaps because of its southerly location on the coast, Dummett's grove survived the devastating freeze of 1835, and he became the source for future citrus stock in the region. The Second Seminole War also did not stop his efforts.

During the war, Dummett served as captain and led a volunteer unit known as the Mosquito Roarers. Dummett was wounded with three others in the hourlong battle defending the Dunlawton Plantation on the Halifax River on January 18, 1836. After the war, with the help of enslaved laborers, Dummett continued to cultivate his groves at Merritt Island, one of the few Indian River settlers who did not abandon his property during the Second Seminole War.

Dummett became well-known for the quality of his citrus, and by 1860 the groves he planted had more than 2,000 trees, with each tree averaging ten to twenty boxes.

With Dummett's success, groves began to be planted up and down the Indian River, and the region's citrus grew in reputation.

Meanwhile, other Florida growers outside the region also labeled their citrus "Indian River." Upset about the mislabeling, growers led by Will Fee of Fort Pierce got the Federal Trade Commission to issue a "cease and desist" order prohibiting the use of the term "Indian River" from being used on citrus not grown in the area that would eventually be established as the Indian River Citrus District.

But it took years for the boundaries of the district to be defined. Finally the US Department of Agriculture determined that Indian River fruit should be separated from interior fruit for regulatory purposes and the economic good of the industry. The district's boundaries include parts of Volusia, Brevard, Indian River, Martin, and Palm Beach Counties and all of St. Lucie County.

The Indian River Citrus League, formed in 1931, says that the quality of Indian River citrus can be attributed to the soil in the region, which is underlain by a formation composed of coquina limestone. During the growing cycle, the root system of citrus trees taps the limestone for essential minerals and nutrients. The flatness of the district and its high water table also provide trees "with enough moisture to obtain the highest quality of texture, shape and flavor."

The league says citrus needs approximately 1 inch of rain per week to produce good citrus, with the average rainfall over the district being 52 inches a year, producing a fruit that is thin-skinned with a high sugar content.

The Citrus League also claims the district has built-in freeze protection because of several factors. It is more southerly than earlier locations and is buffered by the rivers, swamps, and lakes of Central Florida. It's also more easterly. If you draw a longitude line below Jacksonville, Vero Beach—the heart of the district—is actually 100 miles east of the line, placing it closer to the warm Gulf Stream. The region's flat topography allows growers to flood their groves to the level of tree trunk, creating a temporary lake that radiates heat and increases temperatures.

Florida's citrus acreage, along with that of the Indian River region, has declined in recent decades because of diseases such as canker and greening, pressures from development, and changes in market conditions. Florida citrus acreage dropped from 857,687 acres in 1996 to 274,705 in 2024, according to the US Department of Agriculture.

The Indian River Citrus District's premium crop remains grapefruit, with the district providing 69 percent of the state's grapefruit crop in 2021, according to the USDA. The Indian River Citrus District had 13,703 acres in grapefruit production, 11,385 acres in orange production, and 6,226 acres in specialty citrus production in 2021.

At Cow Creek Ranch, turning former pastures and scrublands into Indian River citrus groves proved a success, and eventually a total of 800 acres were planted on the St. Lucie County side of the ranch. None was planted on the Okeechobee side, since the citrus grown in that county couldn't be labeled as Indian River.

Historically, the heart of the region—Indian River, St. Lucie, and Martin Counties—was called the Indian Riverland, paying tribute to its citrus roots and the waterway that runs through the three counties. But in the 1960s, the region came to be promoted as the Treasure Coast after salvage divers and historians confirmed it was where a fleet of eleven Spanish ships carrying silver and gold sank during a 1715 hurricane, scattering treasure in the ocean and onshore.

14

IN THE LIMELIGHT

Discovery *Finds Cow Creek*

The 1960s reached a peak for Tommy and Jo Ann in 1968, when ABC TV came calling. Script writer Joe Hurley, intent on producing a show that emphasized the growth of the cattle industry in Florida and dispelling the notion that all cattle-raising was occurring in the West or Midwest, picked Cow Creek to feature on the *Discovery* television show. Hurley said he selected Cow Creek over several other Florida ranches because of its "progressive program of cattle production."

It probably didn't hurt either that Tommy was the head of the Florida Beef Council and the show was done with the cooperation of the council and the Florida Cattlemen's Association, of which Tommy was vice president and soon would become president.

Hurley spent two weeks at Cow Creek writing the show before a thirteen-member crew descended on the ranch in January 1968, filming over three days at the ranch, along with takes at the Okeechobee Livestock Market.

"I remember they took me out of school to do the filming," said Deroy Arnold, who was ten at the time. Deroy appeared in several key scenes, including one in which he was throwing a lasso while roping a calf and another one in which he dragged his saddle into the barn after a long day's work. Deroy remembered the film crew would review daily takes in the hayloft above the horse barn, which was dark enough to accommodate the viewing.

The filming was exasperating for Kathy. "The directors kept telling me to saddle and unsaddle my horse," Kathy said. "They must have done sixteen takes. I wanted to tell them, 'I know how to saddle and unsaddle a horse.'" Looking back, Debra said it was a fair depiction of life at Cow Creek at the time. "Even if I had to saddle and unsaddle the horse way too many times, it was a good documentary," she said.

The show, titled *Florida: Cowboys, Coconuts and Cattle,* aired nationally at 11:30 a.m. EST on Sunday, March 10, 1968, before 25 million people. The Sloans hosted a huge party at their house for their viewing that included friends, the ranch hands, and their wives.

All of their regular cowboys were featured in the show, including Aubrey and Curtis Arnold, Will'um Thomas, and Earl Story. In the days before all television shows were in color and some were still black-and-white, the show, hosted by Bill Owen and Virginia Gibson, was presented as an ABC color presentation. "Cow Creek's owner thinks of the ranch as a factory and of himself as a manufacturer," Owen said in the introduction. "His product is beef. Tom Sloan and his wife, Jo Ann, have taken a ranch that was a good ranch for three generations and made it a better ranch."

The show opened with the cowboys sitting at a picnic table being served breakfast by Ethel before heading out for a cattle roundup. It centered mostly on Tommy's running of the ranch, with Jo Ann presented in a supporting role. Kathy and Debra, fourteen and thirteen at the time, were also prominently featured. In addition to a cattle roundup, the show featured a segment on the ranch's dipping and vaccination program to prevent disease.

"Behind all this—all the ingenuity, all the devices, all the inventions—are the men and woman who have a solid attachment to the land," Gibson said in one segment. "Added to that, they have a gift for living alongside the animals with whom they share it."

Ending the Decade

Tommy's publicity outreach didn't end with the airing of a national television program depicting him as a model rancher. He soon hosted outdoor writers and editors in a tour to watch ranch operations. After the *Discovery* airing, he also worked with the Florida Department of Agriculture, hosting several events at the ranch and at home for Puerto Rican ranchers visiting Florida. The interaction with the Puerto Rican ranchers led to a deal between them and Tommy to ship Brahman- and Hereford-cross yearlings to Puerto Rico, beginning in 1969, from Vero Beach Municipal Airport. Some were replacement heifers to be bred as cows; others were steers to be raised for slaughter.

Also in 1969, Tommy and Jo Ann, traveling with fellow ranchers Bud and Dot Adams, attended the 72nd Annual American National Cattlemen's Association convention held in Hawaii. Tommy had an even wider international reach in 1969, when he hosted Thai government official Siriwat Sarobo, who observed cattle breeding, feeding, and management at Cow Creek so he could help improve ranch production in Thailand.

Cow Creek Ranch improvements were boosted in 1968 with the arrival of new ranch hand Don Robertson, who had just finished a degree in animal husbandry from Texas Christian University. Arriving with him were his wife, Diane, and their three young children, Robin, Donnie, and Darren.

Don and Diane met at Miami Edison High School—she was a majorette and he was a football player—and married young. At Cow Creek, they lived in one of the ranch-hand houses, and their arrival brought a new dynamic to the ranch. "We went hog hunting almost every Sunday afternoon," recalled Robin, whose last name is now Longstreet.

Don was the son of wealthy bolita kingpin Charlie Robertson and always had a fallback if he grew unhappy in a job. After having kids, Don decided to go to college to study agriculture at Texas Christian University. While he was studying there, Diane and the kids lived at a farm Don's father owned in Georgia. Don got the job at Cow Creek shortly after his graduation from Texas Christian. Diane also began working as a secretary for Tommy at the ranch's corporate office in the Raulerson Building in downtown Fort Pierce.

Added to the mix was a young cowboy named Jimmy Percy, who worked at the ranch as a teen and had met the Sloans through Cathy Browning, the daughter of their friend Dr. John Browning. The smart and handsome Percy showed great promise as a rancher, and Tommy and Jo Ann made him an offer he couldn't refuse when he graduated from high school in 1965: attend college to study agriculture and when he graduated, they would give him a job managing Cow Creek.

"He would stay at the bunkhouse during the summers," said Jamie Percy of Fort Pierce, Jimmy Percy's son. "Then once he graduated from high school, Tommy said, 'If you go to college you can come back and become the general manager of Cow Creek,' so my dad went to the University of Florida for four years."

Jimmy wasn't the only teen on the rise who would benefit from working summers at Cow Creek. One was William H. "Bud" Hallman III, who would become a Sumter County circuit judge. Hallman, a sixth-generation Floridian, was raised in Palm Beach County and was the great-grandson of Robert Roberts, who established the Red Cattle Co. ranches in Hendry County and the Lake Trafford Ranch in Collier County. Roberts eventually amassed 100,000 acres—some of it purchased for three cents per acre—and ran 10,000 head of cattle. After Roberts's death in 1963, his property was split up among his nine children.

Wanting to strike out on his own, Hallman worked as a summer cowboy at Cow Creek in 1970 and 1971. After high school, he continued working at ranches to put himself through college and law school. As a boy growing up at the foot of his great-grandfather, he was awestruck by the opportunity to work with cowboys at Cow Creek that he had heard about such as Junior Mills and Clyde Coker. "I pretty much knew about everybody at Cow Creek Ranch," said Hallman. "When I pulled in there I'd been around quite a bit. That ranch was like any of the famous cattle ranches you'd hear about."

Over the years, Hallman would work at dozens of ranches. In fact, his first job out of law school was not as a lawyer but as a cowboy at Double Diamond Ranch in Okeechobee.

Hallman remembered the hard work at Cow Creek and also the peculiar ranch boss, Tommy: "He had all the toys and things that would have made it look like he should be living in Palm Beach. He lived the life. He took me up in the plane and showed me what was going on. He had a lot of people coming in visiting the ranch, and it seemed like a whole lot of projects were going on."

Hallman said he was especially impressed with Tommy's horse operation, which combined the larger quarter horses with the nimble cracker horses: "It was an A Number One operation. Those days at Cow Creek have stayed with me, and I've compared every place I've been to how that was run. Everything I've done since has brought back memories from these days at Cow Creek. It was the equivalent of any big ranch you've heard of. It was a premier ranch."

The Rodeo

Hallman eventually went to work as an assistant state attorney in the Fifth Judicial Circuit and later in private practice before being appointed by former Gov. Jeb Bush as a judge in the Fifth Judicial Circuit, where he served from 2003 to 2021. Now retired, he has his own herd in Sumter County. Throughout his legal and judicial career, he competed in rodeos and is a two-time Florida state champion steer wrestler. In 1986, he won the Southeastern Region championship and was ranked tenth in the world standings of the International Professional Rodeo Association. He won the Professional Rodeo Cowboys Association Southeastern Circuit Finals when he was fifty-six. At age sixty-nine he was still competing in rodeo steer wrestling competitions. Hallman said his rodeo career was inspired in part by Cow Creek day cowboy Clyde Coker, who was a Florida state champion calf roper.

Besides Coker, other Cow Creek cowboys who competed in rodeo were Junior Mills, who had a brief career as a bull rider before working in the arena; Deroy Arnold, who competed in team roping; and Junior's son, Buddy, who participated in bareback bronc, bull-riding, and team roping.

Growing up at Cow Creek and sharpening his cowboy skills there, Buddy got a full-ride rodeo scholarship to Sheridan College, now Northeastern Wyoming College. He returned to Okeechobee County and was a longtime agriculture teacher at Yearling Middle School, a Future Farmers of America advisor, and rodeo coach at the middle school as well as at Okeechobee High School.

Buddy said competing in the rodeo was a break from the work of the ranch: "It was that challenge of putting my body to the test and the adrenalin rush that you get when you make a really good ride and you hear the crowd roaring." Buddy said the rodeo has changed from the days when ranch cowboys were exhibiting their best skills to featuring many competitors who never worked on a ranch and got hooked on the sport by watching it on television.

The rodeo tradition in Florida began almost as soon as the Spanish began working cattle on the peninsula as a way to both celebrate the end of a roundup and to exhibit the essential cattle-herding skills of roping, riding, and bulldogging, also known as steer wrestling. The word "rodeo" originates from the Spanish word *rodear*, meaning to encircle or round up. At first Florida rodeos were informal affairs held in the open or within cow pens, but eventually they became formal events with dedicated rodeo arenas located throughout Florida's cattle belt.

The Arcadia Rodeo holds the title of "The Granddaddy of 'em All," with the first rodeo there produced in 1929 by a group of American Legion members. Kissimmee in 1944 started the Silver Spurs Rodeos, named after the Silver Spurs Riding Club. The first Okeechobee Cowtown Rodeo was held in 1951 and is produced by the Okeechobee County Cattlemen's Association every Labor Day. Other rodeos in Florida are held in Homestead, Baker, Bonifay, Ocala, Tampa, Indiantown, New Smyrna Beach, and Davie, among many other places.

While Cow Creek is between Okeechobee and Fort Pierce, most of the ranch cowboys had family or social ties to Okeechobee, a close-knit community where the Okeechobee High School Brahman Bulls football team commands fall Friday nights, and one of the biggest annual events is the Okeechobee County Fair, all in keeping with Okeechobee's reputation as Florida's No. 1 county for beef production. Neighboring Highlands and Osceola Counties are second and third, according to 2022 statistics.

On the Homefront

By most outward appearances, Tommy and Jo Ann had the world by the tail in the 1960s. They were a modern ranching couple who worked together to achieve positive results for their ranch and the people it employed. With their large landholdings, newspaper notices, and fancy home and cars, they enjoyed an elevated status in Fort Pierce.

But not everything was roses.

Early in the 1960s, they were confronted with a family tragedy. When Tommy's aunt and uncle were killed, they left behind a high-school-age son, Charles Brantley. With nobody to care for him, Tommy and Jo Ann took up the challenge. "I can remember going to Jacksonville and everybody deciding that Charles would come live with us because we had the most means and opportunity for him," Debra recalled.

Debra said it was not unlike what happened to her mother when, at the age of eight, she became the ward of her grandparents, who concluded that they had better means to take care of Jo Ann than her biological mother.

Charles lived with the Sloans beginning in 1962. That year, the *News-Tribune* reported that Charles, fifteen, accompanied the Sloan family on a 9,850-mile, five-week vacation by car. Stops included Elk City, Idaho; the World's Fair in Seattle; Vancouver; San Francisco; and Disneyland. Kathy and Debra were eight and seven at the time. "According to Mrs. Sloan, the family [was] especially impressed with Disneyland, finding it of interest to all ages," the newspaper brief noted.

Charles lived with the Sloans until shortly after his graduation from Dan McCarty High School in 1965, when he was drafted into the army and served in Vietnam. After his discharge, he returned to Fort Pierce but had a falling out with the family and never saw them again.

Charles Brantley wasn't the only addition to the Sloan family in the 1960s. One day around Christmas 1965, Tommy loaded Kathy and Debra in his Cadillac and drove them to a house in Port St. Lucie. "Right before we got to the house he said, 'I have a Christmas present for you,'" Kathy remembered him saying. "'Y'all have a little brother.'"

And so was their introduction to William Thomas "Tee" Sloan, Tommy's son by his relationship with another rancher's wife. The boy, born November 21, 1963, was raised by his mother, who divorced her husband in 1965, with occasional visits by Tommy. At the request of another of the woman's sons, her name isn't being disclosed.

Debra and Kathy said that the extramarital relationship wasn't Tommy's first and that Jo Ann endured other relationships Tommy had with women besides Tee's mother. The girls say he never strayed far from his ladies'-man image in high school and often flirted with waitresses serving them.

"He never hid any of his indiscretions," Kathy said. "Mother truly loved him because she would never tell him no. She could have told him to hit the highway, but in the 1950s, '60s, and even '70s, divorce was frowned upon, especially for her. She didn't want to start over again. He had a way of making you feel that whatever he said was gospel."

Observed Kent Mills, who grew up at Cow Creek, "Tommy had some good ways about him, but he also had some bad ways, and he had some weaknesses as old as mankind."

Because Jo Ann's father died when she was eight and her grandparents took custody of her, separating her from her mother, Jo Ann had learned to endure almost anything. Raised by her domineering grandmother, she had also learned to stay silent and never publicly show her emotions. Her grandfather Frank was the head of the household and made all of the business decisions, and Jo Ann continued deferring to Tommy on all business matters.

Parental Roles

As parents go in the 1960s, Tommy and Jo Ann were strict. Kathy remembered Jo Ann focusing on speech. "'I don't give a darn. You will not say *ain't* in this house,'" Kathy said. "She was always correcting my English."

While Jo Ann was stressing manners and being a lady to the girls, Tommy spent a lot of time talking to them about life, sometimes incessantly. "I used to beg my dad to beat me [instead of] talking to me for fifteen minutes," Kathy said. "We didn't get too many 'I love yous.' There just wasn't a whole lot of affection."

Kathy said she began using drugs as an early teen and, at fifteen, secretly began dating a man seven years older than she was. She went to the elite private St. Edward's School in Vero Beach in ninth grade and public Dan McCarty High School in tenth and eleventh. "I don't know how I made A's and B's, but I did," she said. "I did a lot of drugs, and everybody I hung around with did. I was not a good kid, but I didn't go to jail or anything."

Debra said, as a parent, Jo Ann did the best she could with the tools she had: "Mother was strict. She wanted things done a certain way, and she wasn't very flexible. I think that had to do with Mother Lou and how she was raised. She was a loving parent as well as she could love, and she got better as she got older."

Jo Ann's exacting standards were always in effect at dinner, which was often served by maids. Silverware had to be set in a certain order, hands had to be in the lap, and the girls had to sit up straight and chew with their mouths closed—"all the things she would want for a perfect child," said Debra, their more obedient offspring. "I was a good child. I didn't give them any problems. I didn't want to get into any trouble."

Mostly, the girls found affection from Tommy's parents, their grandparents Aubrey, whom they called Aubie, and Honey. "I got most of my love and affection from Aubie, and mostly, Honey," Debra said. "She was a sweet woman and good to me. She knew that I didn't get that type of love from Jo Ann or TL."

Debra said Jo Ann had Tommy take care of disciplining the children. She said Tommy only spanked her once, when she told an off-color joke. "The best way I can describe TL's parenting philosophy is that children should be seen and not heard," Debra said. Kathy was more of a problem, and Tommy often beat her, Debra said. "Kathy was kind of wild," said Debra. "She would push the rubber band until it almost broke."

On family car trips, Tommy would smoke his long cigars with the air conditioner on and the windows rolled up, and the girls couldn't complain. "He had an explosive temper and kept it in check more than you would think," Debra said. "But if you hit that button, just watch out."

The girls said that their parents never discussed business in front of them and that they were unaware of family financial matters in the early years.

As 1969 rolled around, Debra was attending St. Edward's School, which at that time ended at ninth grade. As tenth grade approached, she suggested to her parents that she attend Chatham Hall, a girls' boarding school in Chatham, Virginia. Tommy and Jo Ann thought it was too far away and, because the family had relatives in Jacksonville, they compromised by sending her to the Bartram School for Girls in Jacksonville. "It wasn't their decision as much as mine," Debra said. "I wasn't happy at home."

Though apart for most of the year, the girls and Jo Ann reunited in the summer in western North Carolina, where Jo Ann pursued one of her new passions. "We'd hole up in a hotel for about a month," Debra said. "Mother and I were very interested in ruby mining, and Kathy was interested in the guys toting the buckets." As the 1970s approached, Jo Ann's continued fascination with North Carolina intensified, and a drive down a dusty country road would usher in a new era for the family.

15

THE MAKING OF TL

Air of Confidence

As 1970 arrived, the Sloan family was flying high. Tommy had established himself as one of the preeminent cattle ranchers in the nation. He was in line to become president of the Florida Cattlemen's Association, and two years earlier, with wife Jo Ann at his side, he was depicted as a model rancher in a profile on the national ABC television show *Discovery*. An amateur pilot, he spread his wings, using his plane both to manage his ranch and to expand his presence in the region.

The boy who grew up in a modest home by the railroad tracks on Avenue E in Fort Pierce in 1952 had married St. Lucie County's wealthiest maiden, Jo Ann Raulerson, sole heir to all that her grandfather, wealthy cattle rancher Frank Raulerson, had accumulated. The family jewel: his 23,000-acre Cow Creek Ranch spreading over the borders of St. Lucie and Okeechobee Counties.

As Thomas Leighton Sloan approached forty, he was more confident and authoritative. One sign: Both his daughters and many of his friends begin to refer to him as TL, for Thomas Leighton, instead of the more casual Tommy.

Shirts were monogrammed TLS, and, for the cigar-smoking rancher, soon his spittoons—placed in vehicles, offices, porches, and almost wherever he spent any time—were engraved TLS.

"His initials were on everything," said Darren Robertson. "He was a clothes horse. I think he had two pair of any boots that ever had been sold. I don't remember how many suits he had. He had the boots and the belts. That was him. He liked to stand out with the big cigar and the dark glasses, and I don't mean that in any bad way."

For a man of such presence, a lifestyle was needed to match. After purchasing his Cessna and Helio Courier for his own use, he bought a twin-engine Piper Navajo and hired a pilot. He had a second runway installed on the grove side of the ranch, in addition to the one he already had at the headquarters on the south side.

From his time living at the ranch, Darren recalled the wonderful smells coming out of the bunkhouse kitchen in the morning, where he'd eat before heading off to school. He remembered TL landing his plane while he and the other kids ran to the grass runway to greet him.

Besides his planes, TL bought a 48-foot Pacemaker yacht and christened it the *Cow Creek*, with its transom flashing the boat's name in one of the most prominent spots in the Fort Pierce Marina. When not in the marina, the yacht was docked in the Bahamas, a favored spot for TL's fishing excursions.

Change Is Coming

With Aubrey and Ethel's departures and their subsequent divorce, TL and Jo Ann had to find a couple who could both cowboy and cook. Cow Creek had always been known to provide almost every meal to its cowboys, both those who lived on the ranch and the others who worked as day cowboys commuting in.

Junior Mills had worked as a day cowboy at Cow Creek going back to the 1950s, and at the time was working as a day cowboy at a neighboring ranch. He was stricken with polio as a child and walked with a limp, but it never deterred him from outworking other cowboys.

Raised a Pentecostalist, Junior might have been a preacher if not for his love of cowboying and the backwoods. His wife, the effervescent Betty, whom everyone referred to as Miss Betty, was known for her country cooking, especially her biscuits. Betty, who came by her cooking skills genetically, was the daughter of Lula Nichols, creator of Granny Nichols Bar-B-Q Sauce, still produced today by her granddaughter.

Junior Mills was one of the lead cowboys at Cow Creek Ranch from 1970 to 1978. This photo of him atop his horse, Spur, was taken in 1989 during a cattle roundup at a ranch in Indiantown. (Photo by Jon Kral.)

To TL and Jo Ann, Junior and Betty were the perfect replacements for Aubrey and Ethel. When TL and Jo Ann located the couple, they offered them a place to live free at the ranch in one of the three ranch-hand houses, a grocery account, and free gas, in addition to their salaries. Living in town in Okeechobee at the time, Junior and Betty quickly accepted the opportunity to raise their three younger children—Buddy, Kent, and Marty—in the country. Their three older daughters were already grown and out of the house.

The arrival of the Mills family at Cow Creek ushered in a new era and way of doing things. Buddy Mills, Junior and Betty's older son, recalled his parents' first day on the job, with TL driving in from town to have breakfast with the cowboys. With Junior's arrival, TL initiated a new custom at the ranch. "You boys are going to give Junior the courtesy of saying a prayer over our meals," Buddy Mills recalled TL telling the cowboys that morning.

"And he turned it over to Daddy, and Daddy prayed over every meal that I can remember, even on weekends when hunters were out there."

Production Unfolds

For Buddy and Kent, growing up at Cow Creek was like a stage where the production was unfolding minute by minute. Their family lived at the ranch headquarters next to the bunkhouse in the first of three small concrete houses that had been constructed in the 1960s. The headquarters also included the historical Frank Raulerson house Jo Ann and Tommy stayed in, a horse barn, a tractor barn, cow pens, dog pens, and later a house for TL and Jo Ann's friends, Dr. Jack and Sally Wright.

The Mills brothers remember where the cowboys parked their trucks, what their schedules were, which rockers in the bunkhouse they preferred to sit in, which horses they rode, what kind of spurs they wore, what they said, and how they said it.

Not so for sister Marty, who was rarely seen. "When they were gathering cows, I yearned to be out there watching," Marty said. "But, no sir. Daddy didn't allow that because of the offensive language and behavior of cow crews, so his girls were not allowed around that. There were strict rules, and because of pure respect for Daddy, there were no questions. You were told something and you better do it."

Junior worked for Jimmy Percy, who was growing into his role as general manager. Jimmy lived in Fort Pierce with his wife and high school sweetheart, Julie, and their young son Jamie, and later another son, Jason.

Like his boss, Jimmy learned to fly and started using a Piper Cub airplane to help manage the ranch. The plane was especially useful locating cattle in the backwoods that had wandered off from the herd, and just another example of the more modern methods being used to run the ranch.

Meanwhile, at ranch headquarters at the Raulerson Building in downtown Fort Pierce, O. G. Nanney, longtime bookkeeper for Frank Raulerson and a trustee over Jo Ann's estate, held forth. Nanney, known as Ocie, had worked for Frank Raulerson since 1936 and was by his side on virtually every business decision. He was financial advisor to Jo Ann and Tommy after Frank Raulerson's death in 1954 and was one of three people who oversaw the trust that Frank had left Jo Ann.

Nanney's office was in the Cow Creek suite on the second floor of the Raulerson Building, which held the massive safe with the name Cow Creek emblazoned on the doors. Working for the frugal Raulerson, Nanney knew how to eke a small profit out of the narrow margins that could be found in the mercurial business of cattle ranching.

16

LEAVING THE OLD WAYS BEHIND

A New Direction

The promise of the dawning 1970s was shattered with a shotgun blast on the afternoon of February 2, 1970, at the Fort Pierce home of Ocie Glenn Nanney, financial manager of Cow Creek Ranch since 1936. Nanney had just returned home for lunch from Cow Creek's business office in the Raulerson Building when he took his life.

Recently in ill health and discharged from the hospital, Nanney, sixty-four, had been advisor to both Jo Ann and Frank Raulerson. A guiding force in business decisions at the ranch, Nanney was always a welcome sight at Cow Creek, driving the 17 miles from the Raulerson Building in downtown to deliver payroll to the cowboys on Fridays.

Along with lawyer L. O. Stephens and Jo Ann's great-aunt, Grace Lee, Nanney had also been one of the people who oversaw Jo Ann's trust. The trust's greatest assets at the time of Frank Raulerson's death were Cow Creek Ranch and the Raulerson Building, a downtown Fort Pierce landmark with both commercial storefronts and office space. The assets also included the Raulerson's impressive home at Orange Avenue and Eleventh Street and several other smaller properties.

With Nanney executing his directives, Frank Raulerson espoused a program of austere spending at the ranch, reusing staples from old fence posts or frowning on extravagances like dessert for his ranch hands.

When Frank Raulerson died, he was land and cash rich. In the years before his death, the sale of two other ranches the size of Cow Creek created a large reserve of cash. With restrictions on the use of money and the purse strings on the estate held by the financially astute Nanney until his death in 1970, it is likely the estate had grown substantially since Frank's death. Her daughters said Jo Ann's total estate was worth about $11 million by 1970, equivalent to about $90 million in 2025 dollars.

As both personal and business advisor to Jo Ann and TL, Nanney also helped temper TL's free-spending habits. With Nanney's death, all links, limits, and allegiances to the old way of doing things were removed. Tommy and Jo Ann now had full and free access to the estate left to Jo Ann by her grandfather.

Ownership Structure

Trusts are not public record under Florida law, so no record of the trust for Jo Ann Raulerson Sloan was available for review. From newspaper articles and legal ads, it is clear that Frank Raulerson had created the trust with Jo Ann essentially as the sole beneficiary. But at what age the trust ended and Jo Ann—and TL by virtue of his marriage—could control it is uncertain, though her daughters think it was about the age of thirty, or 1960, a time when TL clearly was in control of the ranch operations.

A 1965 legal notice appearing in the *News-Tribune* hinted at a change in structure for the ranch, referred to as the Raulerson Trust Ranch after Frank Raulerson's death. The notice announced that Jo Ann was "desiring to engage in a business enterprise under the fictitious name of Cow Creek Ranch located in the counties of St. Lucie and Okeechobee in the state of Florida." The announcement further noted that Jo Ann "is the sole owner of said business." So at the time, while TL was the public face of the ranch, at least on paper, Jo Ann remained the sole owner. Records from the Florida Department of State show Cow Creek Ranch incorporated in 1972.

Change of Venue

With the arrival of Jimmy Percy on the ranch, TL and Jo Ann spent less time at Cow Creek. Jo Ann had begun spending much of her summers

The Tellico farmhouse, built in 1870, as it appears today. Jo Ann and Tommy Sloan purchased it in 1970. (Photo by Gregory Enns.)

at the old Franklin Hotel in Franklin, North Carolina, ruby mining with Debra and Kathy.

During her time at the Franklin Hotel, Jo Ann had come to know the owner. Their annual visits to North Carolina had prompted Jo Ann to explore buying property there. One day, Jo Ann and Debra took off in their rental station wagon and happened along a remote dusty gravel road that led them to an abandoned house and farm.

"Every time we'd go ruby mining we'd take a jaunt," Debra said. "When Mother came out this way, she saw the farm and the house, and nobody had been in it in a long time. She said, 'This just needs love,' and so they ended up buying the first portion of the farm, 112 acres, for fifty thousand dollars."

And so began TL and Jo Ann's renovation of the rambling farmhouse and farm known as Tellico that, through additional land purchases, would grow to 230 acres.

The Cherokee people had historically inhabited the region, and the word "Tellico" is derived from the Cherokee language. A family named Ramsey was among the first Euro-American settlers in the region and in 1870 built the farmhouse, which once served as a general store, post office, gristmill, sawmill, and blacksmith shop. TL and Jo Ann purchased Tellico from the Ramsey family.

Tellico Creek runs through the property, which is also known for the Tellico white oak, considered one of the largest oaks in the region and a legendary meeting place for the Cherokees.

With the purchase of Tellico, Jo Ann began spending more time in North Carolina than in Fort Pierce, with TL flying in for frequent visits, working on refurbishing the farmhouse—it had no electricity or indoor plumbing—and improving the landscaping at the farm. They also set about a plan to install miles of natural stone walls throughout the property.

Meanwhile, TL was spending less time overseeing Cow Creek. Once overseeing the marking and branding of cattle as the herd's owner, he now allowed others to take on that duty. "I don't know if he lost interest," said Steve Arnold. "He was there all the time, and then for a while it seemed like he wasn't showing up."

Family Secrets Unfold

In 1970, at about the age of fifteen, while visiting Fort Pierce during one of her breaks from the Bartram School in Jacksonville, Debra shared a secret with her parents. Always considered a tomboy and big for her age, she announced to TL and Jo Ann that she was gay. Debra said her father was outraged while her mother was more accepting. "TL's response was, 'You're going to go down and see Uncle Jack and have a talk with him,'" Debra recalled.

Uncle Jack was Jack Wright, the Riviera Beach psychiatrist who had become friends with TL through the orthopedist who treated TL for the severe injuries and chronic pain he suffered to the same leg, first from a car accident in 1959 and then from a bull charging him in a pasture in 1963.

Wright and his wife, Sally, had grown close to TL and Jo Ann and had built a small weekend house next to them on the ranch. Debra said she went down to see Wright as instructed. "We talked, and he said, 'Well, are you comfortable with this?' I said, 'Well, yes, of course I am.' He said,

'Do you think that you would change?' I said, 'No.' It's not like you can change your mind.'"

A New Romance

Debra wasn't the only person in the family keeping a secret in 1970. That was the same year that it came to light that TL and Diane, his secretary and the ex-wife of one of his ranch cowboys, were having a romantic relationship. Diane, who was promoted to Cow Creek financial manager when Nanney died, had divorced Don that January. Kathy Sloan Blanton said her mother's reaction was simply, "Here we go again."

Jo Ann had endured infidelity early in her marriage to TL, including TL's fathering of Tee with another woman in 1963. Kathy and Debra said TL continued seeing the woman after the boy's birth and providing support for her and the boy, including the purchase of a house. "She had basically learned to accept TL's indiscretions," Debra said. "She thought, 'OK, if I'm going to be married to this guy, I'm going to accept that he's not going to be exclusive to me.'"

Her daughters said Jo Ann assuaged her feelings of hurt by drinking. While diving into the work of renovating the North Carolina farmhouse, she often was alone and isolated. Solace also was found in what she was achieving with the property.

"It was the enjoyment of resurrecting an old farmhouse and bringing it up to modern-day amenities like electricity and plumbing," Debra said. "And so for her, it was her little slice of heaven because she didn't have to be down in Fort Pierce in the swirl of whatever TL and Diane were doing."

Another Secret

Kathy also had a secret in 1970: The sixteen-year-old Dan McCarty High junior was in a relationship with John Edgar, a man seven years older than her who lived in an apartment a few blocks north of the Sloan family home on Orange Avenue. "I kept it a secret, but not for long because it's hard to keep a secret in a small town," Kathy said. "I had to be very clever about what I did."

Within a few months, Kathy became pregnant. She was under the legal

This photo of Tommy and Jo Ann Sloan's former compound on Orange Avenue and 11th Street in Fort Pierce shows just a portion of the city block that the compound enveloped. At far left was the new Cow Creek office built by Tommy and to the right is the home built by Frank and Annie Louise Raulerson in 1922. Various Raulerson relatives lived in the houses behind the Raulerson home. The buildings now serve as a treatment center for women with addictions. (Photo by Gregory Enns.)

age of eighteen, and her parents refused to give their permission to marry. In January 1971 she and Edgar eloped to Georgia, where she said she was able to produce a paper driver's license that showed she was eighteen. They had a daughter, Alexis, in June 1971.

Debra recalled that TL initially claimed that he wasn't going to be involved in the baby's life. He felt so strongly that he bet Fort Pierce housekeeper Alice Johnson a million dollars that he wouldn't have anything to do with the girl. But Alice told him that he'd fall in love with her once he held her in his arms and he'd grow close to her. Alice was proved right, and repeatedly joked with TL over the years to pay up on the million-dollar bet.

Kathy said her mother refused to have Kathy raise the baby in Edgar's apartment and allowed them to stay in a garage apartment behind the Sloan home. TL eventually gave money for Edgar to attend a technical school in Tallahassee while Kathy remained in Fort Pierce.

The couple soon divorced, and Kathy began dating Tommy Summerlin, whom she married in 1973. They remained married for twelve years and had three daughters: Tara Leighton, born in 1974; Myrna Anne, born in 1978; and Grace Lee, born in 1981.

Creating "the Compound"

After Diane's divorce, she and her children lived in a home on Peterson Road where Jo Ann's great-uncle, Lucius Raulerson, who died in 1969, had lived. Meanwhile, TL began a campaign to purchase the houses immediately around Jo Ann's ancestral home at 1033 Orange Avenue so that he would own the entire city block.

The family already owned several houses behind 1033 Orange Avenue, where Jo Ann's great-aunts had lived. When the land purchases were completed—except for the purchase of one lot whose owner refused to sell—TL's Xanadu extended between Tenth and Eleventh Streets on the east and west and Orange Avenue and Boston Avenue on the north and south. "He wanted to create a compound where he was the ruler," Debra said.

After the land purchases, he began renovations on some of the houses and added a swimming pool shaped like a cloverleaf—the image of the Cow Creek brand used at the ranch. Other luxuries included the installation of a tennis court, fish pond, and gazebo.

The largest addition was the construction of a two-story corporate office for Cow Creek, complete with an elevator and a downstairs kitchen. The building's size and the fact that it was positioned in the middle of a residential block made it stand out on Orange Avenue. TL had many of the buildings inside what soon came to be referred to as "the compound" painted white with green trim, a color scheme he even extended to the houses and barn at the ranch.

The Sloans eventually sold the Raulerson Building, moving the floor-to-ceiling safe into the new corporate headquarters at 1025 Orange Avenue. Shutters with cloverleafs appeared on the windows of the homes, and cloverleafs were also used in the ironwork leading into the office complex.

When TL was done with the land purchases, he had a concrete wall and chain link fences with barbed wire erected around most of the complex, enabling him to let his growing collection of German shepherds, which started a few years earlier with a single dog named Gunner, loose on the property at night. He always was concerned about security and often had one of the dogs with him in his vehicle.

Unusual Domestic Arrangement

Into the historical Huston house—once home of school superintendent Ben L. Bryan Sr. and just two doors from Jo Ann's family home at 1033 Orange Avenue—TL moved Diane, her three children, and himself. He also eventually moved his mother, Honey, into one of the other houses after the death of Aubie. Diane's mother was moved into another house in the compound.

The historical Raulerson family home at 1033 Orange Avenue remained reserved for Jo Ann and the girls.

This domestic arrangement was highly unusual for the 1970s and perhaps still is even today. Debra and Kathy said Jo Ann was hurt by TL's relationship with Diane, but her upbringing had steeled her into accepting it. Jo Ann's father's death and the separation from her mother at an early age resulted in Jo Ann showing little emotion or expressing her feelings, both as a child and adult. Her daughters said she also clung to the Victorian values held by Mother Lou, deferring to her husband and staying by his side regardless.

"I think in the day and time Mother was raised that you were kind of taught just to stuff it down," Debra said. "You didn't speak your true feelings. It was hard for Mother as an adult to express those."

Jo Ann was also extremely close to TL's parents, Honey and Aubrey, and divorcing TL would mean no longer

The much-loved Honey Sloan, mother of Tommy Sloan, was everybody's favorite relative. (Courtesy of the Robertson family.)

being their daughter-in-law. "She didn't want to start all over again," Kathy said.

Ultimately, said Debra, there was another reason she never sought a divorce. "I think that her love for him just caused her to be blind to the other things."

Divorce Too Expensive?

While Jo Ann's love for TL may have been abiding, Diane's children, Robin Longstreet and Darren Robertson, say it was their understanding that TL and Jo Ann's marriage was over as husband and wife when TL and Diane became a couple.

Kathy, Debra, Robin, and Darren said TL always told them that it would be too expensive to get a divorce, with the marriage of TL and Jo Ann continuing largely as a business arrangement. Debra said that was just a ploy on TL's part: "He just wanted control. He wanted to control her property."

Deeds from the 1970s reveal that the ownership of their ranch—their greatest asset—was not 50/50. The deeds show that Jo Ann owned 77 percent of the largest sections of the ranch, while TL owned 22 percent and Kathy and Debra owned 1 percent.

Despite her majority ownership, however, Jo Ann turned all business decisions over to TL. Jo Ann's daughters say the reason she gave was always the same: "I trust him and I love him."

But Tommy wasn't the only man in Jo Ann's life. During the renovation of Tellico, Jo Ann had become close friends with the contractor, Claude Welch. Debra said she did not know whether they had a romantic relationship.

Dynasty *Family*

While Jo Ann at first was cold about TL's relationship with Diane, she grew to accommodate it. TL and Diane would fly to North Carolina for a visit, sitting down to the dinner table together with her. TL and Diane would also stay overnight at Tellico.

When in Fort Pierce, they would all gather in the kitchen of the Cow Creek corporate building for dinner—always served by housekeepers—with Jo Ann walking next door from the house where she grew up and

TL, Diane, and her three children walking next door from the renovated Huston house where they lived.

"We were *Dynasty* before there was *Dynasty*," said Darren, referring to the 1980s television drama about interwoven family relationships.

"It was an unusual thing growing up," Robin said, "but it worked for them." Robin said neither Diane nor TL were ashamed of their relationship or hid it. TL, Diane, and the children would typically attend services at the First Presbyterian Church on Sundays and then have brunch together at the Hilltop House restaurant on US 1 in Fort Pierce. "We didn't have an inkling of that being a bad thing in our lives," Robin said. "We just were a happy family."

At the annual Cattlemen's Day Parade, Jo Ann no longer participated, and Diane became Cow Creek's most visible rider. Cow Creek won "best ranch unit" in 1972 and 1974, and in 1976 Diane earned the award for "best horsewoman," a title Jo Ann once held.

Both Robin and Darren said they eventually grew to call TL Dad. Their own father, Don Robertson, had moved to Texas, working at the King Ranch, and their brother, Donnie, often lived with him. Don would also work for the Seminole Tribe of Florida, overseeing their cattle programs and transforming their herd into a predominantly Brangus—the cross between Brahman and Angus—breed of cattle.

"We had a good life," Darren said of life with his mom and TL. "I still carry a lot of stuff I learned from him. He was tough, and he wasn't a picnic some days. But there were one hundred times more

Tommy Sloan and Diane Robertson began a romantic relationship around 1970 and remained together for twenty-six years. (Courtesy of the Robertson family.)

In this photo of a Cattlemen's Day Parade in the 1970s, the Cow Creek unit is led down US 1 in Fort Pierce by Diane Robertson, a position Jo Ann Raulerson Sloan once held. (Courtesy of the Arnold family.)

good days than bad days." One thing TL was adamant about was everybody gathering for dinner and arriving by the time it was served at 6:00 p.m. "We eat at six o'clock, not 6:01," he'd tell the kids. "I tell a lot of people if it weren't for him I'd be either dead or in prison," Darren said. "He took me in when I was young. He fed us, clothed us, housed us. Tommy Sloan raised me. He was my dad."

History Buff

One of Robin's favorite memories was when TL, a history buff, took the family on an extended vacation through New England to celebrate the country's bicentennial in 1976. The group included TL, Diane, Robin, Darren, and Tee, TL's son from the previous relationship.

"He was very, very generous," Robin said. "He loved to show us the world. He took us on wonderful family vacations. Like the bicentennial year, we flew from Palm Beach to Boston, went up all through the [New England] states. And we went to all the landmarks you could think of back up to Maine and then back down to New York City and took a train to Washington, DC. And it was a three-week trip. It was wonderful. We did stuff like that all the time. He wanted us to see everything and know about everything."

Darren also appreciated the benefits of being associated with TL. "He liked himself, and he liked nice things," Darren said. "I was along for the ride, so I got to appreciate a lot of nice things."

"The Boss"

Since shortly after their mother and TL came out publicly in a relationship in 1970, Darren and Robin began calling TL Dad. Not so for their middle brother, Donnie. "I called him 'The Boss,'" Donnie said. "I just kind of kept my mouth shut, kept my head down, and went to school. He just didn't really care for me, I guess, because of my dad."

Don Robertson blamed TL for breaking up his family, a position his son Donnie shared. Donnie sometimes lived with his dad in Okeechobee and Texas, and sometimes he lived with his mother and TL at the Orange Avenue compound. His siblings lived full-time with TL and their mom. Donnie said TL would rarely address him directly, instead speaking through his mother.

He remembered going to Okeechobee one Saturday morning to see friends and stopping in to say goodbye to his mother, who was working in the corporate office. "Tommy walked in, saw me, and didn't address me. He asked my mom, 'Why don't you have Donnie clean those leaves out of the pool before he goes?' The pool was wide open [without a screen] and had leaves in it all the time. It was like he had to find something for me to do, and he didn't even address me to do it."

The friction continued for years. Donnie said that when he was attending Texas A&M University, TL saw a friend of Donnie's and told him that Donnie was flunking out of school. "I didn't flunk anything, but that's what he said about me," said Donnie, who in 2023 was running a cutting-edge business in Texas conducting ultrasounds on cattle to determine potential beef quality. "I didn't understand some of the things he did like that."

Brother Darren got along with TL and grew to admire him. Darren said TL gave him a job at the grove and made sure he didn't receive special treatment. "Anytime I was out there he made sure nobody would take it easy on me because I was his son," said Darren, logistics manager for Guettler Brothers Construction in Fort Pierce. "I was there to work. He would provide for you but he wouldn't give us money."

Darren recalled some of the sayings TL drilled into him: "You fight with a skunk you smell like a skunk; a leopard can't change his spots; be polite."

At dinner, Darren said, the boys were told to always stand until all the girls and ladies were seated. And, he said, all those at dinner had to be prepared to engage in conversation: "He would aggravate you to make sure you were in the conversation and had an opinion."

While Robin and Darren had grown to consider TL a father figure, TL's daughters, Kathy and Debra, were growing to view him more as a caricature. Debra recalled how he'd keep a thick money roll in his pocket, with hundred-dollar bills showing on the outside. "I told him, 'Why don't you put them on the inside so somebody doesn't knock you on the head?'" she said. "Having money and being prestigious to TL was his life. That's what he wanted."

Kathy said another difficult relationship TL had was with Tee, the son TL fathered from another relationship. "He wanted Tee in his life, but he never told Tee he loved him," Kathy said. "He always lorded money over him. Nobody was ever good enough for TL."

Donnie, Darren, and Robin said Jo Ann was always gracious to them, with Darren spending one summer working and living with her in North Carolina when she and TL started a trout farm at Tellico in the 1980s. "It was a lifestyle to us, and it was a normal lifestyle to us," Robin said. "Jo Ann never made us feel uncomfortable when we saw her in North Carolina."

Robin said Diane and Jo Ann talked on the phone almost daily. As Cow Creek financial manager, Diane paid the bills for the corporation and the family, including Jo Ann's expenses in North Carolina. Robin said her mother knew intimately about the corporation's financial affairs but did not make decisions.

Endless Money Supply?

To outsiders, the money from the Sloan family well seemed endless.

In the 1970s, TL's list of financial obligations included:

- expenses for Cow Creek Ranch, including the construction of a modern bunkhouse;
- purchase of Tellico land and improvements;
- purchase of land to acquire the Orange Avenue compound and improvements, including the pool, tennis court, and new office complex;
- the planes and yacht;
- Debra's boarding school expenses and later college expenses at schools in Boston and at Western Carolina University, where she would graduate;
- support for Tee Sloan, TL's son from an extramarital relationship;
- support to help Kathy and her new husband as he attended the University of Florida;
- private schools for Diane's kids; and
- new business ventures.

And then there were the incidental luxuries like new cars for the kids when they came of driving age. "At sixteen, he'd say, go down and pick out a car and when you find something call me," Darren said.

How do you support such obligations?

With narrow margins earned from raising cattle, TL was confronted with finding additional ways to raise cash. He expanded his groves, leased property to tomato and other vegetable farmers, and shipped cattle to Puerto Rico. The mining of marl and shell—used in Florida road construction—also brought in revenue while creating a huge reservoir at the northwest corner of the ranch.

Spreading His Wings

In one of TL's first forays outside of ranching, he spread his wings and pursued one of his greatest passions: aviation.

In 1971, he formed a partnership with Charles D. Ellis and Aubrey McCracken, Sun Aviation, and purchased the Piper Aircraft franchise at the Vero Beach airport. He was quoted in a newspaper article as saying the new company includes everything from sales and service of aircraft and equipment to charter flights and flying lessons. He said he got into the business because of his experience flying. Sun Aviation several years later would also begin operating at the St. Lucie County Airport.

With other investors, he began buying and building apartment complexes under the name Southern Properties. These included Cinnamon Tree Apartments in Jensen Beach and Southern Courtyard Apartments, along with townhouses at Eleventh Street and Florida Avenue in Fort Pierce. He also formed a partnership creating a local gas company. He served on the board of First National Bank of Fort Pierce.

Taste of Ranch Life

His image as a rancher was solidified in 1972, when he was elected president of the Florida Cattlemen's Association. And later that year, Cow Creek was featured in a three-part series in the *Palm Beach Post*. The series, by William A. Clark with photos by Ron Smith, gave an insight into Cow Creek operations, as if freezing time.

While the series highlighted TL's ownership and the twenty-five-year-old Percy's management of the ranch, it also profiled the cowboys and cook.

It started out with a profile of day cowboy Clyde "Pop" Coker, whom Clark labeled "Mr. Florida Cowboy" because Coker had been in the saddle fifty-seven of his seventy-two years in Florida. The real cowboying, Coker told Clark, is done in Florida, not "in the West where all they do is rope 'n ride."

"Bring one of those fellows down here," Coker said, "put him in the woods to look for cattle and bring 'em in, and the next thing you know . . . he's lost . . . lost so bad he doesn't know where the barn is."

Junior Mills also was profiled and talked about managing wildlife at the ranch. Among other duties, he was in charge of keeping the ranch's hog population down—the hogs root up ground, making it dangerous for horses and vehicles—and reported that four hundred hogs were harvested in the last three years. The ranch was managed with some thirty horses and eighteen dogs used for herding cattle or recreational hunting.

Also in the series, cowboy Will'um Thomas recalled the days of the open range before the Fence Act of 1949, driving cattle to markets in Fort Pierce or Tampa at a time when a cowboy's pay was about one dollar per day. For the Tampa trips, he said, "You carried 'nuff groceries in your saddle pocket for yourself and your horse to last two, three days or until you met up with

Junior and Betty Mills arrived at Cow Creek Ranch in 1970. This photo was taken of them in the 1980s. (Photo by Jon Kral.)

the chuck wagon. All the cookin' was done over open fires, and you slept rolled up in your blanket."

Life of the Ranch Cook

A big part of one profile focused on Junior's wife, ranch cook Betty Mills, who began every day at 5:00 a.m. cooking for as many as eight men.

On one day of the journalist's visit, she fixed a breakfast of grits, bacon, eggs, and toast. For lunch—the biggest meal of the day—she prepared turkey and dressing, potato salad, baked sweet potatoes, sliced tomatoes, mustard greens, black-eyed peas, lima beans, baked fresh pork ham with barbecue sauce, rice, gravy, biscuits, cranberry sauce, banana pudding, and a choice of iced tea or Kool-Aid to drink.

"You never have two days alike on a ranch," she told the reporter. "The men never have the same type of day they had yesterday. Today, they may build a fence. Tomorrow, they may gather cows. There's always variation."

An Ominous Statement

When ranch owner TL was interviewed, he declined to say how many cattle the ranch had at that time. "That's just like me asking you how much money you have in the bank," he said. But he spoke with pride about the ranch's advancement under his leadership during the last twenty years. "We've developed it [and] mechanized it to the point we have a good professional operation. We're also diversifying—we have orange and grapefruit groves on the northern edge of the property."

In the interview, TL lamented the falling prices of beef and the low margins in the cattle business. "I could take what I have [at the ranch], sell it, and invest in tax-free municipal bonds and make more money."

Because of rising land prices, he predicted fewer ranchers would get into the cattle business, with a small number of ranches producing most of the state's beef.

The statement was ominous.

Like the menacing storm clouds that gather on the ranch in an otherwise sunny summer afternoon, rapid change was on the horizon for the ranch, and it wasn't good.

Too Much Spending

On the outside, the *Palm Beach Post* series may have given the appearance of success at the ranch. But as Jimmy Percy settled into his job as general manager of Cow Creek, he found problems in a different place: the books.

TL and Jo Ann, he concluded, were spending too much money. Profits from the ranch and Raulerson Building rentals were not covering the business and the couple's expenses. "Jimmy told them, 'Y'all can't keep spending like this or you're going to run out of money,'" Debra recalled.

As time went on, the issue grew as a source of conflict, with Jimmy eventually leaving Cow Creek and working at St. Lucie County Bank as a loan officer. With Jimmy gone, TL had to take back management of the ranch at a time when his other businesses were pulling him in a different direction.

TL begged Jimmy to return. "And then Tommy wanted my dad back, and he said he'd come back, and he did, and stayed there for multiple years," said Jamie Percy, Jimmy's son.

The landmark Okeechobee Livestock Market is where ranchers from the Kissimmee Valley and beyond sell cattle and purchase cattle. (Photo by Jon Kral.)

Nevertheless, the return of Jimmy—who gained the title of vice president of Cow Creek—didn't seem to temper TL's spending. But then, as luck would have it, TL had a new card to play in 1973. That's when the prospect of an oil well strike surfaced.

Search for Oil

Shell Oil Co. had been conducting seismic explorations in the region. Soon, with the permission of TL and Jo Ann, the company announced that it planned to drill a test well on the western side of Cow Creek, a quarter mile over the St. Lucie County line into Okeechobee County. A derrick fifteen stories high, visible for miles, was erected with the intention of drilling to a depth of 11,300 feet.

But after months of hope that oil would bring new riches to Cow Creek, the well came up dry. The discovery of oil wouldn't be the Hail Mary TL need to pulled out from his mountain of debt after all.

Darren Robertson said that while some of TL's investments went sour, others came through. Both he and TL's daughters lacked specifics because TL rarely shared details with them. "I think he did well on some stuff and not well on other stuff," Darren said. "But again, he would tell you, 'It's none of your business.'"

Debra had a different take: "With TL supporting three families, mother and our family, Diane and her family, and Tee and his mother, plus Honey, the monetary hemorrhaging was an inevitable fate of the collapse of the 'empire' TL thought he created. It could have been done differently, but the way the money was managed meant that the money that was my mother's was wasted on far too many nonbusiness things. TL never learned to make money work to generate income."

At the same time debt was mounting, TL was also battling medical issues. In 1976, while treating what he thought was an ear infection, he used a solution that was absorbed by his eardrum, which unknowingly had been previously perforated. The episode caused permanent damage and balance issues, prompting him to give up flying and boating. That same year, he was afflicted with Bell's palsy, a neurological disorder that left him paralyzed on one side of his face. He already suffered chronic pain from his leg injuries. Debra said he also had a longtime reliance on the opioid painkiller Demerol.

"When TL broke his leg in '59 and he came back from the hospital in Palm Beach, they sent him home with Demerol," Debra recalled. "And then two years later, he broke the same leg in the same place. There was more Demerol, and so he became addicted. He was an opioid addict. He'd send us to one pharmacy to get one prescription and another to get another one. So that was part of his downfall."

Debra remembered meeting with a tax attorney around their dining room table in North Carolina. TL and Jo Ann were tapped out and needed a way out. On the table: selling part of the ranch.

"TL would go to the bank and borrow a couple hundred thousand dollars, and when that was due, he'd go to another bank," Debra said. "You can run a negative cash flow for a while, but eventually it's going to catch up to you."

Taking Cattle to Market

At the ranch, TL was summoning cowboys more frequently to identify cattle that could be taken to market for a quick cash infusion. "There were times that would occur that he'd say, 'You fellas pull up such and such group and let's get a load or two of them to the market,'" said Kent Mills.

The market was the Okeechobee Livestock Market, which was built in the 1930s by a group called the Dixie Cattlemen. The market, one of just a handful left in the state, sits high above an endless set of cattle pens where a lot, perhaps just one bull or several yearlings, are brought into a small indoor arena, where cattle buyers make the smallest of gestures to bid during daylong auctions every Monday and Tuesday.

The buyers submit a check or credit card payment on the same day an auction deal closes, and the sellers then receive a check, minus a modest 3 percent auction fee.

The Livestock Market had been purchased by ranch owner and former Supreme Court Justice Alto Adams Sr. in 1954, and he sold it to cattleman and rodeo star Otis "Pete" Clemons and Quillie Hazellief in 1961. Clemons's sons Todd and Jeff took over in 1989, and today the fourth generation of the Clemons family is working at the market, which added an online auction component in the 1990s.

Deroy Arnold said at one point the cattle inventory at Cow Creek had nearly been depleted: "In 1972 or 1973, when he was going through money right and left, he about sold out all of his cows just because of having to pay his bills. In 1974 he got down to hardly any. I remember Will'um and Jimmy Percy had to go to South Texas to buy 1,000 head of crossbred cows and move them back here."

Along with these impromptu sales, the herd was growing smaller for another reason. Kent Mills said many of the ranch's bulls were not reproducing, and TL wasn't spending the money to have them tested by a veterinarian so that the less fertile bulls could be replaced. Deroy said the herd by the fall of 1976 had dwindled to about 1,000 from a peak of 5,000.

Ultimately, the painful decision was made to sell 17,000 acres of the 23,000-acre ranch Jo Ann's grandfather had established more than a half century earlier. Bud Adams was interested in buying 3,800 acres, including the Blue Mountain section, and brought investor Charles Vavrus in on the deal to buy the largest chunk, 13,200 acres.

With little notice, the Raulerson/Sloan family ownership of 17,000 acres of the ranch ended on October 1, 1976, when three deeds for separate sections in St. Lucie and Okeechobee Counties were transferred to Vavrus and one deed for sections in St. Lucie County was transferred to Adams Ranch Inc.

Echoing the sentiments of the other children of cowboys at the ranch, Jamie Percy remembered the effect the sale had on his dad, Jimmy, the ranch's general manager. "My dad always said that was the saddest day of his life," Jamie Percy said. "It completely changed my dad's life. He put his heart and soul into that ranch."

Around the close of the sale on October 1, 1976, Buddy Mills remembered Tommy and Jo Ann taking a last drive through the ranch to bid the cowboys farewell and to thank them for their work at Cow Creek. As they concluded their drive and approached the headquarters, they stopped their Chevrolet Blazer to talk to Junior.

"He kind of coasted up there and stopped, and they put down the passenger window. Daddy stepped up there, and he said Jo Ann broke down and went to crying. She told him what it meant to her to have him and Mama and us kids there. And finally, Daddy said she had just got to the point where she got so choked up she couldn't say anything. And that was their last drive through."

17

LIQUIDATION

Selling Cow Creek

Poor business decisions and TL's free-spending habits had put them in the position of having to sell the ranch begun by Jo Ann's grandfather. To the public, the well of money from the estate Frank Raulerson created for his granddaughter seemed bottomless. But the 1976 sale of Cow Creek gave an indication that the money well was drying up and TL was spending too much.

"Tommy was her downfall," said Thomas Kindred Sr., who graduated with Jo Ann in the Fort Pierce High School Class of 1948. "She should have never married that boy. He didn't do anything but spend her money."

TL's primary motivations for selling the main part of the ranch seemed to be to pay off debts he accumulated and to generate cash for investing in his development and aviation interests. "I've only seen Mother cry a few times, but when the papers were signed to sell Cow Creek, she cried," daughter Debra said.

Neighboring ranch owner Bud Adams had negotiated the sale. Adams had met Charles Vavrus, a land developer from Joliet, Illinois, at a cattle conference in Gainesville, Florida. Adams, who coveted the Blue Mountain region of the ranch and purchased it, had been told by TL that he was looking to sell Cow Creek, and Vavrus had told Bud that he was looking to buy land. In 1976, the same year Vavrus bought 13,200 acres at Cow Creek, he purchased 4,673 acres within the city of Palm Beach Gardens to create his Vavrus Ranch.

The cowboys of Cow Creek arranged this photo as a gift for Tommy and Jo Ann Sloan in the mid-1970s. From left and posing in front of Cow Creek swamp are Jimmy Percy, Wil'um Thomas, Curtis Arnold, Junior and Betty Mills, Jack Murphy, and Earl Story. (Photo courtesy of the Arnold family.)

The deeds showed that Vavrus paid $5,281,800 for his sections of Cow Creek while Adams Ranch paid $1,484,500, for a total sale of $6,766,300.

The deeds revealed the ranch had a $3.5 million mortgage in September 1975 from Travelers Insurance and a $1 million mortgage in February 1975 from Equitable Life Insurance, for total mortgages of $4.5 million. The sale, after satisfaction of the mortgages, netted the Sloans $2,266,300. It's not known what was paid for the satisfaction of taxes or other debts. But one other debt incurred by the sale would haunt them for years: a $675,000 tax assessment from the IRS.

The sale included the prettiest parts of the ranch, including Dog Slough, Blue Mountain, and Cow Creek, the waterway of the early Seminoles. It also included the ranch headquarters—the piece first purchased by Frank Raulerson—including the barn and the historical Raulerson weekend house. Vavrus changed Cow Creek's name to V-Bar 2. The Sloans retained ownership of some 2,500 acres on the north side of the ranch along Orange Avenue Extension, at least 800 acres of which had been converted to citrus groves.

With the sale of the big part of the ranch, TL and Jo Ann were confronted with what to do with regard to their longtime ranch hands. One of those hands, Earl Story, who lived at the ranch with his wife and three children, had already gone to work at another nearby ranch.

TL asked grove manager Curtis Arnold to stay on along with Curtis's best friend and brother-in-law, Will'um Thomas, who had been working at the ranch since the late 1940s under Jo Ann's grandfather. TL built a small house for them at the grove entrance on Orange Avenue where they could stay during the week, returning to their wives at their homes in Okeechobee on the weekends. He also built a house for Curtis's son, Deroy, and Deroy's new bride.

Jimmy Percy, who began working at the ranch as a summer cowboy at the age of fourteen and eventually became the ranch manager, stayed on as manager of TL's other operations.

When Vavrus took over the ranch, Jimmy recommended that a relatively new ranch hand, Larry Kesner, take over as foreman instead of longtime ranch hand Junior Mills, who had worked at the ranch from 1970 up until the time of the sale on October 1, 1976.

"Tommy said if you want to stay here this man has promised me he's going to take care of you," Buddy Mills remembered TL telling his father. Though Junior felt slighted by being passed over for the foreman's job as he had raised his kids at the ranch and felt it was home, he decided to stay on under Vavrus and work for Kesner. Mechanic Jack Murphy, who also lived at the ranch with his family, moved on to another job.

TL also had to adjust to life without the ranch, and he appeared to fully dive into his new business ventures. Robin Robertson Longstreet also worked for him at the Cow Creek corporate office he had built at his compound on Orange Avenue, managing his Southern Properties company. She remembered his work ethic in those years. "He was never one to lay around and not do something," Robin said. "He was dressed every morning and in the office or at the ranch working. We were in that office from eight o'clock to five o'clock every day."

One of the goals of Southern Properties was to build affordable housing such as townhouses and duplexes that could attract a workforce to the area. The company's classifieds in the *News-Tribune* boasted: "We have places to rent that can be within everyone's budget."

The strategy of his commuter airline, Golden South Airways, was to connect Fort Pierce with the growing hubs of Orlando and West Palm Beach.

"I thought he was a visionary," said Robin, who named her daughter, Leighton, after TL, whose middle name was Leighton. "The things that have happened in this town were things he talked about and they happened. He was pretty smart."

Things Go South

Debra said TL and Jo Ann continued to defer the $675,000 tax bill from the 1976 Cow Creek sale. "That was pretty stupid because he had enough money; he could pay that tax and be done with it."

The tax bill had serious consequences for TL's Southern Properties investment. One of those investors was Joey Miller, who founded the St. Lucie Battery & Tire kingdom that has multiple stores in St. Lucie, Martin, Indian River, and Okeechobee Counties. In the late 1970s, Miller expanded outside his auto servicing business and partnered with commercial contractor Jim Turner, also founder of Apple Machine & Supply, to build the Southern Courtyard Apartments on Oleander Avenue in Fort Pierce.

The two had purchased 5 acres for the apartment complex and built several of the buildings but then hit a wall. They couldn't get financing to finish the project. They heard TL might be interested in investing. "We had the dirt but not the assets to continue building the apartments," Miller said. "Tommy came in with borrowing power, and we got the job done and finished the project."

For TL's investment and borrowing capacity, Miller and Turner went from 50/50 partners to each owning 25 percent and TL owning 50 percent. Miller recalled that he and Turner had a long initial meeting at TL's new corporate headquarters in the compound on Orange Avenue. "He made a great impression on us because he lived a different lifestyle, had a glamorous two-story office with an elevator, gold fixtures in the bathroom and so forth, so he definitely made an impression us. We thought he was a great businessman, only to our demise later on."

The three formed Southern Properties in December 1981, and Turner's construction company built out Southern Courtyard Apartments to a total of eighty units. Miller said each unit was constructed with firewalls so that the complex could be adapted for condominiums in case they ever decided to sell off individual units. Miller said TL insisted on running Southern Properties out of his corporate office in the complex.

"Our goal was not to just build affordable housing, but we felt like there was a real need for decent housing in Fort Pierce, and we wanted to build something to serve that clientele and also be an asset to Fort Pierce," Miller said.

Miller eventually bought out Turner's share of the company, and he and TL became 50/50 partners. It wasn't a partnership destined to last. Miller soon was informed of TL's delinquent taxes to the IRS: "The straw that broke the camel's back was that one day I got a phone call that the IRS wants to foreclose on our complex. Of course, I went straight to my attorney and found out they couldn't because I was a partner."

To pay the tax debt, TL would have to sell off his share of the Southern Courtyard Apartments. "When the IRS finally came down on Tommy, it was in the middle of a major recession," Miller said. "Tommy had to sell off his share, and the property appraised for less than we owed on it. I went from a 50 percent owner to a 35 percent owner because of the drop in appraisal. The appraisal was terrible, so I took a bath."

TL's share was sold to Peter Busch, a descendant of Anheuser-Busch founder Adolphus Busch. Peter Busch had moved to Vero Beach in 1984 to create Fort Pierce–based Southern Eagle Distributing, the Treasure Coast distributor for Busch, Budweiser, and other beers.

"Peter Busch became my partner, and out of all this turmoil... probably one of the best things that happened was that Peter Busch and I became friends, and we're still friends today," Miller said.

Miller said that after about five years he bought out Peter Busch's share of the Southern Courtyard Apartments and that about five years after that, he sold out. He said he did not know whether TL's tax debt was paid.

"After that, Tommy fell off the radar. I took a lot of financial licks, and I was disappointed. We weren't really friends after that. Tommy was always distant, but after all this turmoil I found out the situation with Tommy. If I knew all the history beforehand, I wouldn't have pulled the trigger with Tommy. He was more of a manipulator than a businessman."

The experience reinforced in Miller the notion that appearances can be deceiving: "My first impression was that he was a very wealthy guy and he could afford his lifestyle, but as time went on, Jimmy and I both found out what the real story was. His lifestyle was way above his earning capacity, I promise you that. He was basically living on the Raulerson estate assets. His finance manager told him that if he didn't stop spending money, he'd go broke, and guess what? He went broke. Tommy manipulated the Raulerson holdings and winded up basically giving them away. His poor wife. She suffered the consequences."

Miller today owns 500 acres of the former Cow Creek Ranch that he purchased in 2006 in a section known as Cypress Creek.

Robin Longstreet said a change in tax laws—the 1986 Tax Reform Act extending depreciating schedules—made the properties unprofitable and they were sold off, often at a loss. Robin also blamed some of TL's financial problems on an accountant's advice on a tax deferment schedule. "When the economy fell out, he couldn't sell his properties. The taxes compounded daily, and it added up."

In addition, the value of property he purchased to create his one-block compound at Orange Avenue, along with other nearby property investments, took a precipitous drop as businesses and churches moved away from the once-thriving Orange Avenue during a time of urban blight. Property values fell. Golden South Airways never really took off, either.

Robin also blamed many of TL's problems on his health issues, which included the two breaks in his legs that left him with a limp and in chronic pain, and the progression of illnesses, including kidney cancer, from which he recovered, and a stroke in 1976.

The illnesses robbed him of the handsome countenance he enjoyed as a young man. He went from occasionally growing a beard to having one all the time to conceal his facial paralysis.

"He had that disability with the ear and his mouth, and it wasn't the same as when he was healthy," said his friend Bill Yates, a well-known Fort Pierce funeral director. "I think it took something out of him."

Another Sale

None of his investments earned enough money to cover expenses, so in 1981—five years after an injection of cash from selling the home ranch—TL and Jo Ann sold the remaining part of the ranch that had been turned into citrus groves. The land was sold for $2,675,000 to Pennsylvania Groves, a company owned by a partnership controlled by Bernard Egan, whose Bernard Egan & Co. became one of the state's largest marketers and shippers of Florida citrus. The sale was the last piece of agricultural land that the Sloans owned in Florida, which in the days of Frank Raulerson had exceeded 70,000 acres.

The sale also meant TL and Jo Ann had to cut ties with their most loyal employees, Will'um and Curtis. Will'um had worked at Cow Creek for Frank Raulerson going back to the late 1940s, and Curtis had worked there almost as long. They had married sisters and were also best friends.

Several of the sons of Cow Creek current and former cowboys had also worked at the grove for Curtis, including Deroy Arnold, Curtis's son; Buddy and Kent Mills, sons of Junior Mills; and Steve Arnold, son of former Cow Creek foreman Aubrey Arnold. Diane's sons, Donnie and Darren Robertson, had also worked for Curtis.

Bernard Egan kept Curtis on to manage the grove and hired Will'um to work there as well.

18

A LITANY OF LOSSES

Raising Trout

With the sale of the grove, TL turned his sights to the North Carolina farm. Tellico had been Jo Ann's haven and had become her full-time home after TL began living with Diane.

In their early years of owning the farm, they raised registered Herefords, but it had been mostly a nonworking, non-income-producing property. However, while recovering from kidney cancer, TL came up with the idea to create a trout farm using the creek that ran through the property. "What he wanted to do was supply processors with fish to make food products," Debra said.

The move required the installation of expensive raceways, a stepped system to house various sizes of trout. The work took several years, but by the mid-1980s the Tellico Trout Farm was established. Construction costs and improvements to the farm totaled $1.3 million.

The opening of the new trout farm made the front page of the *Franklin (NC) Press* on July 3, 1987, and the newspaper quoted TL as saying, "I had no idea when I bought this place that someday I would build a trout farm here, but I wanted to put the farm in a productive mode."

The article said TL designed the facility after visiting other trout farms. His farm included 4,000 feet of concrete raceway, which was terraced into 60-foot and 80-foot holding ponds, with water from Tellico Creek flowing through.

At first, Debra was brought in to manage the gift shop, and she was eventually hired to manage the business. She heard a familiar response when she tried to get TL to work with her to develop a budget for the farm: "He said, 'You know, I've never learned how to live on one of those.' I thought, 'Boy, I'm in trouble.'"

TL and Jo Ann built a house on the property for Debra, which she later purchased from their corporation, Macon County Investments, the technical owner of the farm. TL would make occasional visits from Fort Pierce to check on the farm. Sometimes he would bring Diane and her children and grandchildren.

Sally Richeson, a friend of Jo Ann's from Fort Pierce, said Jo Ann would handle her personal issues such as her husband taking up with another woman and her financial setbacks in the same way.

"She was stoic," said Sally, who also has a home in North Carolina and would visit Jo Ann at Tellico. "It was like you can just keep on kicking me, but I'm not going to give in. She wouldn't cry. I never saw her show any emotion. She would just smile and carry on. She just bore up. Maybe losing your parents at an early age and being raised by elderly grandparents gave her some different backbone. I don't know."

Raising More Children

Besides Debra joining her mother at Tellico, Kathy's four daughters also began living there, while Kathy fought a long-term drug addiction. Kathy later moved there and reunited with her children during her recovery. Around the same time, Debra said, Jo Ann gave up drinking after a health scare.

Fearful for the children because of the drug use of Kathy and husband Tommy Summerlin, Jo Ann and TL in the 1980s went to court to get custody of the four girls and received the judge's order about 1984. The scene was similar to the one that played out when Jo Ann was eight and her grandparents demanded and received custody of Jo Ann instead of her being raised by her mother.

The girls called Jo Ann "Grandma Annie." They called TL "DadDad." They didn't have a nickname for Diane. "I think Grandma Annie and DadDad thought we'd have more stability and it would be better for us," said Tara Summerlin Breeden, Kathy's second-oldest daughter. "I think they thought they could do a better job. It was hard, but I got used to it. They were a little old school."

It was an unusual arrangement. The four girls would live at TL and Diane's home in Fort Pierce first, with Jo Ann making visits. When Jo Ann was in Fort Pierce, they would all meet at the kitchen of the corporate office between the two houses to have dinner. Later, Jo Ann stayed in Fort Pierce for an extended period, and the girls lived in the Raulerson home. Tara remembered she slept in the room Debra had growing up.

Kathy and Tommy Summerlin officially divorced in 1986, though they were separated years earlier. Tommy and Jo Ann sent the three older girls to private Indian River Academy until it closed in 1987. Then they were enrolled in public schools. The youngest, Grace, was just a toddler.

"It was fun living with them," Tara said. "We had the dogs. We had a pool and tennis courts. I had fond memories living there."

But life with her grandparents was exacting. "We had to make our rooms and keep them clean. Grandma Annie was very strict. You had to use proper English. You had to chew with your mouth closed. You had to say, 'yes sir, no sir.' You had to do all the polite things." After school the girls would go over to Honey's home in the compound and stay with her until Diane and TL returned for the day.

About 1988, the decision was made that the girls should go up to North Carolina and stay with Jo Ann full-time. "I just think they thought it would be better to raise us up here because it's a little more laid-back here in terms of lifestyle," said Tara, who continues to live in North Carolina.

TL flew up for frequent visits, sometimes staying for weeks. He slept upstairs while Jo Ann slept downstairs in the master suite, Tara said.

"I do think my grandmother always cared about him, and she would do things for him. She catered to whatever he wanted to eat. I never remember them being affectionate. I think it was just to raise us that they sure did stay married. Growing up, I thought it was normal, but I know it wasn't normal now. He was there to discipline us. He would ground us if we were in trouble."

During the school year, Jo Ann would get the girls up at 5:30 a.m. to catch the 6:30 school bus to make the 15-mile drive along windy country roads into town. As their caregiver, Jo Ann would shuttle the girls to their various activities. Tara was in the school band and ran track: "She was really good at the meals. She was a good cook and had that big kitchen. She was very strict that nobody could help her cook. She had her particular way of cooking."

Even though Jo Ann had a maid, she demanded that the girls clean their rooms every morning. Each of the girls had her own room in the fifteen-room home they called "the big house." One domestic chore Jo Ann always did herself was iron her sheets.

Christmases were always special, with Jo Ann putting up a giant tree. Presents couldn't be opened together; Tommy and Jo Ann demanded that they be opened one at a time.

At sixteen, Tara got a new Ford Festiva. Her older sister, Alexis, got a Ford Escort. If they broke curfew, they couldn't use their cars.

The girls would help build rock walls, mow the lawn, and work at the catch-out pond dealing with customers and cleaning fish. One time Tara picked up 900 pounds of walnuts and bagged them. "Manual labor—DadDad was big on that."

Why did her grandmother stay married to her grandfather?

"I asked her, and she said that she didn't really believe in divorce and didn't want to go through a divorce, and she cared about him. She said she was raised that getting a divorce was something you didn't do. She would have had a lot more if she got rid of him. I loved my grandfather, but he was definitely her downfall."

Tara said her grandmother rarely expressed emotion. "She definitely was a stern woman. I don't remember her crying very much. She was very strong when it came to emotions. She was loving, but she was strict. Her best qualities were she taught us manners and how to act as young lady. She was very smart and very witty. She loved us, and she loved us very much. She took very good care of us. We didn't lack for anything."

Jo Ann always stood by Kathy even when the girls were upset with her. "My grandmother loved her. She said she's your mother, and love her no matter what because she's your mother."

Tara said Debra, who was also managing the trout farm, had to do most of the work to keep things running and the family together. When Jo Ann left North Carolina in 1991 to take care of Honey for nine months during her last days, Debra stayed in the big house and cared for the girls. "She loved my mom, and she loved Debra. Debra had to do most of the work but didn't get credit."

When Tara quit school at seventeen, TL and Jo Ann demanded that she return to complete her education. Tara refused and moved to live with her boyfriend: "I remember the day I left Grandma Annie cried because she wanted me to stay. She felt very responsible for us. She was raising kids all over again."

Tara would later return to the big house to visit her grandmother and apologize. She eventually obtained her GED and attended college. "She took care of us when my parents couldn't do it. My grandmother was more of a mother to me than my mother. I loved my mom, but Grandma Annie was my mother to me."

Losing Honey

In early 1991, TL's mother, Honey, was diagnosed with terminal ovarian cancer. Debra drove down from Franklin to spend time with her in Fort Pierce. After the death of her husband, Aubrey, in 1979, Honey had moved from their home on Rosedale Avenue in Fort Pierce into a home TL had renovated for her inside the Orange Avenue compound.

Honey was the matriarch of the family, the glue that held everyone together and kept things on a light note. Honey also provided Kathy and Debra the affection they didn't get from TL, who was focused more on his own pursuits, and Jo Ann, who was raised not to show emotion. Debra recalled one night during her visit with Honey when the subject of TL came up:

"I just went down there to visit her because I knew she didn't have long. She popped me some homemade popcorn that you pop on the stove. She delighted in doing things like that for people. We were sitting in her TV room, and she just looked at me with a really sad expression and said, 'Your father's not the man I raised.'"

In his fifty-eight years of life to that point, Thomas Leighton Sloan had risen from a humble beginning, the son of Aubrey Sloan, a disabled railroad inspector, and Honey, who spent many of her years as a newspaper motor carrier. Money and power had changed him since his beginnings with Honey and Aubrey in the tobacco country of South Georgia.

As he grew up, Honey had imbued in her only child a sense that he could accomplish anything. His self-assurance extended to his relationships with women. As Honey approached the end of her life and looked back, TL had been her main accomplishment, rising from a clothing store salesman to marry Jo Ann, St. Lucie County's richest eligible young woman.

Honey had loved her son unconditionally. Along with the confidence she had instilled in him, TL had the gift of charisma and achieved much as a young man. "Tommy was a dynamic personality," friend Bill Yates said. "You couldn't help but like him."

But along the way, TL's success, access to money, and self-confidence manifested as narcissism. He not only believed that he could achieve anything, but he also believed that he could have anything: yachts, planes, the best lifestyle, women besides his wife. "I believe that Honey raised a person that had manners and who was kind and caring—that's what she tried to instill in him," Debra said. "But I believe his good looks, his charm, and his lust for women were his downfall, and the other was he had no idea how to run a business."

Nevertheless, TL's faults were tempered with heavy gestures of generosity toward his friends and family. When Deroy got married and was working at the grove, TL built a house for the couple at the grove. When Will'um came down with a mysterious lung ailment, he and Jo Ann arranged to fly him to Duke University Medical Center to be examined. TL and Jo Ann always made sure their ranch hands had three meals a day provided by the ranch and paid them wages above those paid at other area ranches. They also allowed some of the hands to keep their own herds at the ranch.

Buddy Mills said raising the herd and selling it enabled his father, Junior Mills, and mother, ranch cook Betty Mills, to purchase property where they could retire and keep cattle. "People may throw down on Tommy Sloan, but I tell you this, he was good to my mom and dad," Buddy said.

As Honey approached death, she was confronted with what her daughter-in-law had lost over the years at the hands of her son. Because of TL's unfettered spending, Jo Ann had been forced to sell her beloved Cow Creek Ranch, and she had lost her husband in all but name. Worst of all, in the months before Honey's death, there were concerns that her son and Jo Ann were in danger of losing the compound, including Jo Ann's ancestral home, to the bank.

Jo Ann was more than a daughter-in-law to Honey. She was a best friend. In the early years, because of their close relationship, many people mistakenly thought Honey was Jo Ann's mother. Later, as Jo Ann's hair turned gray and Honey's stayed dark, people began mistaking them for sisters.

The two were almost inseparable, with Honey stopping by the house on Orange Avenue almost daily after completing her motor delivery route for the afternoon *News-Tribune*. They sewed shirts together for the Cow Creek ranch unit at the annual Cattlemen's Day Parade. They drank cocktails together.

When Jo Ann began spending most of her time in North Carolina, Honey would travel up there to stay with her for weeks. As Debra's visit with Honey came to an end, Jo Ann arrived in Fort Pierce to care for Honey, spending the next nine months with her. Jo Ann was at Catherine Bailey "Honey" Sloan's bedside when she died on May 30, 1991.

Losing the Compound

Jo Ann's time with Honey would be one of her last visits to Fort Pierce and the Raulerson house, the 1922 home she grew up in. Five months after Honey's death, Citizens Federal Savings and Loan foreclosed on the Orange Avenue compound.

The Raulerson house had been the site of countless post–Cattlemen's Parade parties. When he created the compound, TL also built a large pool in the shape of a cloverleaf, the Cow Creek brand. The compound and pool had been the site for many gatherings of family and friends over the years. Robin and Darren both had their wedding receptions there. "All my birthdays were there because they had that big pool," said Jamie Percy, son of Cow Creek manager Jimmy Percy.

Before the foreclosure, TL and Diane shipped much of the furniture from Jo Ann's grandparents' house, which included bedroom sets, dining tables, oriental rugs, and various other furnishings to North Carolina. Meanwhile, TL and Diane moved to a house in St. Lucie Village, just north of Fort Pierce, that had been purchased in Diane's name.

Jo Ann and TL's last hope to turn around their loss of fortune lay with Tellico Trout Farm. But the cost to run the farm and maintain the 1870 farmhouse in which Jo Ann was living far exceeded any income coming in.

Losing the Farm

Faced with mounting debt, including a $28,000 feed bill when she began managing the farm, Debra said she sold whatever she could to keep the farm going and maintain the house. She first sold a canary diamond ring that TL had given Jo Ann earlier in their marriage, a transaction that yielded $60,000. Then she resorted to selling silver goblets, oriental rugs, and some of the furniture of Granddad Frank and Mother Lou that had been shipped to North Carolina before the eviction from the compound.

When that money was depleted, Debra says she at first leased out the trout farm—with Jo Ann staying in the farmhouse—to two separate companies. When that didn't solve the money issues, Jo Ann filed personal bankruptcy and bankruptcy for Macon County Investments, the family corporation that owned the farm.

"There wasn't any way to keep the farm going, because it wasn't generating any income," Debra said. "It cost $50,000 a year to support the big house. Mother filed bankruptcy because it was the only way to protect her and the farm for as long as possible."

Debra said TL and Jo Ann still had the $675,000 IRS tax debt from the Cow Creek Ranch sale looming as well as outstanding loans from Riverside Bank in Fort Pierce and a $100,000 private loan against the farm. No longer able to get a conventional bank loan, TL had taken the latest loan out from a private individual. "He never filed any bankruptcy because Mother owned the lion's share," Debra said. "I think it was a matter of pride for him."

The financial arrangements between TL and Jo Ann were unusual. Deed records from the sale of Cow Creek showed Jo Ann with a 77 percent interest in most of the sections of the ranch and TL with a 22 percent interest. Debra believed the split in ownership of Macon County Investments was similar.

Even though Jo Ann was the overwhelming majority partner, she always allowed TL to make the business decisions. "It was her money, and she allowed him to use it, which was my issue," Debra said.

Kathy put it more bluntly: "He got away with everything but murder. She could have told him 'no' at any time. He blew an $11 million estate because he had no college or management background or anything like that."

Debra recalled that when Jo Ann filed bankruptcy, TL asked, "'Aren't you embarrassed about the fact that you had to file bankruptcy and all of these things?' She straightened up and looked at him and said, 'I didn't lose the money.' That was the first time I heard her speak her truth to him."

With the farm hanging in the balance, a new farm lessee showed up about 1993. He was successful Atlanta businessman Michael Macke. Macke liked the farm and the family. Before long, he proposed a deal to buy the farm by helping Jo Ann out of bankruptcy and her debts. "When he stepped in, he said he'd just take care of all this," Debra said. "I said that would just be wonderful."

The process took several years before the deal for $660,000 was closed in 1995. Though it yielded no cash for Jo Ann, it resulted in her bankruptcy being discharged and her tax issues being settled. Debra's house and 10 acres on the farm remained under Debra's ownership. "That took Mother out of everything, and she continued to live in the big house a couple more years," Debra said.

When Jo Ann was forced to sell the big house, she stayed on as caretaker, allowed to stay in her master suite and keep her belongings in the house. When the arrangement didn't work out, she had to move to a doublewide trailer, filling five storage units and selling her other belongings. "I remember the day we helped her move," granddaughter Tara Breeden said. "It really took a toll on her, but she handled it. She didn't let us know how much it bothered her."

After the Farm

With the sale, for the first time in her adult life, Jo Ann Raulerson Sloan, once one of the largest landowners in St. Lucie County, didn't own property. Anywhere.

TL, too, was without property, living at the St. Lucie Village home owned by Diane, who was working for a local insurance company and supporting him. Robin said those years were happy for the couple, who she said were in an exclusive relationship throughout their twenty-six years together.

"After it was all over and done with, he always maintained he was never happier in his life than with him and Mr. [Bill] Padrick up there [at St. Lucie Village] drinking rum and fishing in the river," said Darren Robertson. "He said that once he got rid of everything and lost everything, he had never been happier because he didn't have any more worries. They took everything, he didn't owe them anymore and he was going to live out his days."

Thomas Leighton Sloan lived until November 10, 1996. In the days before his death, he had a visit from Jo Ann, who traveled from North Carolina with her granddaughter Grace Lee Summerlin for a visit, staying at the house in St. Lucie Village with TL and Diane.

Before her departure, the sixty-four-year-old TL had a request of the woman who was legally his wife and erstwhile business partner for the past forty-four years. Would she grant him a divorce so he and Diane could get married?

Before, TL and Jo Ann had always told family and friends that it would be too expensive and complex to get divorced because of their joint holdings. "Jo Ann was always very quiet about" TL's relationship with Diane, her friend Sally Richeson said. "She carried on as though she was his wife and never said a word. I said to Tommy one time, 'Why are you doing this? Why don't you divorce Jo Ann and be up front with Diane?' He said, 'Financial.' That was his only comment."

When Jo Ann repeatedly was asked over the years why she stayed married, her response was always the same: She still loved him. But on that visit before his death, given his failing health, she agreed to the divorce and headed back to North Carolina.

The divorce and marriage never happened. Three days after leaving Fort Pierce, a Sunday, Jo Ann received a call from Diane notifying her that TL had just died of an apparent heart attack.

When TL's death was announced two days later in the *News-Tribune*, the obituary listed Diane as his first survivor with her three children and then "his wife, Jo Ann R. Sloan and their children, Kathy Blanton and Debra Ann Sloan, all of Franklin, N.C.; and his son, William Thomas Sloan of Knoxville."

Jo Ann, Debra, and Kathy made their way back to Fort Pierce for the service at Yates Funeral Home and later a gathering at Diane's home. Once a family with the deepest of roots in Fort Pierce, they no longer had any ties there. With TL dead and their property gone, they returned to their lives in North Carolina.

Jo Ann's Last Years

After more than a quarter century of living at the Tellico farmhouse, Jo Ann, in the late 1990s, made the move to a rented doublewide manufactured home in Franklin.

About two years later, Debra heard of a new manufactured home community being developed west of town. She bought the second lot in the development, setting up her mother in the home. "It was a good place for her," Debra said. "She fixed it up, and it was easy for her to get into town."

But that domestic tranquility would only last until 2015. With Jo Ann's only source of income a $770 Social Security check, Debra had to subsidize her mother's expenses. "I was supporting two houses on a state employee's salary," said Debra, who works for the North Carolina Department of Agriculture and Consumer Services. "I couldn't do it."

Debra said she was forced to sell her mother's home at a $30,000 loss and move her into the Grandview Manor Care Center nursing home in Franklin. As always, her mother's reaction was stoic, emotionless. She had lost her parents at an early age. In adulthood, she had lost her beloved Cow Creek Ranch, her ancestral home, her prized Tellico, and ultimately her husband to infidelity and death, so why would her reaction be any different?

"At that point she just flowed with it," Debra said. "I said, 'Mother, I don't want to do this,' and she said, 'Well, we have to. There aren't any other choices.'"

At the nursing home, Jo Ann shared a room with another patient. Debra said Jo Ann got into a group of friends who would play poker and do jigsaw puzzles. "She was kind of social, which was unusual for her, but she was put in a position that she had to be."

She'd also receive visits from her ever-growing family. Kathy's four daughters whom she helped raise at Tellico would produce ten great-grandchildren for Jo Ann. In turn, the great-grandchildren produced eight great-great-grandchildren. The Frank and Annie Lou Raulerson line, once at risk of extinction with Jo Ann the only survivor, was now flourishing with two dozen descendants.

Tara said she frequently visited her grandmother at the nursing home, bringing her one of her favorite foods, a fish sandwich from Burger King. "That was hard to see my grandmother in the nursing home because I don't feel like that's where she should have been in her life at that point."

During her visits with her mother, Debra said she would take her out to eat or go shopping or to stop at a site where they frequently saw bald eagles. The outings became less frequent when Jo Ann began using a wheelchair about 2018. Debra said Jo Ann never complained about the past or expressed any regrets.

But Debra had a lot of regrets about her mother. She wished she could put her in a better facility with her own room. Her mother, she said, deserved better. "There were a lot of things that she lived through that she shouldn't have had to live through."

Debra blamed TL for what her mother endured and, nearly thirty years after his death, still harbored resentment toward her father, something she was trying to work through.

"If I had to sum up Jo Ann, I'd say that she was a woman who was put in situations that most people would not have been able to deal with well, and she dealt with them like a lady," Debra said. "She didn't complain. I think if I were in her position and I knew what was going on, I would have left TL and wouldn't have given him a dime. But she took it all in stride. I think she just kind of learned from Mother Lou and Granddad that you just have to suck it up."

In December 2020, Jo Ann was failing rapidly. The COVID-19 pandemic made visiting Jo Ann difficult. Debra didn't think her mother would make it until Christmas, so she asked a nurse's aide with whom she had grown close to call her when the end was near.

"I told her, 'I don't want my mother to die alone, will you please call me?' She called me about three o'clock in the morning on December 20 and she said, 'Debra, you need to get here now.' I made it in there in record time. Mother was in a coma, and I just held her and told her that her body was worn out and people were waiting for her on the other side. I was encouraging her to let go. I told her we'd be OK."

Jo Ann Raulerson Sloan, ninety, died at about nine thirty that morning.

The obituary in the local paper mentioned her "graceful exit" and began: "Jo Ann Raulerson Sloan was a lady, and a lady always knows when it's time to leave."

19

THE LAST CAMP

Buster

Buster Tommie was restless. Sitting on a wooden plank that was his bed, he swung his foot beneath and looked out to the collection of open-sided, thatch-roofed structures known as chickees that he and his extended family had lived in for the past thirty years.

He was facing the certain prospect of leaving his camp and moving into a block house with family members in town. The owners of the land off Midway Road west of Fort Pierce were planning to turn the camp into a golf course community.

"I like it over here," Buster said. "I grew up over here. It never changed."

The year was 1984, and the fifty-year-old Buster and his family were perhaps the last family of Seminoles in Florida living in chickees outside of any of the five Seminole reservations in the state in Hollywood, Big Cypress, Brighton, Immokalee, and Tampa. Buster and his siblings had grown up at Cow Creek and were descendants from a long line of Cow Creek Seminoles. Their father was Jack Tommie, and their mother was Sally Tommie, granddaughter of Polly Parker. Sally's mother was Polly's daughter, Emma, and her father was Chupco Tallahassee.

Even as it became inevitable that the camp Buster and his family members lived in would be razed, Buster continued staying there after all his other family members—sister Bessie and niece Jennie Bobbie Tommie and her husband and children—had left. Buster had a crop of cabbage, mustard greens, and black-eyed peas and was hesitant to leave it. "I never lived in town," Buster said, "and I don't want to go over to Brighton."

Buster Tommie sits atop a platform he used as a bed during the final days the Tommie family lived at their camp of chickees on Midway Road southwest of Fort Pierce. The camp, one of the last in Florida not within a reservation, was demolished by developers in 1984. (Photo by Jon Kral.)

In keeping with Seminole and Creek traditions, the Midway Road camp was matrilineal, and Sally was its leader. Married daughters and their husbands could live at the camp, while custom also allowed unmarried sons like Buster to live there as well, providing role models for their nephews. Besides Buster, the children who lived to adulthood were daughters Rosalie, Hope [Wilcox], Marie [Gilliam], Bessie, and Minnie [Howard], and the sons were George, Cleveland, Fred, Walter, and Buck.

The camp, located in a pine and palmetto hammock, had nine chickees, some in disrepair. Most were used for sleeping and had cypress platforms for beds. One chickee was used for cooking and another chickee sheltered several rows of theater seats, where the faithful gathered for Baptist services on Sundays.

The only nods to modernity at the camp were a small clapboard building that housed a kitchen and bathroom and the chickee where Buster's niece and her husband lived, which had a bed, television, and electricity.

The camp somehow survived 1979's Hurricane David. "When it was cold, it was cold," said Marty Tommie, who grew up at the camp and is Buster's nephew. "When it was wet, it was wet."

Strong Matriarch

The Tommie family, which had lived at Cow Creek, had been living on the Midway Road land under what they said was an agreement with the property's previous owner, Bill Leeper, that Buster's mother, Sally Chupco Tommie, and her descendants could live on the property as long as they desired.

Jack and Sally Tommie and family began living on the property in the early 1950s. The late John Durham, an artist who knew the Tommies since childhood and had rendered pastel portraits of family members, said in a 1984 interview that the family had lived in the old Blue Mountain region of Cow Creek going back to the 1800s.

The family, listed among Seminoles clustered at Cow Creek in the 1930 Census, left the creek later in the 1930s as game became less available for their subsistence living and more fences went up limiting their movement as Florida's days of the open range ended.

The 1940 US Census showed them living in Martin County in what the enumerator referred to as an Indian reservation. The occupation for patriarch Jack Tommie was listed as entertainer and caretaker at an unidentified Indian tourist camp, and Sally was listed as a seamstress making novelties for the camp. Sons Cleveland and George also were listed as entertainers and caretakers at the camp, and daughter Rosalee was listed as a seamstress who made novelties. Sons George and Buck were listed as laborers.

The 1950 Indian Census showed the family was back living in St. Lucie County on the Belcher Canal bank in what was described as "chickee—thatched roof."

Their traditional way of living no longer being possible, the family had become migrant farmworkers, following seasonal crops where work would take them. They built chickees for housing at each stop. For a long time, they were employed by Leeper, who allowed them to make his Midway Road property their home base. While waiting for the next harvest, they would stay at the camp doing what jobs they could, including collecting and sorting palm fronds to sell to churches for Palm Sunday services.

Family members said Leeper agreed to allow Sally Tommie and her descendants to live on 10 acres of the property as long as they desired. The document outlining the agreement was lost when Sally Tommie's trunk was stolen from the camp in 1977, family members said. Leeper died in 1967, and the property was sold in the 1970s, with the Tommies still living on it without disruption until their eviction in 1984.

"Stern but Loving"

Sally Tommie, a well-known figure in Fort Pierce even though she spoke little English, died in 1978 at the age of ninety-eight. In her later years, she made a living sewing traditional Seminole garb, weaving sweet straw baskets, and creating Seminole dolls.

Described by *Palm Beach Post* writer Mary Jo Tierney as "a stern but loving woman who didn't want to change," Sally Tommie demanded that her grandchildren address her in Creek and stay close to their Seminole values. "She did what she had to do along with Jack Tommie, my grandfather, to go out into the woods, to find food to bring back and feed the family, to build chickee huts so that we could have shelter, to do the things that needed to be done so that we would survive," Sally Rene Tommie, her granddaughter, told the *Seminole Tribune* in 2014.

"She stood very tall," her granddaughter said. "She carried a shotgun and a bull whip and a stick. Anytime she needed to use it, she used it. She had no fear."

Sally Rene Tommie, who grew up at the camp, worked in tribal government for nearly thirty years and opened an art gallery in Hollywood in 2002 and started a national media advertising agency, Red Line Media Group, in 2003. In a note on her company's website, she said the lessons learned at the camp from her grandmother, aunts, and mother, Minnie Tommie Howard, were essential to her success.

> As a child, many laughed at the thought when I shared the vision of the future that I saw for myself, as if my ambitions were not achievable. My grandmother, mother and aunties, encouraged me and reinforced that failure is not an option, for me. This little Seminole girl growing up in a traditional camp ... dreamed of the day that she would represent her Native American bloodline and exemplify her tribe's legacy of being unconquered. I have remained inspired by strong matriarchs, often

Shamy Tommie sits astride a horse at the Fort Pierce Reservation. (Courtesy of Indian River Magazine.)

reflecting on my humble beginnings of being raised in a community of close family, each residing in their own chickee; we honored the land, while being immersed in the rich culture and ancestral heritage of the Seminole Tribe of Florida.

While Sally Rene Tommie eventually retired as chief of staff to the chairman of the Seminole Tribe in 2010, some of the Tommie family often felt like outsiders to the tribe. Sally Chupco Tommie's daughters married African Americans. Shamy Tommie, Sally's grandson and Sally Rene Tommie's brother, said in a 2007 interview that the taunts he received as a "half breed" as a child spurred him on to learn more about Seminole culture and pass it on. With his grandmother Sally demanding that he speak Creek, Shamy emerged as an adult speaking the language of his ancestors while other Seminoles his age could not.

Seminoles and African Americans had mixed marriages in the early 1800s as Seminoles living in then Spanish-held Florida took in Black people escaping slavery. But the tribe later considered outlawing such mixed marriages. Today, only people who are 25 percent Seminoles are recognized as tribal members. "I got picked on by both sides, the Black side and the Indian side," Shamy said.

Signed with an X

Over the years, family members departed the camp either to live at the Brighton Reservation or in Fort Pierce. Buster and his niece, Jennie Bobbie Tommie, and her husband and children were the last living there.

With their claim to the property in dispute, the new owners, HHHP Properties, had Buster and his niece sign a document relinquishing any claim to the property in exchange for three hundred dollars for Buster and one thousand dollars for his niece. The document, which was signed with an *X* for Buster's signature, said they agreed to "hereby vacate and abandon our rental tenancy to use the property as of June 1, 1984."

Jennie had left several weeks earlier. Buster was moved off the property on May 31, 1984. The family's chickees were razed two weeks later.

"All I can say is that it's another case of the white man's failure to appreciate an enduring culture," Rufus Alexander Sr., an African American community activist who had known the family for decades, said at the time. "What they have allowed to be done angers me. The Indians have once again been betrayed by the white man."

After leaving the camp, Buster moved into town and lived in a concrete block house with relatives. "He doesn't like to stay in that house he's in now, but he doesn't have any choice," his sister Hope Wilcox said at the time. "He didn't ever like the regular house. He wouldn't move out to the reservation either. He just doesn't feel right. He's usually outside working in the garden. Now he's stuck inside the house."

By the time of his death in 1995 at the age of sixty-seven, Buster had moved to the Brighton Reservation, where brother Cleveland and sister Bessie had also moved. Surviving sisters Hope Wilcox, Marie Tommie Gilliam, and Minnie Tommie Howard lived in Fort Pierce.

The year Buster died, the US Department of Interior designated 50 acres

Chupco's Landing is a modern subdivision for residents of the Seminole Tribe's Fort Pierce Reservation. (Photo by Gregory Enns.)

of land on the south side of Okeechobee Road west of Fort Pierce as the sixth reservation of the Seminole Tribe of Florida, to house about two dozen families that were descendants of Sally Chupco Tommie.

The reservation is called Chupco's Landing, an $11 million gated community of 2,500-square-foot concrete block homes surrounded by wetlands. The reservation also has a rodeo arena and barn called the Chupco Youth Ranch and a $5 million arena, the Chupco Community Center, that opened in 2014. The community center houses a clinic, fitness center, gym with basketball and volleyball courts and retractable bleachers, classrooms, and offices for Family Services, Administration, Police, House, and Culture and Education Departments.

When Chupco's Landing was dedicated in 1996, only one of Jack and Sally Tommie's thirteen children, Bessie, was still living. She died in 2023 at the age of eighty-four.

"The grandkids are now enjoying what the elders waited and fought for," Shamy Tommie said.

EPILOGUE

The Creek

Splashing around in the waters of Cow Creek swamp is one of my earliest childhood memories. I was about four years old, and my dad loaded my two older brothers and me in a Jeep for a ride around Cow Creek Ranch. As we drove down a lane along various pastures, we approached Cow Creek crossing, a narrow swath where cypress trees and their knees had been cleared so you could drive through the creek.

On most days—as I later learned—the old Willys Jeep could pass through the creek. You merely had to stop the Jeep, put it in four-wheel drive, and trudge through, the Jeep's muffler often gurgling in the water. But there were certain days after heavy rains that you simply couldn't cross the creek. It became a matter of judgment when to take the chance, and my dad, who spent most of his time in the army in Korea driving a Jeep in the motor pool, was a pretty good judge of when you could make it through.

On this day of my introduction to Cow Creek, rains had swollen the crossing to 4 or 5 feet, and my dad made the wise decision not to make the crossing. It was a hot day—perhaps in summer—so instead of crossing the creek, Dad pulled the Jeep over, and we went swimming. It was before I knew about or had a fear of alligators, so I happily played in those tea-colored waters, squeezing my toes in the creek's white sandy bottom.

Ever since, I've always associated the name Cow Creek Ranch with the image of that creek crossing, despite our family making many other trips to the ranch and crossing the creek countless times with ease.

The Cow Creek Ranch of my childhood was 23,000 acres of cow pastures, oak and cabbage palm hammocks, citrus groves, and pure fun. The ranch, equally situated between Okeechobee and St. Lucie Counties, was so large that once you entered the main gate, you had to drive 4 miles through the ranch just to reach the headquarters, which in those early days consisted of a horse barn, cow pens, dog runs, two barns for Jeeps and tractors, a bunkhouse, a weekend house for the Sloan family, and three small houses for the ranch hands.

A Vast Treasure

How my family, which consisted of my mom and dad and seven siblings, had come to enjoy unlimited access to this vast treasure probably started with my mother, Katie. As she recalled it, she had met Jo Ann Sloan at a garden club event in the 1950s. As they talked and got to know each other better, they learned that they had something in common: They were both born on the same day and year, July 22, 1930. They became fast friends and dubbed themselves the "birthday twins." Despite the wide economic gap between Jo Ann and my mom, they shared an undying friendship for the next sixty-five years.

I imagine their early friendship led to an invitation by Jo Ann to visit the ranch. I'm sure my dad, Bob, an editor at the *News-Tribune*, jumped at the chance. He was a country boy at heart and had grown up at Ten Mile Creek west of Fort Pierce.

He always qualified that he had lived in the country up to the age of fourteen because at that age, he and his family moved into town, an event, at least in his mind, of monumental displacement. In the thirty years that I knew him, he always seemed to long for his country life, despite his college education and white-collar job. He was happiest in the woods, and it seemed to provide him a certain interior peace.

After several visits to the ranch with Jo Ann and Tommy, Dad somehow wrangled himself into becoming a volunteer cowboy at the ranch one day a week. As a newspaper editor, he always worked Saturdays to put out the big Sunday paper. That left him with Sunday and Monday off. He occupied his time with family on Sunday, but he needed something to do on Mondays. Why not be a day cowboy?

While he was pretty smart about the ways of the Florida backwoods, as far as I know he had no experience being a cowboy. But I'm sure the cowboys out there at the time—Will'um Thomas, Earl Story, and brothers Curtis and Aubrey Arnold—didn't mind the extra hand. And, after a while, he became proficient enough that he proved of some value. He even rode in the Cattlemen's Day parade with them and appeared in the *Discovery* segment galloping across the screen on the old gray gelding Matthews during a roundup.

The payoff was that he could go hunting at the ranch and could bring the family to enjoy it as well. Tommy and Jo Ann generously allowed Dad and a few close others to use Cow Creek, without qualification. You didn't need to call ahead or ask permission. You had a key to the main gate, and once you entered, you simply respected the place and the resource that it was.

Over the next two decades, whenever inspired, my dad would write columns for the *News-Tribune* about Cow Creek. "My favorite sport, in case I haven't told you, is rounding up cattle at Cow Creek Ranch," he wrote in one column. "Cow Creek has to be one of the prettiest corners of the universe."

Getting Back to Cow Creek

In my childhood days visiting the ranch, I didn't know how Cow Creek Ranch came to be. The old horse carriage in the barn gave a clue that it had been around a long time. I learned only the broadest outline of a story: that Jo Ann's grandfather, Frank Raulerson, had founded the ranch and that he and Jo Ann's grandmother raised Jo Ann after her father died when she was a young girl. Jo Ann then inherited the ranch when her grandfather died.

It was only after a lifetime in journalism and the deaths of Jo Ann in December 2020 and my mom just a month later that I started to fill in the details and work in earnest on the story that has resulted in this book. It was a story my mom had been urging me to write ever since my return to the Treasure Coast in 2006 to launch my own magazine.

For years, I had longed to return to Cow Creek, wondering what might've happened to the homeplace and ranchlands. I also yearned to go through the Cow Creek crossing, see its cathedral of cypress, and find the old moss-covered tangerine trees my father said Seminoles planted on the south side of the ranch.

In the decades since the Sloans sold the lands, the ranch has been carved up into seven separate ranches, with two of them carrying the Cow Creek name. It took a while, but somehow I managed to revisit much of the Cow Creek holdings, with Buddy Mills blazing the trail.

Back with Buddy

Buddy had followed in his dad Junior's footsteps and always kept his cowboy roots close to him, from growing up at Cow Creek, to working as a day cowboy in his early years, teaching agriculture and coaching rodeo in the school system, and still today raising his own herd.

Our first meeting was at his home in Basinger in Okeechobee County. It's nestled in an oak-covered hammock that looks out to a pasture where deer and turkey appear frequently. Buddy provided a big spread of pork ribs, barbecued chicken, greens, and, best of all, swamp cabbage he had harvested from a palmetto that morning. After lunch, Buddy introduced me to thirty-six-year-old Spur, the last horse his dad rode. He also showed me the cow whips he was working on, a well-known tradition begun by his dad that Buddy continues today.

Buddy took me around to the old Basinger Cemetery where his parents, Junior and Betty, are buried. Nearby were the graves of Will'um and his wife, Punk. Through my reporting, I would learn that, except for former ranch cook Ethel Durden, all of the Cow Creek folks I knew from my parents' and Tommy and Jo Ann's generation were deceased.

The large headstone for Buddy's parents has a cowboy hat on one side for Junior and a nurse's cap on the other side for Betty, who was the ranch cook during her days at Cow Creek. Junior went out about as well as a cowboy could, with his boots on. Instead of a hearse, his coffin was mounted on bales of hay and transported inside a horse trailer to where the service was held at the Okeechobee County Agri-Civic Center.

At his parents' gravestone at the Basinger Cemetery, Buddy shared how his mom earned her licensed practical nurse degree after leaving Cow Creek. She initially worked at Raulerson Hospital in Okeechobee but found her work as a nurse at the Okeechobee County Jail far more rewarding. "I can't tell you the number of people who were in jail who told me they turned their lives around because of my mother," Buddy said.

After decades away, Alfred Norman, *left*, Buddy Mills, *center*, and Deroy Arnold returned for a visit to Cow Creek in 2022. (Photo by Gregory Enns.)

Catching up with Deroy

Buddy had kept in touch with Deroy Arnold, who was a continuous witness to Cow Creek from his birth in 1957 to 1981, when the Sloans sold their final parcel of the ranch. Deroy's dad, Curtis, had worked under Frank Raulerson going back to the late 1940s, and Deroy's father-in-law, Alfred Norman, was the son of John Norman, Frank Raulerson's longtime foreman who helped establish Cow Creek Ranch.

Deroy invited me to visit them at Triple S Ranch, where Deroy has been foreman since 2017. Before Deroy, Alfred, then eighty-six, had been foreman of Triple S since the 1960s; he still lives at the ranch. During my visit to Triple S, Alfred recalled the early days of Cow Creek, how his father had to transform rough Florida scrublands into pastures, and shared memories of Frank Raulerson and his penchant for Tampa Nugget cigars and Cadillacs.

As I talked to Deroy, I realized that if Cow Creek had an exemplar, it would be Deroy, who spent his earliest days at Cow Creek, learning to ride horses and herd cattle. Essentially, everything Deroy learned as a cowboy he learned at Cow Creek. Deroy's Uncle Will'um and his dad, Curtis, were best friends and, except for army stints, they had spent their nearly entire cowboy careers working for Frank Raulerson and then the Sloans.

Back at the Ranch

Buddy, Deroy, Alfred, and I had gotten the okay to visit the old homeplace at Cow Creek from ranch co-owner, Travis Larson. I hadn't set foot on the ranch since the Sloans sold it in 1976, and Buddy had not been out there in almost as long. Deroy and Alfred had been out there about twenty years before, working cattle for previous owner Vernon Smith.

We drove in through a new entrance and across pastures until reaching the main ranch road. It was familiar and virtually unchanged. We stopped by the gate to Sandy Lane, the big ranch thoroughfare where you could see pastures for miles and flush out wildlife. We passed by the "county line oak," the milestone for the separation between Okeechobee and St. Lucie Counties.

Continuing on, Buddy and I recalled the small citrus grove on the south side of the ranch road planted by Seminoles. Whenever my family would pass by it and the fruit was in season, my dad would turn in to find some towering and ancient moss-draped trees that produced some of the sweetest tangerines I ever tasted.

We stopped, and Buddy, Deroy, and I got out and walked south in search of the old grove to find out whether the old trees still were there or had rotted or been bulldozed. After several minutes of foraging through the woods we found no evidence of the grove—our search literally turned up fruitless—but I discovered something else. I realized how connected I was to Buddy and Deroy through our love of Cow Creek and the mutual respect our fathers had for one another.

"We could go anywhere we wanted anytime we wanted," Buddy said during the search for tangerine trees. "We thought it was going to last forever. But nothing lasts forever. I thank God every day for the memories I've got, and as long as I'm alive that's my forever, on this property right here."

"Oh, yeah," Deroy interjected, as if in a church service.

In a way, it was a church service. I know my dad considered Cow Creek heaven on Earth, and if there was one place his restless spirit might roam around it would be Cow Creek.

Seeing the "Homeplace"

Next, we headed to the homeplace, or headquarters. Remarkably, even after nearly fifty years, almost everything was in practically the same condition: the home Frank Raulerson built, the old horse barn, the cow pens, the Jeep barns, houses for the ranch hands, and the little house Tommy and Jo Ann's friends the Wrights built. Even the old cypress tables in the barns were still there and the same pot used for scalding.

It was as if the place had been preserved in time, with much of it still in the same white paint and green trim Tommy used to match his compound in town. The only exterior changes that could be detected were the tin roofs Travis had added to several of the buildings to keep them from deteriorating. The only thing missing was the house in which the Millses lived, which had been destroyed by fire.

During an interview with Travis, and later in an interview at the ranch with his dad, Woody, also a ranch co-owner, I happily learned that Travis and his wife, Colleen, were in the process of restoring the homeplace. Talking to Travis, I realized how much he values the historical nature of the land and the homeplace.

"The original Cow Creek Ranch . . . is one of the few pieces of property that you'll find in Florida that really sums up the way Florida was," Travis told me. "It has the big cypress domes, the pine flatwoods, the oak hammocks also the old tomato grade pastures and a lot of native pastures and big Bahia grass pastures as well as palmetto flats."

The Larsons shared the news that they had received a conservation easement for 3,280 acres of the ranch, on the Okeechobee County side. "It's going to stay the same and is going to look just like this," said Travis. And it's likely the ownership will stay in the same hands. Travis and Colleen have two children interested in agriculture.

The easement, a legally binding agreement between a landowner and the state, protects the land from future commercial and residential development and keeps it in agricultural and open space uses, protecting the wildlife habitat. The state paid the Larsons $5.92 million for the easement for the Okeechobee County side of the property. The easement excludes the 20 acres around the homeplace. The Larsons in 2023 received $11,637,500 for an easement on 3,521 acres on the St. Lucie County side.

The Larsons are better known for raising dairy cows than beef cattle. Woody Larson's dad, Louis "Red" Larson, founded Larson Dairy in 1947. While Larson Dairy continues to operate as an umbrella company for various descendants of Red Larson, Woody and his brother, John, operate separate farms, as do Woody's sons, Travis and Jacob. Woody expanded to beef cattle in the 1990s when he converted his Dixie Ranch in Okeechobee County from raising dairy heifers to beef cattle.

In 2011, Woody and Travis were made aware of the lease opportunity for Cow Creek, then owned by former Riverside Bank president Vernon Smith and under the threat of foreclosure. They began leasing 6,800 acres—with about half the acreage on the Okeechobee side and half on the St. Lucie side—and continued to lease the ranch under several subsequent owners until purchasing the property from Sunbreak Farms in 2016 for $22 million.

To swing the deal, the Larsons sold two farms and refinanced other properties. And while conservation easements typically involve property held by families over multiple generations, Woody said he and Travis purchased the Cow Creek property with the intention of getting it put under a conservation easement. Meanwhile, they had to service a huge mortgage for six years.

"It was a real stretch to be able to acquire the property," Woody said. "But we did it with conservation in mind and wanted to keep it as a ranch."

The Larsons acquired the property under the name Cow Creek Ranch Land, a limited liability corporation. The principals are Woody and his wife, Grace, and Travis and his wife, Colleen. Travis runs his cattle at the ranch under the name Cow Creek Cattle LLC.

Woody has a keen interest in the history of the ranch and shared his discovery of an early 1960s map of St. Lucie County showing the main ranch road as the Old Basinger Road, an indication that the ranch road may have been the main road between Fort Pierce and Basinger, before State Roads 70 or 68 were constructed. If so, the road would have gone right through the Cow Creek Ranch headquarters, which would explain why the headquarters is so far away from either of those roads today.

I pretty much concluded that the story of the homeplace of Cow Creek Ranch has a good ending, and that the land is in the hands of people with a vision for the future of agriculture.

Up the Creek

After our visit to the homeplace, we headed for the Cow Creek crossing, which Buddy and Deroy assured me would not be the same as I remembered.

Driving along, Buddy pointed to a dike where a barbed wire fence runs alongside it. Buzzards were perched on the fence, an ominous sign. "That's it," Buddy said. "That's Cow Creek."

My heart sank. Where once was the creek crossing—a large swamp with a swath cut through a cathedral of trees—is now merely a dike that you drive over, with culvert pipe carrying the creek underneath. Buddy explained that Charles Vavrus, who bought Cow Creek from the Sloans in 1976, and his manager, Larry Kesner, had diked the creek and harvested and sold the abundant cypress in its waters.

The creek, which seemed almost as wide as a football field in the rainy season, always had presented an obstacle to getting from one side of the ranch to the other, and the dike certainly solved that problem. But removing the creek crossing robbed the ranch of its soul and South Florida of one of its most scenic vistas.

We parked the trucks where the creek once was and got out. Deroy, Buddy, and Alfred talked about the days of driving cattle through the creek. "I remember this, right here, you could swim your horse across it," said Alfred, who dropped out of fourth grade in the 1940s to work as a full-time cowboy at Cow Creek.

Deroy recalled a day when tin cups were hung from the cypress trees so cowboys could use them to scoop up water from a creek so clean you could drink it. He remembered catching perch out of the creek and frying it up right away.

It was an emotional day for all of us. Though the creek crossing was gone, we were greatly comforted that many other parts of the ranch remained, and the news of the conservation easement meant much of the wildlife areas would be protected forever.

As Buddy was driving back across the ranch back to the main gate on State Road 70, he told me how important Cow Creek was to him and how it formed him as a man. "It was the best of any world that anybody could dream of: the freedom, the beauty, the knowledge you learned from being

Cattle are driven across Adams Ranch, which today includes many sections of the old Cow Creek Ranch. (Photo by Jon Kral.)

here," he said. Then he turned to the many cowboys he learned from and looked up to over the years.

"The number-one thing I picked up from all of them was the appreciation they had for the land and the animals," he said. "The land is important—you didn't destroy or take from it without giving back or trying to protect it."

When I asked him what the day meant to him, he choked and couldn't get any words out. There was a long silence. He apologized. No need. The moment reaffirmed the hold Cow Creek has had on so many lives.

Back to Blue Mountain

After the visit to Cow Creek, I called my friend Robbie Adams, co-owner of the neighboring Adams Ranch. I knew the eastern part of Cow Creek ran through the property the Adamses had purchased from the Sloans in 1976, so I asked him if we could take a ride to Blue Mountain.

I met him at the ranch office early one morning, and his brother, Mike Adams, president of Adams Ranch, was there. I asked Mike about the vitality of Cow Creek and its relationship to ranches in the region. Mike told me the problems diking the creek caused during the Vavrus years. The dike broke during heavy rains in 1991, putting part of Adams Ranch underwater.

"It probably helped them harvest all that cypress by holding that water back," Mike said. "If you look at the creek at their dam, all the cypress to the west has died out. It doesn't look anything like it should."

Mike said water from Cow Creek, which originates in Okeechobee County and runs east into St. Lucie County through Adams Ranch, comes from the seepage of a sand ridge rather than from a spring. The constant seepage allowed the cypress to grow in and around the creek. "It's great habitat for a lot of birds and animals," he said.

He has been working with the South Florida Water Management District to improve water flow at the creek. For example, a weir was recently installed at the creek at Adams Ranch to hold back water when needed. The water flow is essential to the health of cypress trees—sensitive to both too much water and too little—that grow in and along the creek.

Where Cow Creek was once a natural free-flowing waterway going through only a few ranches, today it travels through multiple ranches with each owner having his own approach to managing the creek.

Mike said properly managing the creek's flow could also reduce the amount of water that runs into the C-25 Canal, which discharges into Taylor Creek and the Indian River, and the C-24 Canal, which empties into the St. Lucie River.

After talking to Mike, Robbie and I headed for Blue Mountain, one of the prettiest parts of the old Cow Creek Ranch and one of my dad's favorite spots to hunt. We drove his truck off road and came upon Cow Creek. It's relatively dry, and in some places the creek bed is just a swampy area with a trickle. But the cypress are abundant, in contrast to the lack of cypress where the creek had been diked.

Blue Mountain is an illusion and is actually a large stand of cypress trees that looks like a blue mountain in the mist. Seminoles had once lived at the site, the last evidence being the base of a wrought iron sewing machine in a raised area before the land gets swampy. Robbie said shards and glass bottles have been discovered at the site. Robbie pointed to an area of raised elevation at the edge of the swamp that had been built up by the Seminoles and where sour citrus trees, used for cooking by the Seminoles, still grow on the edge of the swamp.

Back to "the Compound"

During my reporting for *Cow Creek Chronicles*, I also revisited "the compound," the one-block area on Orange Avenue between Tenth and Eleventh Streets where Frank Raulerson built his Mediterranean Revival–style house in 1922. Raulerson had hired noted architect William Hatcher to design his impressive Raulerson Building downtown about the same time, and it's likely Hatcher designed Raulerson's home as well. Many of those details—such as the barrel-tile roof—are gone, but the arches remain.

The block—which includes the Raulerson house, the old Cow Creek corporate office, the house Tommy and Diane lived in, and various other houses—today is owned by the Brackett Family Limited Partnership.

The partnership was founded by Bob Brackett, who sparked a renaissance in downtown Fort Pierce by renovating 214 Orange Avenue, the old McCrory's building on South Second Street, and then the Arcade Building on US 1, now known as Kraus Square. Brackett, who lives in Vero Beach, also renovated the Theatre Plaza, Pueblo Arcade, Courthouse Executive Center, Seminole Building, and the Seminole Courtyard in Vero Beach.

After Tommy and Jo Ann lost the compound to foreclosure in 1991, it went through several owners before the Brackett family partnership bought the property from Alpha Health Services in 2001 for $335,000. Today, the property has an estimated $1,039,400 market value, according to St. Lucie County property records. Since purchasing the property, the Brackett family has leased it to Counseling and Recovery Center Inc. (CRC), which runs the Village of CRC there, a residential center for women with substance abuse issues or recurring mental health disorders.

The management of CRC gave permission for a tour, and Brackett met me at the compound one morning to show me around. We climbed up the stairs to the old corporate office, where the focal point remained the big Cow Creek safe Tommy had moved from the Raulerson Building. Other signs of the old Sloan days were the iron gates in the shape of the Cow

Creek cloverleaf brand, shutters decorated with the brand, and, of course, the giant swimming pool in the shape of the brand.

Downstairs was a great room with kitchen and dining areas and a massive fireplace Tommy had built, which seemed like it would be more in place at a Montana lodge than a corporate office in Florida.

We went inside the old Raulerson house, where an entry under the staircase was once used as a hideaway during Prohibition. Few changes or permanent adaptations have been made to the house in the last fifty years.

I could tell by the friendly banter between the staff and Brackett that relations are good between landlord and tenant, and I suspect that a break on their rent has allowed Counseling and Recovery Center to stay there so long.

While much of *Cow Creek Chronicles* is a story of loss, walking through the CRC Village that morning and seeing what was being done for the women treated there made me realize that good things were coming out of the ashes. I thought of the hundreds of women who had been treated at the center, many of them recovering, and of Kathy Sloan Blanton, who had her own struggle with addiction and grew up in the house now used as a dormitory for recovering women. Good was coming from the compound Tommy and Jo Ann built.

Bound for Carolina

After having visited many sites on the Treasure Coast for *Cow Creek Chronicles*, I felt I needed to visit North Carolina and see Kathy and Debra in person.

In the summer of 2022, my wife, Gretchen, and I were driving north to New England, so we stopped to visit Debra and Kathy, whom I hadn't seen in fifty years. Because they were several years older, and Debra went to boarding school at thirteen and Kathy married young, I hadn't had much interaction with them. But conversation flowed as easily as if we'd been keeping up with each other for years.

Kathy had eventually moved to North Carolina and reconciled with her family. During our visit, it was apparent that Debra and Kathy remained close despite their differences and experiences. Sometimes when addressing

Kathy, Debra called her Lou, after her middle name. Born Kathryn Louise Sloan, Kathy acquired her middle name in honor of her great-grandmother Annie Louise.

After walking around the Tellico farmhouse, Kathy and Debra took us over to an old white oak tree said to be the largest in North Carolina. Kathy encouraged us to get close to the trunk to get the best view looking up to the tree. She sat down on a rock slab, as if taking the energy from it. She talked about the crucifix that can be seen in a white dogwood flower. It made me think of how, spiritually, she's connected to the land, a connection that probably began at Cow Creek.

We drove down along the creek to see the raceways, where trout of various sizes are kept in concrete containment areas, with the largest fish at the top of the creek and the smaller ones at the bottom. It's an impressive operation. Most of the fish are sold to stock recreational ponds in the region, but the operation also has a small pond at the bottom of the property where tourists can fish for a fee during summer.

Debra started the fee-fishing when she managed the farm as a way to bring in extra revenue. Debra, who now counsels entrepreneurs such as aqua farmers in her job with the North Carolina Department of Agriculture and Consumer Services, talked about how farmers can often improve their revenue through agri-tourism.

It made me realize that her own experiences—as manager of the trout farm and watching her father's various ventures fizzle out—help her in her job of counseling farmers. She said her father had vision but lacked the business skills needed to make an enterprise successful. The availability of Jo Ann's inheritance didn't force him to live within a budget, and eventually he depleted their assets entirely.

"I don't believe Mother knew the money train was about to crash," Debra said. "TL, on the other hand, knew he was digging a hole deeper than he could get out of. That's why we lost the ranch and sold the grove."

Though it had been more than a quarter century since her father died, Debra keenly remembered what her mother endured and how she had to live the final years of her life penniless after her husband ran through her estimated $11 million estate.

The final lost asset was the 220-acre Tellico farm and farmhouse, which was sold in the 1990s in a break-even deal that paid off Jo Ann's debts but yielded no money to sustain her in retirement. In the transaction, Debra got to keep the 10 acres of Tellico where she was living and had built a house after paying off the mortgage.

Atlanta businessman Michael Macke bought the farm from Jo Ann for $660,000, and Macke still owns it. "I'm glad Mike owns Tellico because he loves it as much as I do," Debra said.

Why?

In our conversation that day visiting Kathy and Debra and in several subsequent phone conversations, Debra asked me, "Why do you think Aunt Katie wanted you to write the story?"

I didn't have a good answer. At first I think I told her, "Because she thought it was a good story." But knowing what a romantic my mother was and having all those conversations with Jo Ann over the years, I think she was amazed that Jo Ann stayed in love with Tommy until her death despite his betrayals and the loss of her fortune.

It was an unusual love story because it involved a litany of losses for Jo Ann: the loss of her parents at an early age, the loss of her husband's fidelity, the loss of her beloved Cow Creek, and the loss of Tellico.

I think my mom was also impressed that, as unconventional as it was, Jo Ann lived life on her own terms and always with the utmost grace. "My mother lived her life with such grace, no matter what happened to her," Debra said. "She was pretty amazing. I don't think other people could do what she did."

Like Jo Ann, Tommy also lived life on his own terms. Though flawed, Tommy was charismatic and good at enlisting people in his causes. And though he grew apart from Kathy and Debra in his later years, he developed a strong bond with two of Diane's children, Robin and Darren, who considered him a father and credit him with many of their important life lessons.

When I started *Cow Creek Chronicles*, I wondered whether Jo Ann, emotionally vulnerable because of her upbringing, was victimized by Tommy. But my research revealed that Jo Ann was always in majority control of their assets. The Cow Creek Ranch sale in 1976 showed Jo Ann with a 77 percent share of the ranch and Tommy with a 22 percent share, and Debra said the arrangement was similar with other assets, including the property in North Carolina.

I don't think Jo Ann ever thought of herself as a victim. She was a strong woman who had the control of the family assets at her fingertips. She trusted her husband to handle the finances, and that trust was misplaced. But in some ways, she was a victim of a time when women were not generally viewed as capable of running a business. Thus, instead of her grandparents preparing Jo Ann to run Cow Creek, they put their hopes in her marrying a man who would run it for her. "She always had majority control on paper in any kind of business matter, but she didn't actively make the decisions, which was her downfall," Debra said.

Keeping land through generations requires the long view from the generation controlling it. For the Seminoles, Cow Creek was a sacred hunting ground, refuge, and dwelling space to be honored in its natural state. For Frank Raulerson, it was something that could be cleared and fenced and passed to future generations. To Jo Ann, it was an heirloom she thought she'd never lose. To the ranch hands, it was the means by which they could make a living while also maintaining their treasured way of life. To Tommy, who acquired his ownership of Cow Creek through marriage, the land was a commodity from which he could achieve his immediate goals.

While the story of Cow Creek provides a glimpse into how early Florida cattle ranches were established, it also shows that this accomplishment caused the displacement of the Seminole people. Through the erection of wooden fences and later barbed wire, which eliminated the days of the open range and the traditional style of Seminole living, ranches were instantly created. It took years of hard labor clearing brush to maintain grazing grounds for cattle herds, along with the creation of irrigation systems to drain the lands. The cleared pastures seen throughout much of South Florida today weren't always thus, and instead were mostly marsh or hard scrub during the open range.

Though Tommy and Jo Ann's story is unusual, the story of Cow Creek Ranch isn't unique. I suspect that there are hundreds of ranches across the Florida landscape where hardworking people are living out lives like those at Cow Creek. They are close to the land, close to nature, and close to the Creator.

The only difference between Cow Creek and the other ranches is that

Gregory Enns rides Matthews at Cow Creek Ranch around 1972. His earliest childhood memories are of Cow Creek. (Photo by Michael Enns.)

what transpired at Cow Creek has been documented, first with my dad's stories and columns about Cow Creek going back to the early 1960s, then with the *Discovery* feature on ABC television in 1968, and now with *Cow Creek Chronicles*.

In telling the story of Cow Creek, I hope I have provided a window into the history of Florida, from its earliest days as a collection of coral reefs, to its use as a grazing ground for prehistoric animals like mastodons, to the arrival of the first humans and appearance of native groups like the Ais, to the days of Spanish colonization, to the formation of what would become the Seminole people, and to the arrival of the first Euro-Americans and creation of the communities we know today.

I set about telling the story of Jo Ann, and in the process learned that her story and that of her ancestors the Raulersons helped tell the wider story of the settlement of Florida, a story that came at the expense of Native Americans. As a child growing up in Florida, my school textbooks from the 1960s and 1970s overlooked my native state's history. Narratives focused on the English settlement of Jamestown in 1607 or the arrival of the pilgrims in Plymouth in 1620 while paying scant, if any, attention to the far earlier settlements by the Spanish of Pensacola in 1559 or St. Augustine in 1565. Florida's history is essential to the story of America. Barring archaeological evidence that the Vikings traveled beyond Newfoundland a millennium ago, Florida was the site of the first Euro-American settlement in what today is the United States. It also was the birthplace of what would become the nation's cattle culture.

Greater attention should also be paid to the story of the Seminoles, who from 1816 to 1858 and during three wars were engaged in the longest continuous conflict against the US government fought by any Native American tribe. They were also the only tribe never to sign a formal peace treaty with the government. Their efforts at resisting forced relocation, including Polly Parker's heroic escape with a handful of other Seminole women from the steamer *Grey Cloud* and return to their homeland near Lake Okeechobee, ensured that the tribe remained in Florida for generations to come.

Florida's history is rich and important to the story of America. Let's share it.

ACKNOWLEDGMENTS

Imagine being able to take your favorite memories from your childhood of long ago and vividly bring them back to life.

That's what I was able to do in constructing *Cow Creek Chronicles*, thanks to the generosity of people I hadn't seen in a half century. Because I lost contact with them after much of the ranch was sold in 1976, I often wondered if my memories from Cow Creek were real, and they confirmed for me that indeed they were, as they shared many of the same memories themselves. They also helped me tell the story of Cow Creek.

I'd like to thank my late dad, Bobby Enns, for introducing me to the wonders of Cow Creek at about the age of four, and to my mom, Katie, who in her last two decades urged me to write about the remarkable life of her friend Jo Ann Raulerson Sloan.

Deepest thanks also go to:

Jo Ann and Tommy's daughters, Debra Sloan and Kathy Sloan Blanton, who didn't make any question off-limits and never held back during our multiple interviews. They also shared multiple photos. Even though I hadn't seen or talked to them in more than five decades, we renewed our friendship, and they became like sisters to me. Sadly, Kathy died in October 2022, while I was writing the *Cow Creek Chronicles*. I still can't bring myself to delete the voicemails she left me.

Buddy Mills, who carries on the cowboy tradition of his father, Junior, and who was my passport back into the world of Cow Creek.

Deroy Arnold, with whom as a child I first shot a BB gun and rode a minibike, for reconnecting and sharing memories and photos. Like Buddy, he also continues the cowboy tradition of his father.

Alfred Norman, who shared his memories of early Florida cattle ranching and the days of Cow Creek going back as far as the 1930s, and his sisters Bertice Harper and Josephine Glenn for sharing their family photos and memories of Uncle Frank and Aunt Lou. Bertice's daughter, Susan Flint, proved invaluable during the fact-checking process.

Ethel Durden, Steve Arnold, and Patty Arnold Boney for sharing their memories and photos.

Woody Larson and Travis Larson for allowing me to revisit Cow Creek headquarters. Woody and his wife, Grace, also helped educate me on cattle ranching. Through purchasing a large part of the old Cow Creek Ranch and putting it under conservation easements, Woody and Grace and Travis and his wife, Colleen, have ensured that the property will always remain a part of unspoiled Florida.

Robbie and Mike Adams, who generously allowed me to return to Cow Creek's Blue Mountain several times, provided photos and background about the Cow Creek waterway, and read the manuscript and made suggestions. I am proud to continue the friendship our families have had for more than a century.

Sport Pickering, for sharing photos and providing crystal-clear memories in interviews and delivering a wonderfully written account of his Cow Creek days.

Frank H. "Speedy" Fee III, descendant of one of Fort Pierce's first families and a font of historical knowledge, read the manuscript and provided a detailed and thoughtful written analysis. He also provided me with guidance in interpreting land transactions.

Willard Steele, former historic preservation officer for the Seminole Tribe of Florida Inc., who read the manuscript, provided a written review, and made important suggestions.

Retired Judge Bud Hallman, for sharing his memories as a Cow Creek summer cowboy and his own family's ranching history and providing the insight of a rodeo cowboy.

The Clemons family of Okeechobee, for their hospitality in letting me spend an afternoon at their Okeechobee Livestock Market and for sharing its rich history.

My childhood friend Allen Osteen, who went into the magazine business with me twenty years ago, allowing me to indulge myself in writing about Treasure Coast history. I wouldn't have been able to tell the story of Cow Creek without his willingness to be my business partner.

My other colleagues at Indian River Media Group—Michelle Moore Burney, Lauren Shott, Patricia O'Neill Durham, and Ian Love—who took up the slack when I focused on the book. Michelle also helped with the design of the magazine series and curated the photos used in the book.

My friend, the late Phil Strazzulla, whose endless knowledge and list of contacts resulted in a visit to the north side of Cow Creek, and to our schoolmate Greg Nelson of Bernard Egan & Co. for letting us roam the property.

Rick Modine for his friendship, suggestions, and help in researching the history of the Florida CowBelles.

My old newspaper colleague Craig Pittman, who provided essential guidance for getting the book published and marketed.

Barbara Drondoski and Frances McGlenn, for reading proofs and making suggestions for changes.

Bob Brackett, for giving me a cook's tour of the complex Frank Raulerson began and Tommy and Jo Ann Sloan expanded.

My old karate teacher Jon Kral, who happened to become one of Florida's preeminent photographers, for allowing us to use his outstanding images.

Rose Marie Kenton Anderson, for giving us the rights to produce the images of her father's Cow Creek paintings for use in the book.

Harry Quatraro from the St. Lucie County Regional History Museum, who good-naturedly accedes to my never-ending requests for photos.

My editor Sian Hunter, assistant editor Carlynn Crosby, copy editor Susan Murray, book designer Mindy Basinger Hill, marketing director Rachel Doll, marketing assistant Şevval Erçin, Michele Fiyak-Burkley, managing editor Marthe Walters, and all the folks at the University Press of Florida who helped shepherd the book into publication.

My aunt, anthropologist Susan Stans, who lived at Brighton Reservation while getting her PhD, and long ago connected me with the Seminoles.

My brother, Michael, who presciently took photos of our Cow Creek days during his early years as a photographer and somehow kept the negatives all these years.

My children, Lucie, Nick, and Alex, who read the manuscript and made thoughtful and honest suggestions.

And finally, but above all, my wife, Gretchen, who continually proves to me that it's not where you go but who you go with.

NOTES ON SOURCES

Introduction

Jo Ann's early days at Cow Creek are based on my 2023 interviews with three siblings of Ephraim Norman: Alfred Norman, Bertice Harper, and Josephine Glenn.

Jo Ann's interactions with the Seminoles are based on my 2007 interview with her as well as my 2022 interviews with her daughters, Debra Sloan and Kathy Sloan Blanton.

The history of a portion of the tribe tracing their lineage to Emateloye Estenletkvte/Polly Parker is found in Cathy Salustri, *Florida Spectacular* (Gainesville: University Press of Florida, 2024), 127.

Material on Florida geological history is found in "Florida's Geological History," https://tampabay.wateratlas.usf.edu/upload/documents/257_Florida_Geological_History.pdf.

Information on the creation of Lake Okeechobee is found at "A Brief History of Lake Okeechobee: A Narrative Conflict," https://www.journaloffloridastudies.org/files/v010109/lecher-brief-history-lake-okeechobee.pdf.

1. The Earliest Arrivals

Research on early human arrival in Florida is found at Jessi J. Halligan et al., "Pre-Clovis Occupation 14,550 Years Ago at the Page-Ladson Site, Florida, and the Peopling of the Americas," https://www.science.org/doi/10.1126/sciadv.1600375.

Material on Paleo-Indians is found at "Prehistoric Native People," https://dos.fl.gov/florida-facts/florida-history/prehistoric-native-people/.

The edition of Dickinson's 1696 narrative referenced is *Jonathan Dickinson's Journal or, God's Protecting Providence; An Early American Castaway Narrative,* ed. Amy Turner Bushnell and Jason Daniels (Cocoa: Florida Historical Society, 2023).

Information about Florida demographic history in the early 1800s is found at James Cusick, "Florida in 1821—A Small but Diverse Population," https://pkyonge.uflib.ufl.edu/2021/08/20/florida-in-1821-a-small-but-diverse-population/.

Background on the sources of early cattle stock can be found in *History of Florida Cattle Ranching: Five Centuries of Tradition* (Kissimmee: Florida Cattlemen's Foundation); John Anthony Caruso, *The Southern Frontier* (New York: Bobbs, Merrill, 1963), 17; and L. B. Copeland and J. E. Dovell, *La Florida: Its Land and People* (Austin: Stick Col, 1947), 14–17.

The quotations from Joseph A. Ackerman Jr. are from *Florida Cowman: A History of Florida Cattle Raising* (Kissimmee: Florida Cattlemen's Association, 1976), 2, 12.

Information on Cracker horses is found at https://floridacrackerhorseassociation.com/about-us/.

Seminole history is sourced at https://www.semtribe.com.

Background on Seminole tribe community histories is sourced from "A Very Brief History of the Seminoles," by Andrew K. Frank, https://guides.lib.fsu.edu/fsuandseminoles/briefhistory.

Analyses from Jason Herbert are sourced from his doctoral dissertation, "Beast of Many Names: Cattle, Conflict, and the Transformation of Indigenous Florida, 1519–1858" (University of Minnesota, 2022), quotations on 6–7.

Seminole cattle history is sourced at "Cowkeeper's Legacy/A Seminole Story," Seminole Tribe of Florida Tribal Historic Preservation office, 2023, https://stofthpo.com/wp-content/uploads/2023/12/Cowkeepers_Legacy_Web01223.pdf.

The progression of Tallahassees to Cow Creeks is found at Mark Boyd, "Asi-Yaholo or Osceola," *Florida Historical Quarterly* 33, no. 3 (1954), https://stars.library.ucf.edu/cgi/viewcontent.cgi?article=2551&context=fhq.

The quote from Harry A. Kersey appears in *The Florida Seminoles and the New Deal, 1933–1942* (Gainesville: LibraryPress@UF, 2017), viii, https://ufdcimages.uflib.ufl.edu/AA/00/06/13/84/00001/AA00061384_00001.pdf.

Material on the Cow Creek Seminoles is sourced from Clay MacCauley, *The Seminole Indians of Florida* (1887; Gainesville: University Press of Florida, 2000), 508.

Research and analysis from Kristalyn Marie Shefveland is from her book *Selling Vero Beach: Settler Myths in the Land of the Ais and Seminole* (Gainesville: University Press of Florida, 2024), 160–61, quotation about Tom Tiger's portrayals on 62.

Details on the Battle of Econfina are sourced at https://www.georgiaencyclopedia.org/articles/history-archaeology/seminole-wars.

Biographical information on Chupco is found at Spessard Stone, "Chipco: Tallahassee Chief," https://sites.rootsweb.com/~crackerbarrel/Chipco4.html.

Information on the Dade Massacre is from https://www.floridastateparks.org/parks-and-trails/dade-battlefield-historic-state-park/history and https://vlp.cah.ucf.edu/vlpedia/UCF-VLP-VLPedia-DadeBattle.pdf.

Alexander Spoehr writes about the Cow Creek Seminoles at Alexander Spoehr, *Kinship System of the Seminole*, Anthropological Series, Field Museum of Natural History, vol. 33, no. 2, February 19, 1942, 97, https://archive.org/details/kinshipsystemofs332spoe/page/n6/mode/1up?view=theater.

Tom Tiger's grove ownership and the sale to Eli Morgan is found in *Florida Agriculturalist* (DeLand), July 26, 1899, 5.

Biographical information on Tom Tiger and Frederick Ober's description of him is from Deanna Butler, "Tom Tiger's Camp: The First Seminole Tourism Enterprise," Florida Seminole Tourism, https://floridaseminoletourism.com/tom-tigers-camp-first-seminole-tourism/.

The Seminole Tribe says Tom Tiger was the first Seminole to take a white person to an American court (see https://www.semtribe.com/history/historic-seminole).

2. The Settlers

Much of the genealogical research on the Raulerson family was conducted through ancestry.com.

Early Georgia cattle history is found in Mart Stewart, "Whether Wast, Deodand or Estray?': Cattle, Culture, and the Environment in Early Georgia," *Agricultural History* 65 (Summer 1991): 1–28.

South Carolina cattle history is found at "Cattle Ranching," *South Carolina Encyclopedia*, https://www.scencyclopedia.org/sce/entries/cattle-ranching/.

Much of the history of Jacob Raulerson was based on "The Knabb Brown Raulerson Families" report compiled by Loyce Knabb Coleman and Paul K. Knabb, https://www.seekingmyroots.com/members/files/G003907.pdf.

Details on the Georgia land lottery are found at Jim Giganto, "Land Lottery System," https://www.georgiaencyclopedia.org/articles/history-archaeology/land-lottery-system/.

3. Florida Migration

Agnes Norfleet's brief marriage to Wade Raulerson is documented at Loyce Knabb Coleman and Paul K. Knabb, "The Knabb, Brown, Raulerson Families" (Jacksonville, FL: H. & W.B. Drew, 1964), https://www.seekingmyroots.com/members/files/G003907.pdf.

Details on the Land Act of 1820 are from Heather Michon, "Land Act of 1820," *Economic Historian*, May 22, 2021, https://economic-historian.com/2021/03/land-act-of-1820/.

Details on stump clearing are at Marilyn Salzl Brinkman, "For Pioneers, Farming Started with Stump Clearing," *St. Cloud (MN) Times*, https://www.sctimes.com/story/life/2015/02/14/pioneers-farming-started-stump-clearing/23418141/.

4. Fort Pierce Beckons

Keightley Raulerson biographical information from 1896 to 1903 is based on reports in the *Florida Star*. Details of Keightley and Frank Raulerson from 1903 to 1920 were found largely in the *Fort Pierce News* and the *St. Lucie County Tribune*. Details of Frank, Annie Louise, Alfred, and Jo Ann Raulerson and Tommy Sloan after 1920 are based largely on reports in the *Fort Pierce News-Tribune*.

5. Polly Parker (Emateloye)

The biographical information about Polly Parker attributed to James W. Covington is found at James W. Covington, *The Seminoles of Florida* (Gainesville: University Press of Florida, 1993), 111, 139.

Abner Doubleday's narrative of Polly is at David Ramsey, "Abner Doubleday and the Third Seminole War," *Florida Historical Quarterly* 59, no. 3 (1980): 330, Article 6, https://stars.library.ucf.edu/fhq/vol59/iss3/6.

Details of Emateloye/Polly Parker's seizure by William S. Harney and subsequent transport to Fort Brooke are found in Cathy Salustri, *Florida Spectacular* (Gainesville: University Press of Florida, 2024), 124.

The Seminole references to Egmont Key are at https://www.semtribe.com/stof/docs/default-source/default-document-library/egmont-key-a-seminole-story.pdf?sfvrsn=b72df140_2. The Seminole references to women accompanying Emateloye/Polly Parker are found in https://www.semtribe.com/stof/history/the-long-war.

The number of Seminoles in Florida after the Third Seminole War is found in "Seminole History, A Brief History of the Seminole People in Florida," Florida Department of State, https://dos.fl.gov/florida-facts/florida-history/seminole-history/the-seminole-wars/.

Accounts of Polly Parker at the Sun Dance Festival are found in "Oldest Seminole at Sun Dance," *Tampa Tribune*, March 11, 1922, 15; and "Oldest Seminole in Sun Dance Parade," *Miami Metropolis*, March 3, 1922, 1.

The report of Polly Parker's death was sourced from the *Vero Press*, August 3, 1922, 3, quoting the account from the *Sebring White Way*.

James Billie's column is at James E. Billie, "Emateloye's Escape Gave Birth to Today's Tribe," *Seminole Tribune*, December 9, 2004, https://seminoletribune.org/emateloyes-escape-gave-birth-to-todays-tribe/.

6. Frank at the Fore

The purpose of the state cattlemen's association formed in 1916 is found in Joseph Ackerman, *Florida Cowman* (Kissimmee: Florida Cattlemen's Association, 1976), 251.

Details on the use of tar and pitch and naval stores are in James P. Barnett, *Naval Stores: A History of an Early Industry Created from the South's Forests* (Asheville, NC: US Department of Agriculture Forest Service, Southern Research Station, 2019), https://research.fs.usda.gov/treesearch/58160.

7. The Open Range

J. P. Platt's interview is in John S. Otto, "Open-Range Cattle-Ranching in South Florida: An Oral History," *Tampa Bay History* 8, no. 2 (1986), Article 4, https://digitalcommons.usf.edu/tampabayhistory/vol8/iss2/4.

Punta Rassa's place as a destination from which to ship cattle is in the James E. Ingraham Papers and the Chase Collection in the Special and Area Studies Collections Department of the University of Florida Digital Libraries, https://www.uflib.ufl.edu/spec/ingraham/expedition/18920313.htm.

The full interview with Teet Holmes can be found in Joseph A. Ackerman Jr., *Florida Cowman: A History of Florida Cattle Raising* (Kissimmee: Florida Cattlemen's Association, 1976), 164–66.

Information on Raulerson's purchases is sourced from "Raulerson Co. Acquires All Miller Cattle," *Fort Pierce News-Tribune,* November 12, 1928, 1.

The history of Florida cattle during the Civil War is in Lewis L. Yarlett, "History of the Florida Cattle Industry," *Rangelands,* October 1985, 206, https://journals.uair.arizona.edu/index.php/rangelands/article/viewFile/11974/11247.

9. Seminoles Leave Cow Creek

Roy Nash's 1930 description of the Seminoles living at Cow Creek is found in Harry A. Kersey Jr., *Florida Seminoles and the New Deal, 1933–1942* (Gainesville: Library Press@UF, 2017), http://ufdcimages.uflib.ufl.edu/AA/00/06/13/84/00001/AA00061384_00001.pdf.

Alexander Spoehr's description of the Cow Creek Seminoles is at Alexander Spoehr, *Camp, Clan and Kin Among the Cow Creek Seminole of Florida,* Anthropological Series, vol. 33 (Chicago: Field Museum of Natural History, 1947) 11.

The Seminole transition to the use of chickees is described by James W. Covington in *The Seminoles of Florida* (Gainesville: University Press of Florida, 1993), 96–97.

13. Ranch Improvements

Most of the background on cracker cattle came from the Livestock Conservancy, https://livestockconservancy.org/florida-cracker-cattle/.

Background information on cow/calf operations was provided by Woody and Grace Larson, current owners of Cow Creek Ranch and Larson Dairy.

Florida's beef production status is in Hannah Baker, "Florida Cattle Market Update," UF/IFAS Range Cattle Research and Education Center, February 2024, https://rcrec-ona.ifas.ufl.edu/media/rcrec-onaifasufledu/pdf/2024_02_FCMU.pdf.

The history of Indian River Citrus is based on information from the Indian River Citrus League, http://ircitrusleague.org/history/; and the Florida Citrus Hall of Fame, https://floridacitrushalloffame.com/inductees/douglass-d-dummitt/.

14. In the Limelight

Locations of Florida rodeos are in https://www.artswfl.com/festivals-2/film-festivals/bonita-springs-international-film-festival/biff-2021/documentaries-biff-2021/state-of-rodeo/state-of-rodeo-explores-500-year-history-of-rodeo-in-florida/state-of-rodeo-explores-500-year-history-of-rodeo-in-florida.

19. The Last Camp

The Tommie family's last camp is based on my interviews and reporting while a journalist at the *Fort Pierce News-Tribune* in 1984.

INDEX

Page numbers in *italics* refer to illustrations.

ABC TV, 141
Ackerman, Joseph A., Jr., 12, 69, 72, 93
Adams, Alto, Sr., 55, 104, 174
Adams, Alto Lee "Bud," Jr., 55, 104, 105, 133, 134, 143, 176
Adams, Cara, 106
Adams, Dot, 143
Adams, Mike, 212
Adams, Robbie, 106, 211, 212
Adams-Onis Treaty, 27
Adams Ranch, 41, 55, 106, 134, 174, 177, *211*, 212
Ahaya, 14–15
Ais people, 11, 217
Alachua Lions Club, 127
Alderman, Effie Morgan. *See* Raulerson, Effie Morgan Alderman
Alderman, Lee, 41–42
Alderman, Morgan, 43, 97
Alderman, Robert, 97
Alderman, Ruddy, 96
Alderman, Ruth, 42
Alderman, "Teet," 69, 71
Alderman, Thelma, 97, 98
Alderman, William, 71
Alexander, Rufus, Sr., 200
Allen, Beulah, 97
Alligator, Florida, 27
Alligator Clan, 91
Along These Waters, 113, 128
Alpha Health Services, 213
American Braford Registry, 134
American Brahman Breeders Association, 132
American Hereford Association, 134
American Legion, 146
American National Cattlemen's Association, 143
American Red Cross, 113, 125
Andalusian cattle, 12, 133
Andalusian horses, 81
Angus cattle, 134, 135, 164
Anheuser-Busch, 180
Apalachee people, 11, 13
Apple Machine & Supply, 179
Arcade Building, 213
Arcadia Rodeo, 146
Armed Occupation Act of 1842, 29
Arnold, Aubrey, 115, *116*, 117, *118*, 121, 142, 151, 152, 182, 204
Arnold, Curtis, 114, 117, *118*, *119*, 121, 137, 142, *177*, 178, 182, 204, 206
Arnold, Deroy, 77, 113, 118, 121,*128*, 133, 141, 145, 174, 178, 182, *206*, 207, 210
Arnold, Ethel. *See* Durden, Ethel
Arnold, Patty, *116*
Arnold, Steve, *116*, 117, 121, *128*, 158, 182

Arnold, Vena "Vee" Raulerson, 117
Ashley, John, 22, 75, 88

Baggett, Joe, 104, 106
Baggett, W. C., 104
Bailey, Beetle, 109
Barbed wire, 65, 78–79
Bartram School for Girls, 149, 158
Basinger, Florida, 27, 44, 46, 76, 77
Basinger Cemetery, 205
Bass, Oscar, 95
Bassett, Harry Hood, 95
Battle of Econfina, 17, 18
Battle of Horseshoe Bend, 17, 19
Bear Clan, 91
Beef Institute, 129
Beefmaster cattle, 135
Beef Round-Up, 130
Bell, Emily Lagow Bell, 52
Bell, J. F., *39*
Bend, The, 46
Bernard Egan & Co.
Big Cypress Reservation, 16, 195
Biggs, Nancy, 26
Bigtown Clan, 91
Billie, James E., 56
Billy, George, 88
Billy, Willy, 88
Bird Clan, 90
Blanton, Kathy Sloan, 99, 100, 101, 102, 103, 108, 110, 111, 112, *122*, 123, 125, 128, *129*, 141, 142, 147, 148, 149, 157, 159, 160, 163, 167, 168, 184, 185, 186, 187, 190, 192, 193, 214, 215
Bluefield, 20, 42, 88
Bluehead Ranch, 134
Bowers, Andrew Jackson, 87
Bowers, Joe (Seminole), 5, 87, 88, 92, 93
Bowers, Lena. *See* Morgan, Lena

Bowers, Richard, 55
Bowlegs, Billy, 50
Boyd, Mark, 15, 16
Brackett, Bob, 213, 214
Brackett Family Limited Partnership, 213
Braford cattle, 133, 134
Brahman cattle, 132, 133, 134, 135, 143
Branding cattle, 13, 24, 64, 71, 73
Brangus cattle, 135, 164
Brantley, Charles, 146–147
Breeden, Tara Summerlin, 161, 184–187, 191, 193
Brighton Reservation, 50–51, 54, 86, 90, 92, 93, 195, 200
Brown, A. V., 54
Brown, Sheriff B. A., 64
Browning, Cathy, 143
Browning, Dr. John, 143
Bryan, Ben L., Sr., 162
Buffalo in Florida, 14
Busch, Adolphus, 180
Busch, Peter, 180
Bush, Gov. Jeb, 145
Buster, Billy, 20

Cahow, C. E., 63
Calusa people, 11. 13
Capt. Richard Walker's Wayne County Mounted Volunteers, 25
Carr, Robert, 55
Cason, Hillery, 31
Castillo de San Marcos, 18
Catfish Lake, 16, 19
Cattlemen's Day Parade, 112, 123, 124, 125, 164, *165*, 189, 204
Center, Bruce, 109
Chacato people, 11
Chai, 49
Charolais cattle, 135

Chatham Hall, 149
Cherokee people, 157, 158
Chickees, 4, 6, 55, 86, 91–92, 93, 195, *196*, 197, 198, 199
Chipco, Dennis, II, 20
Chisca people, 11
Chupco, Echo Emathla, 16, 17, 19, 47
Chupco's Landing, *201*
Chupco Tallahassee, 195
Cinnamon Tree Apartments, 169
Citizens Federal Savings and Loan, 189
Civil War, 16, 28, 29, 34, 52, 72
Clark, William A., 169
Clay, Henry, 132
Clemons, Jeff, 174
Clemons, Otis "Pete," 174
Clemons, Todd, 174
Coats, J. G., 54
Coats, W. L., 46
Coffee, Gibon, 36
Coker, Clyde "Pop," 144, 145, 169
Compound, the, *160*, 161, 162, 166, 168, 178, 179, 181, 185, 187, 188, 189, 190, 213, 214
Cone, Capt. William, 25
Consolidated Naval Stores Company, 66
Copinger, Polly, 18
Counseling and Recovery Center Inc., 213, 214
Courthouse Executive Center, 213
Covington, James W., 49
Cow/calf operation, 81, 132, 135–136
Cow Creek brand, 77, 189
Cow Creek Cattle LLC, 209
Cow Creek Ranch: 1920s, 6; 1930s, 7, 66, 67, 74, 77, 93; 1940s, 1, 76, 83, 132; 1950s, 113, 114; 1960s, 2, *3*, 123, *124*, 125, 133, 141, 142, 143, 144, 202, 204, 205; 1970s, 8, 139, 150, 155, 156, 158, 167, 168, 169, 172, 174, 176, 177, 181, 216; 1980s, *152*, *170*, 182, 188; 1990s–2000s, 181, 188, 190, 193, 202, 204, 206, 207, 208, 209, *211*, 212, 215; 2000s, 137, 139, 217, 220
Cow Creek Ranch Land, LLC, 209
Cow Creek Seminoles, 6, 15–22, 49, 50, 51, 75, 86–93, 195
Cow Creek waterway and swamp, *ii*, 4, 8, 11, 15, 19, 47, 53, 69, 78, 93, *116*, 134, 177, 202, 210, 211, 212
Cow Creek Yacht, 151, 168, 199
Cowkeeper. *See* Ahaya
Cow whips, 69, *119*
Cracker cattle. *See* Scrub cattle
Cracker horse, 12, 81, 137
Crain, Jack, 125
Creek people, 13, 17, 25, 26, 91

Dade, Brevet Maj. Francis, 19
Dade Massacre, 19
Dania Reservation, 89, 90
Dan McCarty High School, 112, 147, 159
Dark Hammock Ranch, 77
Davis, Floyd, 101
Debogory, Progar, 86–87
Deer Clan, 90
De Molay, 104
Demoral, 173
Dennison, Mary Ann, 26
Deseret Ranches, 134
De Soto, Hernando, 12
DeVane, Albert, 49–51
Dickinson, Jonathan: *Journal*, 11
Discovery television show, 141, 142, 150, 204, 217
Disneyland, 147
Dixie Cattlemen, 174
Dixie Ranch, 67, 76, 77, *82*, 85, 95, 209
Doubleday, Capt. Abner, 49
Double Diamond Ranch, 144

Duke University Medical Center, 188
Dummett, Douglas, 137, 138
Dunlawton Plantation, 138
Durden, Ethel, 115, *116*, 117, 142, 151, 152, 205
Durham, John, 197
Dynasty television show, 164

East Coast Cattle Co., 38, 40, 41, 43, 57, 58, 59, 73
Edenfield Jewelry, 63
Edgar, Alexis, 160, 186
Edgar, John, 159, 160
Egan, Bernard, 182
Egmont Key, 50
Elks Club, 125
Ellis, Charles D., 168
Emateloye. *See* Parker, Polly
Enns, Bobby, 122, 202, 203, 204
Enns, Gregory, 202–217, *218*, *238*
Enns, Katie, 203, 204, 216
Esing, Christopher M., 28
Evangeline, 17, 51–52
Everglades, 8, 22, 49, 51, 54, 72
Evers, Sherrod, 120

Farm Supply, 125
Feaster, J. T., 38
Federal Trade Commission, 138
Fee, Frank H., 126
Fee, Judge Fred, 42, 43
Fee, Will, 138
Feeder beef operation, 132, 135
Fee-Gaa-Pee. *See* Tiger, Lucy
Fellsmere Farms, 67, 76
Fence Act of 1949, 65, 169
Festival of Florida Foods, 130
First National Bank of Fort Pierce, 122, 169

First Presbyterian Church of Fort Pierce, 164
First United Methodist Church of Fort Pierce, 63
Fisheating Creek, 16, 49
Flagler, Henry Morrison, 37
Florida Artists Hall of Fame, 127
Florida Beef Council, 126, 127, 130, 141
Florida Cattlemen's Association, 125, 126, 129, 133, 141, 150, 169
Florida CowBelles, 130
Florida: Cowboys, Coconuts and Cattle, 142
Florida Cracker Cattle Association, 133
Florida Cracker Trail Association, 85
Florida cur dogs, 69–70
Florida Department of Agriculture, 133, 142
Florida East Coast Railway, 37
Florida Legislature, 65
Florida Senate, 64
Flournoy, John T., 22
Ford, Willie Mae, 98
Fort Brooke, 19, 49
Fort King, 19
Fort Marion, 18
Fort Moultrie, 19
Fort Pierce, 37–38
Fort Pierce Amphitheater, 113, 128
Fort Pierce Armory, 130
Fort Pierce Cemetery, 106
Fort Pierce City Council (later Commission), 6, 59
Fort Pierce City Hall, 63
Fort Pierce Golf and Country Club, 63
Fort Pierce Marina, 151
Fort Pierce Memorial Hospital, 63
Fort Pierce News, 41, 63
Fort Pierce News-Tribune, 63
Fort Pierce Woman's Club, 128

Franklin Hotel, 157
Friends of the Florida Seminoles, 21, 53
Funk, Lawrence S., 63
Future Farmers of America

Gates Building, 63
Geneva, Florida, 6, 34–36
Georgia Military Academy, 96
Gibson, Virginia, 142
Gilliam, Marie Tommie, 196, 200
Glenn, Josephine, 75, 82
Golden South Airways, 179, 181
Gorham, Vinnie, 122
Gorham Construction, 122
Grandview Manor Care Center, 193
Granny Nichols, 151
Granny Nichols Bar-B-Q Sauce, 151
Green Corn Dance, 16
Grey Cloud, 50, 51
Guettler Brothers Construction, 167
Gunner, dog, 127, 161

Hallman, Judge William H. "Bud," III, 144, 145
Hardee, W. R., *39*
Harney, Gen. William S., 50
Harney Cove. *See* Geneva, Florida
Harper, Bertice Norman Waldron, 75, 76, 82, 83, 84, 85, 104
Hart, Mary Ann, 33
Hart, William B., 33
Harvey & Clarke, 63
Hatcher, William, 63, 213
Hazellief, Quillie, 174
Helio Courier, 127, *128*, 151
Helsel, Paul, 95
Henry, Arch, 69
Herbert, Jason, 14–15
Hereford cattle, 125, 132, 133., 134, 135, 143

Hichiti, 13
Hill, Harry, *48*, 53, 54
Hill, Tommy, 20
Hilliard, Kyle, 69
Hilltop House, 164
Hollywood Reservation, 89, 195
Holmes, Addie, 97
Holmes, Hazel, 97
Holmes, Henry, 73, 75
Holmes, Mary Louise, 73
Holmes, Minor, 73
Holmes, Nathan "Teet," 69, 72–73, 75, 93
Holmes, R. D., *39*
Holmes, Ruth, 97
Homestead Act of 1862, 29, 87
Howard, Minnie Tommie, 196, 198, 200
Huckabee, Tantie, 46
Hudgins, Edgar, 133
Hull, Harmon, 20
Hungryland, 20, 22
Hurley, Joe, 141
Hurricane David, 196
Hutchinson, Bill Roy, 73

Immokalee Reservation, 195
Indian Hills Country Club, 103
Indian River Academy, 185
Indian River citrus, 137–140
Indian River citrus label, 138
Indian River Citrus League, 139
Indian Riverland, 140
Indian Riverside Park, 11
Indian territory, 5, 49, 50, 91
Indiantown, 20, 22, 89, 93, 146, *152*
Ingraham, James E., 72
International Braford Association, 134
International Professional Rodeo Association, 145

Jacobs, Dorcas, 39
Jacobs, Joshua, 39
Jacobs, Mary, 39
Jacobs, William, 39
Jaycees, 125
Jece, 11
Jernigan, Howard, 122
Jernigan's Pond, 8
Jesup, Gen. Thomas, 18
Jim the cow skinner, *83*
John B. Orr Company, 62
Johns, Edie, 88
Johns, Hilliard, 88
Johns, Laura, 88
Johns, Willy, 88
Johnson, Alice, 160
Jones, Collie, 88
Jones, Judge M. S., 21
Jones, Mussie, 88
Jones, Sam, 88, 90
Jororo people, 11
Josh, Johnny, 89
J. R. Edwards Cattle Co., 95
Jumper, Betty Mae, 22
Junior Chamber of Commerce, 113

Kennedy Space Center, 138
Kenton, E. L. "Buster," 127
Kersey, Harry A., 53, 54
Kesner, Larry, 125, 178, 210
Kindred, Thomas, Sr., 104, 106, 176
King Ranch, 164
Kissimmee River, 8, 44, 45, 46, 73, 76
Knight, Abraham M., 31
Kraus Square, 213
Kroegel, Paul, *39*

Lake Geneva, 35
Lake Harney, 35

Lake Istokpoga, 50
Lake Okeechobee, 8, 10, 11, 19, 20, 22, 46, 51, 86, 90, 134
Lake Trafford Ranch, 144
Lake Wales Ridge, 7
LaMartin, Robert, 46
Land Act of 1820, 28–29, 32, 34
Land Remembered, A, 72
Lanier, Mose, 54
Larson, Colleen, 208
Larson, Grace, 209
Larson, Jacob, 209
Larson, John, 209
Larson, Louis "Red," 209
Larson, Travis, 207, 208, 209
Larson, Woody, 208, 209
Larson Dairy, 209
Laurel Grove Cemetery North, 93
Lee, Grace, 102, 111, 155, 161
Lee, Pete, 102
Leeper, Bill, 197
L'il Abner, 129
Limousin cattle, 135
Livestock Sanitary Board, 6, 63, 64, 67
Longfellow, Henry Wadsworth, 52
Longstreet, Robin Robertson, 143, 163, 164, 165, 166, 167, 178, 179, 181, 189, 191, 216
Lykes Ranch, 134

M., Susie, 20
MacCauley, Clay, 15, 16, 52, 91
Macke, Michael, 190, 216
Macon County Investments, 184, 190
Macy, Gerald Underhill, 96
Macy, Ida, 96
Mansion at Tuckahoe, 11
Maraca people, 11
Martin, Charlie, 20
Martin, Emma, 20

Mayaimi people, 10, 11
McCall, Joyce Palmer, 101
McCracken, Aubrey, 168
McCrory's, 213
McQueen, Peter, 15, 17, 18, 19, 25
Meserve, Faith Raulerson, 46, 53
Miami Edison High School, 143
Micco, Holata. *See* Bowlegs, Billy
Miccosukee, 13, 14, 20, 50
Miccosukee Tribe of Florida, 14
Mickler, Capt. Jacob E., 49
Mikasuki, 13
Miley, Charles S., 99
Military Bounty Lands Act, 28
Miller, Joey, 179–181
Miller Bros. 101 Ranch, 73
Mills, Betty, 118, 151, 152, *170*, *177*, 188, 205
Mills, Buddy, 137, 145, 152, 153, 175, 178, 182, 188, 205, *206*, 207, 210
Mills, George Harrison "Junior," 118, 121, 125, 137, 144, 145, 151, *152*, 153, 169, *170*, 175, *177*, 178, 182, 188, 205
Mills, Kent, 118, 119, 147, *152*, 153, 173, 174, 182
Mills, Marty, 152, 153
Mizner, Addison, 61
Moore-Willson, Minnie, 21, 42
Morgan, Eli O. (Pioneer) 20, 42
Morgan, Ely (Seminole), 90
Morgan, Jake, 88, 89
Morgan, Leacy, 42
Morgan, Lena, 5, 42, 55, 87, 92
Morgan, Shelie, 88
Mosquito Roarers, 138
Mount Olive Missionary Baptist Church, 111
Murphy, Jack, *177*, 178
Muskogean, 13
Muskogee, 13 15, 16, 19, 47, 75

Nance, 52
Nanney, Ocie Glenn (O. G.), 111, 153, 154, 155, 156, 159
Nash, Roy, 89, 90, 92
Nicholson, Homer, 36
Norman, Alfred, 72, 75, 76, 77, 78, 79, 80, 81, 83, 84, 85, 113, 132, *206*, 207, 210
Norman, Anzie Josephine. *See* Glenn, Josephine
Norman, Anzie Morgan, 76
Norman, Bertice. *See* Harper, Bertice Norman Waldron
Norman, Ephraim, 1, 3, 4, 75, 76, *82*, 83, 104
Norman, George, 75
Norman, Jack, 75
Norman, John, 1, 5, *74*, 75, 76, *82*, 85, 95, 115, 206
Norman, Julia Roberts, 75
Norman, Lewis, 75
Norman, Margaret, 75
Norman, Rachel, 75
Norman, Stella, 75
North Carolina Department of Agriculture and Consumer Services, 193, 215
Northeastern Wyoming College, 145

Ober, Frederick, 20
Oconee people, 14
Okeechobean Sea, 8
Okeechobee, 1, 3, 10, 27, 46, 53, 54, 76, 84, 90, 95, 98, 115, 118, 144, 146, 152, 166, 178, 205
Okeechobee City Hall, 63
Okeechobee County Agri-Civic Center, 205
Okeechobee County Fair, 146
Okeechobee County Jail, 205

Okeechobee High School, 63
Okeechobee High School Brahman Bulls, 146
Okeechobee Livestock Market, 141, *172*, 174
O'Laughlin, L. A., Jr., 130
Old Basinger Road, 76–77, 209
Open range, 6, 22, 35, 59, 64, 65, 66, 67–73, 78, 131, 197
Osceola, 17–19
Ott, John S., 68
Otter Clan, 90
Owen, Bill, 142

Pacemaker Yacht, 151, 168, 188
Padrick, Bill, 191
Palm Beach Post, 169, 171, 198
Panther Clan, 90
Parker, Argie, 89
Parker, Courtenay, 88
Parker, Dan, 89, 90
Parker, Henry (Seminole), 52
Parker, Henry L. (Settler) 44, 52
Parker, Polly, 5, 17, 22, 47, *48*, 49–56, 87, 88, 89, 92, 99, 195
Partin, Henry O., 133, 134
Partin ranching family, 70
Payne's Prairie, 15
Peace River Historical Society, 50
Pearce, J. C., 95
Pearson, Samuel M., 31
Pelican Island, 11
Pennsylvania Groves, 182
Pensacola people, 11
Percy, Jamie, 143, 153, 171, 175, 189
Percy, Jason, 153
Percy, Jimmy, 121, 143, 153, 156, 171, 174, 175, *177*, 178, 189
Percy, Julie, 153

Perry Smith and Sons, 117
Pickering, Sport, 120–121
Pierce, Lt. Col. Benjamin, 37
Pierce, US President Franklin, 37
Pioneer Drug Store, 62
Piper Aircraft, 168
Piper Cub, 153
Piper Navajo, 151
Platt, J. P., 68, 73
Platts, Mrs. Clyde, 128
Pleasant View Inn, 103
Poinciana Garden Circle, 113, 128
Polly's Hammock, 55
Ponce de Leon, Juan, 12
Potano people, 11
Powder Puff Beauty Shoppe, 63
Powell, Billy. *See* Osceola
Public Land Survey System, 66–67
Publix, 130
Pueblo Arcade, 213
Punta Rassa, 72

Raulerson, Adeline, 46
Raulerson, Agnes Elizabeth Norfleet, 31, 32
Raulerson, Alfred Keightley, 7, 40, *83*, *94*, 95, 96, 97, *98*, 99, 100, 101
Raulerson, Annie (wife of Herschel Raulerson), 41
Raulerson, Annie Louise (Mother Lou), 1, 2, 3, 39, 60, 82, *83*, 95, 96, 98, 99, 101, 102, 103, *105*, 106, 108, 109, 110, 148, 160, 162, 190, 193, 194, 215
Raulerson, Arabell Carter, 117
Raulerson, Archibald, 44
Raulerson, Arizona "Punk." *See* Thomas, Arizona "Punk" Raulerson
Raulerson, Catharine Frances Hart, 33–35, 39, 40, 87

Raulerson, Christopher Herschel, 35, 36, 38, 41
Raulerson, Claudius (Claude) Algernon, 34, 35
Raulerson, Cornelius, *45*, 46
Raulerson, Courtney Keightly Stewart, 26
Raulerson, Cyrus Franklin. *See* Raulerson, Frank (Granddad)
Raulerson, David (son of Jacob Raulerson), 31
Raulerson, David (son of Noel Raulerson Sr.), 44
Raulerson, Effie Morgan Alderman, 41, 42, 43
Raulerson, Eleanor, 28
Raulerson, Elizabeth Moore, 27
Raulerson, Elizabeth Randolph, 38, 40–41
Raulerson, Faith. *See* Meserve, Faith Raulerson
Raulerson, Fanna, 27
Raulerson, Frances "Fanny," 24, 25, 28
Raulerson, Frank (Granddad), *viii*, 1, *3*, 4, 5, 6, *7*, 23, 25, 26, 31, 35, 38, 39, 87, *106*; 1907–1920, 40, 43, 56–59, 69. 86, 97; 1920s, 60, *61*, 62–64, 66, 73, *83*, *94*, 98, 213, 217; 1930s, 67, 68, 81, 86; 1940s, 76, 80, 82, 83, 93, 97, 99, 101, 102, 103, 106, 133, 136; 1950s, 85, 95, *105*, 106, 110, 111, 123, 127, 148, 150, 153, 155, 156, 176, 177, 182, 190, 193, 194, 204, 206, 207, 208
Raulerson, Hardy, 28
Raulerson, Harley, 77, 117
Raulerson, Harmon, 46
Raulerson, Ida Kate, 35, 36
Raulerson, Jackson, 28
Raulerson, Jacob, 24, 25, 26, 28, 31
Raulerson, James, 24, 31, 32, 34
Raulerson, Jo Ann. *See* Sloan, Jo Ann Raulerson

Raulerson, Kathryn Louise (Jo Ann Sloan's sister), 99
Raulerson, Keightley Braxton (K. B.), 34, 35, 37–38, *39*, 40–43, 57
Raulerson, Lewis, 46
Raulerson, Lillian Courtney, 35
Raulerson, Louisiana Chandler, *45*, 46
Raulerson, Lucius Adolphus, 35, 85, 110, 161
Raulerson, Mae Pearce, 3, 98, 99, 100, 101
Raulerson, Mary Sevenah, 35, 36
Raulerson, Mattie, 46
Raulerson, Melville, 46
Raulerson, Moses, 28
Raulerson, Nichabod, 28, 31
Raulerson, Nimrod, 24, 25, 28
Raulerson, Noel, 24, 25, 26, 27, 28, 31, 44
Raulerson, Noel (Rabun or Rabe), Sr., 25, 27, 44
Raulerson, Noel Rabun, Jr., 25, 27, 44, 45, 46, 117
Raulerson, Peter, 27, 44, *45*, 46, 53
Raulerson, Russell, 31
Raulerson, Ruth, 32
Raulerson, Tempa "Tempie" Whidden, 44
Raulerson, Thorp, 28
Raulerson, Vena "Vee," 117
Raulerson, Wade Hampton. 25, 26, 31–35, 39, 40, 44, 87
Raulerson, Walter, 117
Raulerson, William (Continental soldier), 23
Raulerson, William (son of John Rawlinson), 24, 25, 27, 28
Raulerson, William (son of Noel Raulerson Sr.), 44
Raulerson, William Bartholomew, 34, 35
Raulerson Building, 6, *61*, 62–63, 111, 143, 153, 154, 155, 161, 171, 213
Raulerson Cattle Co., 66, 73

Raulerson Cemetery, 25, 27
Raulerson Grocery Company, 40, 43, 44, 62
Raulerson home, 60, 61–62
Raulerson Hospital, 205
Raulerson Trust Ranch, 156
Rawlinson, Avis Ann, 24, 26
Rawlinson, Benjamin, 23
Rawlinson, Benjamin, II, 23
Rawlinson, George, 23
Rawlinson, John, 23, 24, 25, 26, 28, 30
Rawlinson, Richard, 23
Rawlinson, William, 23
Reade, Stephen F., 97
Red Cattle Co., 144
Red Cross, 125
Redline Media Group, 55
Red Sticks, 15, 17
Reichter, Robert, 95
Reynolds, Wiley, 95
Richeson, Sally, 184, 192
Rieta's Gown Shop, 63
Riverside Bank, 209
Roberts, Robert, 144
Robertson, Charlie, 143
Robertson, Darren, 107, 109, 111, 113, 120, *128*, 143, 150, 151, 163, 164, 165, 166, 167, 168, 172, 182, 189, 191, 216
Robertson, Diane, 130, 143, 159, 161, 162, 163, *164*, *165*, 167, 168, 173, 182, 183, 184, 185, 189, 191, 192, 213, 216
Robertson, Don, 143, 164, 166
Robertson, Donnie, *128*, 143, 164, 166, 167, 182
Robertson, Robin. *See* Longstreet, Robin Robertson
Rodeos, 112, 145–146
Rollins College, *104*, 106
Rollinson, John. *See* Rawlinson, John

Sacagawea, 47
Sandy Shoes Festival, 112, 123, 125
Saturiwa people, 11
Scrub cattle, 65, 68, 81, 131, 132, 133
Sebastian Elementary School, 63
Second Seminole War, 28, 37, 44, 47, 49, 138
Seminole Building, 213
Seminole Courtyard, 213
Seminole Indians of Florida, The, 15
Seminole Tribe of Florida, 13, 14, 22, 55, 164, *199*, *201*
Seville, Florida, 32–33, 34, 35, 38
Sharfschwerdt, Hetty, 42
Shefveland, Marie, 16, 21
Shell Oil Co., 172
Sheridan College, 145
Shorthorn cattle, 135
Silver Spurs Riding Club, 146
Silver Spurs Rodeo, 146.
Sloan, Aubrey "Aubie," 107, 112, 148, 162, 187
Sloan, Catherine "Honey," 107, 112, 114, 125, 148–149, *162*, 173, 185, 186, 187–189
Sloan, Debra, 95, 98, 101, 102, 103, 106, 107, 109, 111, 114, *122*, 123, 125, 128, *129*, 142, 146–149, 157, 158–163, 167, 168, 171, 173, 176, 179, 183–194, 214–217
Sloan, Jo Ann Raulerson: childhood, *viii*, 1–7, 83, 83, 95, *98*, 99, *100*, 101–103, *104*; 1950s, *105*, 109, *110*, 111–116 1960s, 117, 118, *122*, 123, 125, 127–130, 142–143, 146–149; 1970s, 150–153, 155–159, *160*, 161–164, *165*, 167, 171–176, *177*, 178, 179; 1980s, 182–186; 1990s–2000s, 187–194, 203, 204, 208, 213–217
Sloan, Kathy. *See* Blanton, Kathy Sloan
Sloan, Tommy (TL), 1950s, *104*, 107, *108*, 109, *110*, 111–114, 115; 1960s, 117, 120, 121,

240 · Index

122, 123, *124*, 125–127, *128*, 130, 131, 134, 137, 141–144, 146–149; 1970s, 150, 151, 152, 153, 156, 158–159, 160, 161–163, *164*, 165, 166–169, 171–173, 175, 176, *177*, 178, 179; 1980s, 180–186; 1990s, 187–192, 203–205, 208, 213, 214, 216, 217
Sloan, William Thomas "Tee," 147, 159, 165, 167, 168, 192
Smiley, Nixon, 51
Smith, Billy, 22, 88
Smith, Dick, 89
Smith, Hansel, 99
Smith, Morgan, 89, 90
Smith, Patrick, 72
Smith, Ron, 169
Smith, Tom, 89
Smith, Vernon, 207, 209
Smithsonian Institution, 15, 22
Snake Clan, 22, 90
Southern Courtyard Apartments, 169, 179, 180
Southern Eagle Distributing, 180
Southern Properties, 169, 178–180
South Florida Pioneers, 71
Spanish colonial period, 11
Spencer, Lucien, 89
Spoehr, Alexander, 20, 90
St. Andrew's Episcopal Church, 97
St. Edward's School, 148, 149
Steele, Willard, 49
Stephens, L. O., 111, 155
Stetson University, 96–98
Stewart, Mrs. Josephine, 41
St. Lucie Abstract and Title Insurance Company, 62
St. Lucie Battery & Tire, 179
St. Lucie County Agriculture Building, 130
St. Lucie County Airport, 167

St. Lucie County Bank, 122, 171
St. Lucie County Cattlemen's Association, 63, 113
St. Lucie County CowBelles, 129, 130
St. Lucie County Fair, 128
St. Lucie County Tribune, 41, 63
St. Lucie High School, 63
St. Lucie Ice Company, 58
St. Marks, Florida, 50, 51
Story, Earl, 118, 121, 142, *177*
Story, Joan, 118
Story, Little Earl, 118
Story, Mordy, 118
Story, Nancy, 118
Stracke family, 73
Summerlin, Clarence, 87, 89
Summerlin, Grace Lee, 161, 185, 192
Summerlin, Jacob, 27, 72
Summerlin, Mary (Mrs. Clarence), 52, 86–89
Summerlin, Myrna Anne, 161
Summerlin, Ned, 53
Summerlin, Tara Leighton. *See* Breeden, Tara Summerlin
Summerlin, Tommy, 160, 168, 185
Summerlin Road, 87
Sun Aviation, 168
Sunrise Theatre, 62, 101

Tallahassee (town), 15
Tallahassee, chief, 17, 19–20, *21*
Tallahassee clan, 90
Tallahassee Seminoles, 13, 15, 18
Tallassees, 15
Talmuches Hadjo. *See* McQueen, Peter
Tampa Reservation, 195
Taylor, Zachary, 46
Taylor Creek Ranch, 67, 76, 85, 95
Taylor Creek waterway in Fort Pierce, 212

Taylor Creek waterway in Okeechobee, 46
Tellico Creek, 159, 183
Tellico farmhouse, *157*, 158, 163, 167, 168, 183, 184, 189, 191, 192, 193, 215, 216
Tellico Trout Farm, 183, 189
Tequesta people, 11, 13
Terry, Bob, Sr., 122
Texas A&M University, 166
Texas Christian University, 143
Texas longhorns, 133
Theatre Plaza, 213
Third Seminole War, 20, 44, 47, 49, 50
Thomas, Arizona "Punk" Raulerson, 117, 118, 205
Thomas, Floyd, 85
Thomas, Will'um, 85, 113, 117, *118*, 121, 123, 125, 142, 169, 174, *177*, 178, 182, 188, 204, 205, 206
Tierney, Mary Jo, 198
Tiger, Ada, 22
Tiger, DeSoto, 22, 88
Tiger, Lucy, 22, 51, 52, 55, 88, 92
Tiger, Martha, 20
Tiger, Naha, 22, 88, 90
Tiger, Tom, 17, 20, *21*, 22, 88
Tommie, Bessie, 195, 196
Tommie, Buck, 196
Tommie, Buster, 195, *196*, 197, 200
Tommie, Cleveland, 196, 197, 200
Tommie, Fred, 196
Tommie, George, 196
Tommie, Howard, 55
Tommie, Jack, 88, 90, 195, 197, 198
Tommie, Jennie Bobbie, 195, 200
Tommie, Marty, 196
Tommie, Rosalie, 88, 196
Tommie, Sally, 88, 195, 196, 197, 198, 199, 201
Tommie, Sally Rene, 55, 198, 199

Tommie, Sam, 88, 90
Tommie, Shamy, *199*, 200, 201
Tommie, Walter, 196
Trail of Tears, 18, 50
Treasure Coast, 11, 140, 180, 204, 214
Treaty of Payne's Landing, 18
Triple S Ranch, 206
Trowel, Nathan, 39
Trowel, Seventh C., 39
Turner, Jim, 179, 180
Tuscanuga, 52
Tushlanee. *See* Bowers, Joe (Seminole)
Tustenuggee, Mary Tiger, 22

University of Florida, 106, 144, 168
Upper Creeks, 13, 15, 25
US Bureau of Land Management, 29, 32, 34
US Department of Agriculture, 138, 139, 142
US Department of the Interior, 29, 200
Utina people, 11

Vanderbilt, Gloria, 100, 101
Van Landingham, Kyle, 71
Vavrus, Charles, 174, 176, 177, 178, 210
Vavrus Ranch, 176
V-Bar 2 Ranch, 177
Vero Beach Municipal Airport, 143
Village of CRC, 213
Volstead Act, 62

Waldron, Stanley, *82*, 83, *84*, 85
Walters, Bucky, 121
War of 1812, 17, 26
Warren, Gov. Fuller, 65
Washington, William "Old Folks," 119
Welch, Claude, 163
Western Carolina University, 168

White City Elementary School, 63
Wilcox, Hope Tommie, 196, 200
Wilcox, Mrs. Van Brunt, 35
Wilkinson Treaty, 26
Williams, Ada Coats, 113, 128
Willingham, Belle, 20
Wind Clan, 91
Woodward, Gen. Thomas W., 18
World's Fair, 146
Wright, Ben, 111
Wright, Christine, 111
Wright, Dr. Jack, 122–123, 153, 158
Wright, Evelyn, 111
Wright, Jervene, 111
Wright, Rose Ann, 111
Wright, Rosetta "Rogie," 111
Wright, Sally, 122–123, 153, 158
Wynne Ranch, 76

Xanadu, 161

Yaholo. *See* Osceola
Yates, Bill, 181, 188
Yearling Middle School, 145

Gregory Enns is a fifth-generation Floridian who spent a twenty-five-year career working as a reporter and editor at newspapers in Florida and Alabama. In 2006 he founded Indian River Media Group, a company based in his native Fort Pierce that publishes magazines on the Treasure Coast and Space Coast of Florida, including its flagship *Indian River Magazine.* He is the founder of the Treasure Coast History Festival, held every January at the St. Lucie County Regional History Center in Fort Pierce. Enns and his wife, Gretchen, live in Vero Beach, Florida, and Gilford, New Hampshire, and are the parents of three grown children. Reach him at enns@indianrivermedia.com. See additional photos and read more about Cow Creek at cowcreekchronicles.com.

www.ingramcontent.com/pod-product-compliance
Lightning Source LLC
Chambersburg PA
CBHW031807220426
43662CB00007B/560